THE AUTOCRATIC PARLIAMENT

Modern Intellectual and Political History of the Middle East
Fred H. Lawson, *Series Editor*

For a full list of titles in this series,
visit https://press.syr.edu/supressbook-series
/modern-intellectual-and-political-history-of-the-middle-east/.

THE
AUTOCRATIC
PARLIAMENT

Power and Legitimacy in Egypt, 1866-2011

IRENE WEIPERT-FENNER

Syracuse University Press

∞ The paper used in this publication meets the minimum requirements
of the American National Standard for Information Sciences—Permanence
of Paper for Printed Library Materials, ANSI Z39.48-1992.

For a listing of books published and distributed by Syracuse University Press,
visit https://press.syr.edu.

ISBN: 978-0-8156-3678-6 (hardcover)
        978-0-8156-3688-5 (paperback)
        978-0-8156-5501-5 (e-book)

Library of Congress Cataloging-in-Publication Data

Names: Weipert-Fenner, Irene, author.
Title: The autocratic parliament : power and legitimacy in Egypt, 1866–2011 / Irene Weipert-Fenner.
Description: First edition. | Syracuse, New York : Syracuse University Press, 2020. | Series: Modern
    intellectual and political history of the Middle East | Includes bibliographical references and
    index. | Summary: "Weipert-Fenner has created a comprehensive study of Egypt's parliamentary
    history from 1866–2011, using a systematic empirical analysis, to explore and explain the public
    outcry that followed the December 2020 election"—Provided by publisher.
Identifiers: LCCN 2019058854 (print) | LCCN 2019058855 (ebook) | ISBN 9780815636786 (hardback) |
    ISBN 9780815636885 (paperback) | ISBN 9780815655015 (ebook)
Subjects: LCSH: Legislative bodies—Egypt—History. | Egypt—Politics and government.
Classification: LCC JQ3854 .W45 2020 (print) | LCC JQ3854 (ebook) | DDC 328.6209/04—dc23
LC record available at https://lccn.loc.gov/2019058854
LC ebook record available at https://lccn.loc.gov/2019058855

Manufactured in the United States of America

To Benjamin

Contents

Illustrations

Figures

Tables

Acknowledgments

This book is a substantially revised version of my PhD thesis, but, beyond that, it is the result of a much longer endeavor that started with my first trip to Cairo in 2004. What was initially planned as a six-month stay to improve my Arabic—funded by the German Academic Exchange Service—turned into an academic passion that has now gone on for fifteen years. Fascinated by contemporary Egypt as much as by its incredibly rich political past, upon my return to university, I began exploring the nineteenth century, a period in which political institutions and ideologies such as nationalism and Islamism evolved. At Friedrich-Alexander-Universität Erlangen-Nuremberg, I received a great deal of support and inspiration from Thomas Philipp during my study of the first parliament of Egypt in the context of imperialism and local resistance. He was also one of the first to comment on the manuscript for this book. Sadly, he passed away before he could see the final version. His support will always be remembered and missed in the future.

After initially identifying an active role of parliamentarians in political developments in the Egyptian monarchy of the nineteenth century, I then wanted to know more about parliaments in autocracies in general. While developing my PhD project on this topic in Erlangen, I was lucky to work with Thomas Demmelhuber, Peter Lintl, Christian Wolff, Ulrike Frank, and Tina Zintl. I am particularly indebted to Christoph Schumann, who guided me throughout my doctoral studies but tragically passed away before my thesis defense. His support and friendship will never be forgotten.

While working as a lecturer at the University of Bamberg, I profited enormously from the support provided by Thomas Hildebrandt, Andreas

Pflitsch, and Rotraud Wielandt as well as my exchanges with them. I also valued the inspiring atmosphere during the seminars I gave; it was here that I got to know many enthusiastic students who pushed me forward in their drive to understand the Middle East and North Africa.

In 2010, I was accepted as a PhD student at the Cluster of Excellence "The Formation of Normative Orders," a research cluster at Goethe University Frankfurt funded by the German Research Foundation that, inspired by the philosopher Rainer Forst, tried to understand a political order by analyzing how it is both justified and criticized. Understanding a normative order by looking at justifications and criticism—exactly the kind of debate one usually finds in parliaments—became the central idea for my analysis of parliamentary minutes. At the same time, I was lucky to be able to work with great international relations scholars, including my PhD supervisor, Christopher Daase, and the director of my graduate program, Nicole Deitelhoff, along with their teams. Together we addressed the problem of how to study nondemocratic political institutions (be they international organizations or institutions in autocracies) in regard to questions of legitimacy and co-optation, which proved to be extremely stimulating. The "Normative Orders" cluster provided me with a monthly stipend, travel grants for field research, funding to attend conferences and, just as important, academic and moral support from fantastic colleagues. I would particularly like to thank Caroline Fehl, Julian Junk, Judith Mohrmann, Ben Khamis, Michael Lidauer, Carolin Retzlaff, Verena Risse, Thorsten Thiel, and Christian Volk for being such great company in both good times and bad.

During my field work, I received immense support from my Egyptian colleagues and friends. Given the current circumstances, I prefer not to mention any names. You know who you are and that you can count on my support whenever you need it. I would also like to thank the numerous politicians and political activists who were willing to share their insights with me.

I am extremely thankful to the German Middle East Studies Association for Contemporary Research and Documentation (DAVO) for providing excellent networks with flat hierarchies in research on North Africa and the Middle East. I am also grateful for the DAVO Dissertation Award

I received in 2014. It was through DAVO that I was able to meet fantastic scholars who went on to become my friends and mentors. Among those, I would like to particularly mention Holger Albrecht, who provided me with all kinds of support, including eternal wisdom about academic life (such as to put all my effort into revising my PhD thesis, for "how many times in your life will you hold a book manuscript in your hands?"—so true). Another unofficial mentor I would like to thank, who supported me in my work, was Janine Clark: over the years, she always dedicated time to guide me on my path, to motivate me, and to provide critical feedback when needed.

I also benefited enormously from comments and suggestions that I received at numerous conferences. I would like to particularly highlight the panel on authoritarian regime stability organized by Johannes Gerschewski and Wolfgang Merkel at the European Consortium for Political Research (ECPR) general conference held in Reykjavik in 2011. Another inspiring event was the workshop on the emergence of parliamentarianism at the 2014 ECPR joint sessions in Salamanca, where I had the chance to discuss my concept of the autocratic parliament with experts on parliaments in democracies. Special thanks goes out to the organizers, Hanna Bäck and Bjørn Erik Rasch, and to Kaare Strøm and Torbjörn Bergman for their valuable comments on my paper.

I was happy to spend part of the time during which I was fully developing this book at the Center for Near and Middle Eastern Studies at Marburg University. I worked as a postdoctoral research fellow at the research network "Re-configurations: History, Memory and Transformation Processes in the Middle East and North Africa," which was funded by the German Ministry of Education and Research. I was lucky to always have the opportunity to present and discuss parts of my book while engaged in new projects. I would like to thank Anne-Linda Amira Augustin, Thorsten Bonacker, Andrea Fischer-Tahir, Igor Johannsen, Rachid Ouaissa, Achim Rohde, Laura Ruiz de Elvira, Christoph Schwarz, Dimitris Soudias, and Alena Strohmaier. I am particularly grateful to Mariam Salehi for persistently pushing me to keep on going with this book project.

Since 2014, I have been working at the Peace Research Institute Frankfurt, where I have had the chance to develop in countless ways. I am thankful to all my colleagues, particularly Jonas Wolff, who helped me solve problems I had been struggling with for years, and Carmen Wunderlich for her friendship and support.

I thank Nick Gemmell for his language editing work, which was generously funded by the Cluster of Excellence "The Formation of Normative Orders," the research network "Re-configurations: History, Memory and Transformation Processes in the Middle East and North Africa" at Marburg University, and the Peace Research Institute Frankfurt. Many thanks also to Cornelia Hess for her support during the final stages of preparing the manuscript.

I very much enjoyed working with Suzanne Guiod and Peggy Solic at Syracuse University Press. Many thanks also to the anonymous reviewers who gave incredibly constructive feedback.

Support from my family has also been something I appreciated immensely throughout the years. Birgit Fenner and Peter Triefenbach never declined to read and comment on my manuscript. I counted on moral support from Franziska Fenner so many times. I thank my father, Reinhard Weipert, for believing in me, no matter what. It was from him that I learned the stubbornness it sometimes takes to keep on going, along with the passion to dig deeper.

In 2004, I fell in love twice: with Egypt and also with Benjamin. According to his accounts, I have been talking about this book project from the very beginning of our relationship. I guess he must be just as happy as I am that this part of our journey has now come to an end—and hopefully with many more to come. I dedicate this book to him.

Abbreviations

ASU	Arab Socialist Union
CAO	Central Auditing Organization
COMESA	Common Market for Eastern and South Africa
CPA	Competition Protection Authority
FJP	Freedom and Justice Party
GDP	Gross domestic product
IMF	International Monetary Fund
MP	Member of Parliament
NDP	National Democratic Party
SAP	Structural adjustment program
SCAF	Supreme Council of the Armed Forces
SCC	Supreme Constitutional Court
UAR	United Arab Republic

The Autocratic Parliament

Introduction

Why would one study the parliament in an authoritarian regime? I was recurrently asked this question when I mentioned my topic while doing field research in Cairo in the first half of 2010. Many people tried to convince me not to spend too much time focusing on Egypt's parliament because, as I was repeatedly told, parliament cannot possibly matter in a country that is not a democracy. But when a new Egyptian parliament was elected in December 2010, there was a huge outcry that these were the most fraudulent elections ever witnessed under the Mubarak regime. Former opposition members of parliament (MPs) founded a shadow parliament for the first time in the history of modern Egypt, and a considerable level of frustration fueled a general feeling of discontent that ultimately led to the mass uprising in January and February 2011. Why did these particular elections cause such outrage at the time, considering that votes had never been cast freely and fairly at any previous time? In 2005, in response to US pressure for democratization, opposition MPs were allowed to assume 25 percent of seats in parliament. Yet although that year's elections were still marked by a massive degree of vote buying and brutal repression at the polling stations, the 2005 elections did not garner much public criticism. Public reactions to the elections of 2005 and 2010 might appear contradictory upon first consideration; all the more so since the parliaments of authoritarian regimes are usually regarded as meaningless, democracy-imitating institutions that only serve the ruling elite as an instrument for co-optation and legitimization. So why would any Egyptian have bothered to criticize the parliament elected in 2010?

To provide a short answer, it was because, for years, private business-men, as one part of the ruling elite, had been unwilling to share power

1

and benefits with other groups within the broader ruling coalition. They had also miscalculated the consequences of violating the norms of state-economy relations, which were deemed essential by a large portion of the Egyptian elite and public during a time of growing socioeconomic protest. The actions of these businessmen in parliament had contributed to a growing legitimacy crisis that spread from the economic policies in place to the identities of political actors and institutions. The manipulation of the 2010 elections was a manifestation of the unbalanced manner in which they wielded power, silencing opposition MPs as well as critical voices from within the ruling party and violating the norms of representation that had been developing for decades.

After the uprising of 2011, former members of the ruling elite spoke publicly about the intra-elite conflict.[1] Yet it would have been possible to predict this crisis beforehand by analyzing parliament's nature as an intermediary institution, in terms of its relations with the public and constituencies on the one hand, and its relations with the government and the head of state on the other. Understanding these relations in an authoritarian context provides us with a new theoretical approach for understanding the *autocratic parliament* that can serve as a key for assessing power relations and legitimacy beliefs in an authoritarian regime. A closer look at two crucial developments that occurred in Egypt in the 2000s illustrates the major arguments proposed here.

(1) Parliament and socioeconomic protests. In 2004, a wave of protests erupted in Egypt that would expose the growing discontent with the political regime and a socioeconomic situation marked by increasing prices and stagnating wages (Bush and Ayeb 2012; Abdelrahman 2014). During the world financial and economic crisis of 2008, Egypt was hit hard by skyrocketing prices for basic goods, accompanied by a shortage of subsidized bread. The latter had been a sensitive issue with regard to regime stability ever since the 1977 bread riots, which broke out when

---

1. Interviews conducted in Cairo in June 2011 with political experts, journalists, and new and old politicians.

President al-Sadat announced an increase in bread prices. Since then, the Egyptian flatbread 'aysh baladi had remained heavily subsidized, albeit not always with the desired result of ensuring food security. In addition to the fraud and corruption plaguing the system of flour distribution, many poor people used bread as a substitute for rice and beans and for feeding their livestock. In 2008, increased demand for subsidized bread forced people to wait in long lines for hours in front of bakeries, some even being compelled to leave empty handed. Public anger eventually mounted, and occasional outbursts of rage brought the army to intervene by producing bread at military-owned companies and deploying soldiers to distribute it on the streets and in public view.

The increase in prices not only led to contentious actions by the very poor, but also mobilized parts of the lower-middle class, whose fixed income had not risen in proportion with consumer prices. Moreover, this was all occurring in the context of working and living conditions that had been deteriorating since the late 1990s, when economic restructuring programs reduced the resources available to support the public sector, public services, and the education and health systems. Added to this is the fact that the private sector suffered from minimal worker protections as well as low wages. The official representative for labor interests, the Egyptian Trade Union Federation, was completely state controlled by that time, and it had become less and less responsive to the needs of Egyptian workers (El-Mahdi 2010; Abdalla 2015). As a result, the only way blue- and white-collar workers could assert their demands was through wildcat strikes, mainly in form of sit-ins. Up until 2010, an estimated two million workers had actively engaged in protests and strikes throughout the country (Beinin 2010; Beinin and Duboc 2013).

From 2008 onward, sit-ins were more frequently staged in front of the parliament, with several groups often present at the same time, seated right next to one another. The first protest near the assembly on Majlis al-sha'b Street was carried out by real estate tax collectors on Husayn Hijazi Street in front of the council of ministers' building (Bishara 2018, 66). Other workers quickly came to realize just how much media attention they could attract by staging protests in the government district in the middle of Cairo, which was in close proximity to television and newspaper offices.

Soon, workers who lived hours away from the capital started to come to the parliamentary building in downtown Cairo to raise their demands (Weipert-Fenner 2013b). Through these actions, parts of the Egyptian populace were coming into closer contact with their parliament, voicing their claims in front of the representatives of the people. But what did this mean for the Mubarak regime? Did the assembly serve as a "safety-valve" that allowed people to let off steam, a function often ascribed to elections in authoritarian regimes (Brownlee 2007, 8; Buehler 2013)? Would it really be possible to ignore the protests completely? Or would the protests be channeled into parliament and influence political decisions in order to appease the public, as Jennifer Gandhi has argued (2008, xviii)? In this book, I will show that this balancing function does not occur automatically but rather greatly depends on the actors in parliament and how they actually react to public claims. Generally speaking, this means that members of parliament possess agency. More specifically, one could observe that, in Egypt over the centuries, a low degree of responsiveness to widely shared norms about socioeconomic issues has been a frequent reality and has led to political crises time and again. In our present case, the lack of parliamentary responsiveness owed to an incremental power shift within the ruling elite.

(2) Parliament and power relations. Politics in Egypt in the 2000s were marked by the rise of a group of private business elites around Gamal Mubarak, one of the sons of President Husni Mubarak. They first assumed powerful positions in the newly created policies secretariat of the ruling National Democratic Party (NDP), which was tasked with setting up the NDP's future policies (el Tarouty 2015). In the cabinet of Prime Minister Ahmad Nazif, they then took over powerful positions in the government while also expanding their influence in the People's Assembly, with their most visible figure, Ahmad 'Izz, becoming head of the budget and planning committee. These business elites accelerated the aforementioned restructuring of the Egyptian economy toward liberalization, privatization, and the state's withdrawal from welfare functions. What was officially called a transformation from a state-led economy to a free market economy in reality developed into a system of crony capitalism. Private

businessmen with close ties to the regime profited from the privatization of state-owned companies either by retaining control of the profitable businesses and establishing cartels to ensure their position or by reselling the companies at a much higher price than they had originally paid to the state. Some individuals became publicly visible through their political careers and turned into symbols of the generational change that appeared to be paving the way for the time after Husni Mubarak's rule, with his son Gamal as the most likely successor.

While most international attention at the time focused on the new "technocratic," "modern" elite, the issue most often debated in the national media was the relation between the new and the old guard of the ruling party. The conflict lines proved even more complex than the generational aspects, including different approaches to organizing support for the party along with rivalries and conflicts within the respective groups (Arafat 2009; Stacher 2012, 106). The general question at hand, however, was how the rise of a new group that was pushing through neoliberal reforms that suited their world view and interests would affect other influential groups or individuals whose power was built upon a strong state as a welfare provider. Would the old elites simply abandon their positions? This development coincided with a disintegration of party cohesion, most clearly visible in the phenomenon of the "NDPendent" assembly members—a large portion of the parliamentary bloc from the NDP comprised of parliamentarians who had run as independent candidates despite belonging to the NDP (Koehler 2008). Their electoral success proved that they no longer relied on the party to access parliament. At the same time, obtaining a parliamentary seat, especially among urban constituencies, increasingly depended on a candidate's financial resources for outright vote buying, financing the party headquarters, or directly funding the president's electoral campaign (Blaydes 2011; el Tarouty 2015). While attention was turned toward internal party developments (Brownlee 2007), the repercussions for parliament were overlooked.

For this book, I closely analyzed parliamentary activities between 2005 and 2010 on the basis of parliamentary minutes. Although the actual decision-making process undoubtedly happened behind the scenes, this analysis of the parliament's activities allowed me to observe which groups opted for what policies in the beginning, as well as which positions won out in the end. Through this lens, the rifts within the NDP became clearly visible. Besides exhibiting no willingness to compromise politically, the businessmen also started to justify their actions less and less. This is all the more remarkable considering that, at the same time, the analysis revealed that overall pressure was being exerted on members to justify even the most arbitrary decisions made by the ruling party. In this sense, the new elites were also violating procedural norms, which negatively affected perceptions of their political identity and, ultimately, parliament as a whole. This observation helps to explain why the prominent businessmen were the first to be removed from the political stage after the ouster of Mubarak. This is just one example of how exercising power in a completely arbitrary manner can come at a high cost and how parliamentary activities can provide insights into the mutual dependencies that exist among political actors, changing power relations and actual belief in their legitimacy.

Generally speaking, all of these observations concerning the parliament reveal two things that have been underestimated in previous research. First, they show that the institution itself, along with its relation to the public and to the executive, is dynamic and subject to change. Further, although they all point to internal conflicts and struggles that have the potential to further destabilize the regime, they also hold the possibility that parliament could become the place of mediation between the different sides. Although there is no simple causal relationship between the existence of parliament and regime stabilization, as the literature on authoritarian resilience has argued, neither is there a causal relationship between parliament and regime *de*stabilization, as assumed in the literature inspired by the transitions that took place under the "third wave" of democratization (Huntington 1991) based on the idea of the democratic nature of parliament (Baaklini, Denoeux, and Springborg 1999). In contrast, I show that there are several possible trajectories that depend on how actors behave and interact in relation to the institution of parliament. All of these observations do move away from explaining why political institutions and legislatures exist in the first place, which has been the general tendency in comparative political studies on authoritarian regimes since the 1980s. These studies often assume that institutions work according to the logic they were designed for by the ruling elite—ensuring regime stability—and the dictator could simply dissolve the institution if it no longer fulfilled its desired function. I tend to agree with Lagacé and Gandhi, who state that there is a gap in our knowledge about how institutions actually operate, and that we need new, creative approaches for how to study and understand institutions in authoritarian regimes (2015, 286–89). I present my suggestion for a new approach to understanding the parliament in an autocracy in the next section.

Introducing the Autocratic Parliament

This book identifies five characteristics of autocratic parliaments across various authoritarian regime subtypes:

1. Autocratic parliaments work according to the logic of an authoritarian regime (and should therefore not be regarded as a dysfunctional democratic institution).
2. Autocratic parliaments can grow stronger within a given political system (either incrementally, driven by internal processes, or quickly in the case where rights are granted by the executive).
3. Autocratic parliaments can become contentious when norms regarding policies, political actors, and institutions are violated on a large scale or at a fast pace. These fields of legitimacy beliefs are interconnected, meaning that negative evaluations in one field can spill over to others. (Most important, a parliament can turn against the executive when parliamentary rights are withdrawn or when socioeconomic norms are violated.)
4. Institutional as well as interinstitutional actions are shaped by asymmetric power distribution but never by a power monopoly held by one side. They involve constant bargaining processes based on power assessments of actors and institutions (which can be incorrect or have unintended consequences).
5. Low parliamentary responsiveness to broadly shared norms can contribute to a regime crisis.

When speaking of the parliament in an authoritarian regime, I opt for a new term, "autocratic parliament," to identify these recurrent characteristics rather than relying on terms generally found in academic literature, such as "non-democratic" legislatures. My aim here is to establish a concept of autocratic parliaments as a genuine part of autocratic regimes and to escape the trap of using only democracy as a benchmark for analyzing such regimes, as doing so leads to the tendency of highlighting only the aspects that a legislature under an autocracy has failed to fulfill. Moreover, this reliance on the term "non-democratic" brings with it the danger of comparing an idealized version of democracy with the real-world political practices in an autocracy. Parliamentarians in democracies are, for example, assumed to represent the people because they are elected in free and fair elections. Parliamentarians in autocracies, by contrast, are generally seen as manipulators of elections, or elected by a specific support group that they must satisfy by offering services and resources in return. In Egypt, a member of parliament used to be pejoratively referred to as *na'ib al-khidmat*—a deputy of services. However, MPs in democracies also lobby for services, jobs, and resources for their electorate, which, as Loewenberg describes, creates a tension with the widespread ideal of the "gentleman" (and "lady," one should add) who operates independent of interests and parties and is only guided by a "sense of general welfare" (Loewenberg 2016, 13).

In fact, parliaments in autocracies, surprisingly, share similar "image problems" with their democratic counterparts. Whether they serve any purpose at all is continually questioned in both regime types. Since the late nineteenth century, scholars have often proclaimed that the power of legislatures was in decline (Martin, Saalfeld, and Strøm 2014, 3). This was understood to have various causes: the rise of political parties (early twentieth century), the welfare state and its powerful executive apparatus (1950s–1960s), neocorporatist arrangements between government and business (1970s), and Europeanization or globalization (1990s–2000s). As such, when considering specific practices and paradoxes, the line between democracies and autocracies becomes blurred at times. In this sense, the autocratic parliament is not the "complete other" in relation to its democratic counterpart, but rather is imbued with its own roles and dynamics on the basis of its constitutive relations, which are autocratic. Although the logic of authoritarian elections and appointments differs from that of democracies, as I will explicate in detail, varying degrees of liberties and freedoms—especially in regard to freedom of assembly and speech—do, of course, affect the public and its relations with the parliament (see Linz's "limited pluralism" [1975, 264]). On the other hand, one finds an executive and core elite with final decision-making power and control over the security apparatus. While power is always relational and never absolute, constitutive relations are generally characterized by power asymmetries in favor of the executive. The theoretical approach for understanding the autocratic parliament proposed here offers a way to systematically study how the characteristics of a regime affect political practices. While taking into account power asymmetries in autocracies, it leaves space for the agency of actors beyond the core elite. At the same time, the approach opens the door for further studies that may compare the practices of democratic and autocratic parliaments to further explore differences among the regimes, in spite of observed similarities.

I also avoid referring to the parliament as a "nominally democratic" institution, which is used interchangeably with the adjective "non-democratic" (e.g., Gandhi 2008; Schedler 2009). The term "nominally democratic" links an institution to a specific function one assumes it should fulfill, namely, creating a democratic façade to enhance regime legitimacy. Although I will argue that the logic of the autocratic parliament historically predates the claim of democratic representation, this is not to say that ruling elites refrain from using the parliament for such purposes. As the reference to "democracy" or "the sovereignty of the people" is part of almost all constitutions in the world today, authoritarian elites may intend to use the parliament to bolster their legitimacy in the eyes of both international and national audiences. I will show that this claim of legitimacy is just one of many within the political discourse, and it can come under direct attack when it clashes with practices resulting from authoritarian regime logic. As I intend to show, parliaments within autocratic regimes are more than merely a democratic fig leaf.

Finally, I consciously use the term "parliament" instead of "legislature," though they are often applied synonymously. The latter has even developed into an overarching term, and the relevant scholarship is called "legislative studies," whereas "parliament" is taken to be one example of a local name for a legislature (Martin, Saalfeld, and Strøm 2014, 1). The basic definition of legislature ("a body created to approve measures that will form the law of the land" [Norton 2013, 1]) indicates that lawmaking is a central function of legislatures, but whether legislatures play this role in autocracies is heavily disputed. Do these institutions merely serve a "rubber-stamp" function while legislation is de facto the prerogative of the executive? How much decision-making power these institutions have is a major topic of research, and the question remains far from being definitely answered. In contrast, the term "parliament" highlights the function of deliberation and debate, which is historically older than its lawmaking function (Loewenberg 2007, 57). The origins of today's democratic parliaments were the feudal assemblies of medieval, predemocratic Europe, where influential individuals representing social classes or local constituencies had the opportunity to bargain with the monarch, who in turn sought to secure access to their money and military conscripts (Loewenberg 2016, 8). As I will later show, this fundamental logic of parliament as a representative, consultative assembly also applies to the autocratic parliament of Egypt from the nineteenth century until today. In Egypt, legislative powers, as well as other rights of control that constrain the executive, have repeatedly been developed and subsequently withdrawn. As such, if we seek to understand how parliament works, we must start by analyzing what parliamentarians do; namely, talk—to the executive as representatives of the people or of particular constituencies.

The specific nature of parliament as such lies in its being an *intermediary institution* between the represented and the executive. This is also relevant for authoritarian regimes, as revealed by literature on co-optation and authoritarian elections, albeit without further elaborating on the consequences for parliament. The specific importance of parliament becomes evident when we take full account of who obtains a seat and how, and what consequence this has for the functioning of the parliament. Scholars of authoritarian regimes usually refer to the concept of co-optation when explaining how institutions give incentives to powerful groups for their cooperation with the regime. One type of incentive is rent distribution. In the case of parliament, while such rents do not appear to be of a financial nature at first sight, they do entail privileges that may pay off monetarily, including preferential access to state tenders, contact with decision-making incumbents, and legal immunity (Albrecht and Schlumberger 2004, 383). Studies dealing with co-optation beyond the mere exchange of loyalty and benefits have considered more complex processes of power sharing in parliament. They view co-optation from the perspective of how it further bolsters regime stability. The co-opted may actually exert an influence on the decision-making process itself; as decisions by the assembly must be supported by the majority, policy proposals would have to be moderate—and thus easier to implement—leading, in turn, to improved decisions by the core elite (Wintrobe 2007, 379). Giving in to the demands of parliamentarians is also thought to improve the investment climate in the country by taming the arbitrary power of the dictator and lending more credibility to his or her commitment to respecting property rights. It is also of interest to the dictator that this potential increase in investments might have a positive effect on overall economic development: when there is more money in the country, there is more for the dictator to take (Wright 2008, 325).

As Lagacé and Gandhi (2015) point out, however, if institutions are actually supposed to have the effects mentioned here—because they truly share in the decision-making process—then this also comes at a considerable risk. What if conflicting interests arise among the opposition parties within the assembly and, even more important, within the ruling party? What if the outcomes of decision making are not moderate policies but rather favor for one political position at the expense of others? And one might wonder if and how active opposition or street protests (or both) could affect ongoing conflicts within the ruling elite. What kind of impact could these conflicts have on institutional behavior and interinstitutional relations?

We gain an even more complex understanding of co-optation when looking at the ways in which the actual co-optation processes take place. In the past decade, studies on the phenomenon of "electoral" (Schedler 2006) or "competitive" (Levitsky and Way 2002) authoritarianism have shown how elections, as an institution, function based on authoritarian regime logic and ensure that "the right actors" are integrated into the political system. Elections can be regarded as a tool for managing broader circles of elites by leaving space for competition: the elites who are best able to mobilize voters are the most powerful actors, and their support and loyalty are more vital to secure through a legislative seat. For the core elite, elections therefore serve as a source of information about the current distribution of power among elite groups (Magaloni 2006, Kechavarzian 2009). They also "outsource" the problem of inclusion and exclusion in terms of resource distribution: by creating a market-like situation, core elites escape being blamed by those who are excluded (Blaydes 2011).

The basic aim of ruling elites is to ensure that the actors who gain access to parliament are worthy of the benefits tied to co-optation. Often, electoral manipulation ensures that the preselected candidates will ultimately win. It can also be understood as a more consensual process of deliberation taking place among an influential group of actors—be they businessmen, members of the military, state employees, trade unionists, or powerful families and clans (e.g., Arafat 2009; Chen 2015, 242). They choose an individual whom they perceive to be most suitable for representing the respective group's interests, which can include rents and services directed to a specific locality or group, or influence on political decision making in favor of these interests. Selected candidates can attain power through formal means, such as campaigning in an election, or informal ones, such as buying votes, providing collective goods, or rallying support among different elite groups (Blaydes 2011). The means available depend on the sort of capital the candidate can mobilize. Economic capital enables a candidate to buy votes directly in exchange for money, food, or other material resources distributed on or shortly before election day. Social capital provides support among certain groups (such as families and clans) and can also raise prospects for future bargains made by parliamentarians in the interest of the groups that selected the candidate.

A closer look at these methods highlights the fact that there are specific *expectations* that members of parliament would have to meet by making use of the agency granted to them through their parliamentary seats. These expectations might be based on individual cost-benefit calculations in terms of recouping the money spent for vote buying, but they could also encompass the needs of the electoral college and the local or functional group interests they represent. Whether these expectations are met has an important impact on relationships with support groups that need to be observed over time. Temporality in general is a relevant factor in research on clientelism and patronage—a conceptual debate that has not yet been sufficiently integrated into the study of legislatures in autocracies.[2] Such studies reveal that *iteration* is an important characteristic of patronage and clientelist relations, one that should also inform the understanding of the autocratic parliament. These relations persist over some period of time, which means that loyalty, along with an exchange of benefits, rests on trust that one will receive something in return at a future date (Hicken 2011, 292). Trust can, however, be lost if expectations are not met within an anticipated timeframe. Even a client, though in a less powerful position, can find alternative patrons or a means to pressure a patron to fulfill their side of the deal. This means that there is a reciprocal relationship between the patron (as a member of parliament) and the client (a member of the support group or inhabitant of the constituency). The same holds true when one regards the member of parliament as a broker: they take the resources offered through the parliamentary seat from the core elite and, in exchange, provide the regime with their loyalty and a relevant base of support. Again, we find a reciprocal relationship marked by mutual dependency in spite of obvious power asymmetries. This relationship is monitored by both sides over time according to expectations in terms of returns. If negative assessments prevail in the long run, the relationship as such may be dissolved or replaced. If a considerable number of intermediaries break off their relationship with the core elite and withdraw their loyalty, this can result in a crisis or even the breakdown of the regime.[3]

To establish a new theoretical approach to studying parliament in autocracies, it is crucial to take these dependencies created by the election and selection of parliamentarians seriously. These dependencies help

2. Some treat these terms as synonyms while others regard patronage as a subtype of clientelism tied to either the distribution of public sector jobs or the patron being a public office holder (Hicken 2011, 295).

3. For a more detailed discussion of this conceptual approach to clientelism and patronage, see Ruiz de Elvira, Schwarz, and Weipert-Fenner (2018).

to explain why the legislature and parliamentarians matter in a political regime whose power is concentrated with the core elite, or rather, with the head of state and the head of state's closest allies. The short answer is that parliament matters because its members are—in potentially varying ways—relevant to the core elite and thus belong to the circles of the ruling elite (Perthes 2004). In a multiparty system, this applies to parliamentarians from the ruling party;[4] in all cases, parliamentarians grant their loyalty to the core elite in exchange for services or specific policies that promote either their personal interests or those of the group they represent. To keep the groups and individuals tied to the regime, the distribution of goods, services, and privileges, as well as general political decisions, need to be balanced among the integrated actors. This process is continuously ongoing and involves what Lagacé and Gandhi (2015) call the trade-off that autocratic institutions require. In contrast, I place greater emphasis on the agency that the co-opted actors possess: the core elite has to consider what the specific actors believe is right or wrong—or to live with their discontent, which might threaten compliant or cooperative behavior and even lead to contestation in the long run. This means that, in a systematic analysis, an autocratic parliament should be studied as the center of a web of relations: when one string moves, the whole web quivers. Figure 1 depicts this web: the dotted arrows show that all of the elements are interconnected, whereas the five solid arrows represent the relationships that constitute autocratic parliaments.

All arrows point in two directions, signifying that the relations are mutually shaped. Although this is likely self-evident with regard to the relationships that the parliament has with other institutions or the public, it does require more explanation in terms of what the arrow between parliament and parliamentarians indicates. How I conceptualize the relationship between institutions and actors is explicated in the next section,

---

4. The integration of the opposition and the taming effect explained by Ellen Lust-Okar (2005) are valid points and play a role, yet I show that the opposition is not constitutive for the autocratic parliament, as one can find similar patterns of parliamentary development without oppositional parliamentarians.

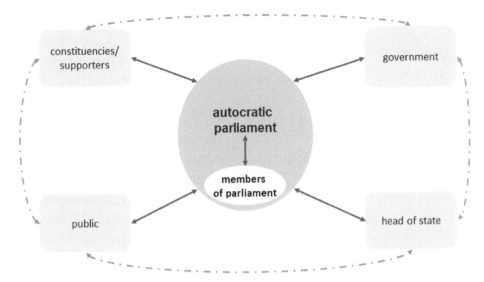

1. The constitutive relations of autocratic parliaments.

where I lay out the type of neoinstitutionalism that inspires my theoretical approach to the autocratic parliament.

Theoretical Background: What Type of Neoinstitutionalism Is the Best Fit?

The entire discussion and critical debate surrounding different forms of neoinstitutionalism—rational choice institutionalism, sociological institutionalism, and historical institutionalism (Hall and Taylor 1996), along with a recent suggestion of a fourth type called constructivist or discursive institutionalism (Bell 2011; Schmidt 2010, 2012)—has produced a substantial amount of literature.[5] However, most studies on authoritarian institutions have made use of rational choice institutionalism, as Schuler and Malesky's (2014) overview of the research about legislatures in autocracies

5. Explicitly constructivist institutionalists are Blyth (2002), Hay (2004), and Schmidt (2010). In contrast to Bell (2011), I see Vivien Schmidt's (2010) discursive institutionalism, especially her argument of how well it fits with historical institutionalism, as fairly similar to what I understand of constructivist historical institutionalism.

demonstrates. Rational choice institutionalists assume institutions to be a solution to a collective action problem brought about by the relevant actors. These actors agree on a set of rules that constrain their behavior and obey them as long as the result of coordination serves their interests (North 1990). Applied to parliaments in an autocracy, the relevant actors that define the institution are seen to solely exist among the core elite. Their overall interest, and the function that the institution has to fulfill, is regime stabilization. The institution in itself is regarded as a source of equilibrium (e.g., Magaloni 2006; Gandhi and Przeworski 2007): change either entails the breakdown of equilibrium or a shift to another equilibrium. As I will demonstrate, such logic is meaningful, especially at the moment when the institution is newly introduced into a political system. Yet it cannot be used to explain the ensuing institutional developments and dynamics and how they matter to the regime as a whole.

The second approach, sociological institutionalism, was developed in the context of organization theory. By providing the actors with cognitive scripts and models, the institutions were regarded as influencing the scope of action and even the identity of the actors. The scripts or templates that tend to be implicit in the institution help the actor define a situation and offer ways to deal with it (March and Olsen 1984). That does not exclude the possibility that actors might still behave strategically to attain their goals, as rational choice institutionalists suggested. Sociological institutionalism just raises the awareness that preferences, rationality, and other concepts exist only in specific situations and cannot be defined without taking into account the cultural and social framing. In addition, the actor-institution relation becomes interactive, in that scripts, like all social conventions, need to be reinforced by actors referring to them and making use of them (Hall and Taylor 1996, 946–50).

Under the umbrella of the third influential type of neoinstitutionalism, historical institutionalism, one can find two different approaches. The first is rational choice–oriented historical institutionalism (Pierson 2000; Mahoney 2000; Katznelson and Weingast 2005; for authoritarian regimes, see Brownlee 2007), which deals with history through the concepts of path dependency and critical junctures: as soon as a certain path is chosen, the actors are locked in and must modify their strategies accordingly. Only during moments of crisis does agency come back in, and changes to or of institutions are made. Over time, these concepts were gradually developed and opened up to different forms of change, first induced exogenously (Streeck and Thelen 2005) and then endogenously (Mahoney and Thelen 2010).

The second approach, which I would characterize as a constructivist variant of historical institutionalism (first outlined by Thelen, Steinmo and Longstreth in 1992), pays greater attention to the complexity of the relations among context, institution, and actors, and, most important, the potential for conflicts. Various institutional arrangements can simultaneously make up a polity; institutions are thus interdependent, and change within one of them will affect others (Thelen 1999, 382–83). In addition, the most powerful actors are not the only ones who matter in politics; "losers" are also influential in political conflicts. They do not just disappear, leaving the new institution to those who established it. Instead, even as they adapt to the new situation, they stick to their own goals, either waiting for their chance to alter the rules of the game or actively subverting the new order from inside or outside the institution (Thelen 1999, 385).

Historical institutionalists give a special emphasis to power asymmetries in institutions, distancing themselves from rational choice theorists, who tend to see individuals as similar units. This also distinguishes them from sociological institutionalists, who refer to social templates, models, and scripts, and may thereby overlook the role of individual and group behavior, which is interest driven, potentially contentious, but also creative. Behavior, therefore, might strengthen, weaken, repeat, or invent institutional arrangements, as an intended or unintended consequence. Instead of focusing on only a single outcome of an institution (stabilization or destabilization of the regime), institutional and interinstitutional relations can bring about different patterns of conflicts and frictions, as well as cooperation (Thelen 1999, 382–83).

The important role actors play in fighting over which norms and scripts are seen as appropriate was further developed by constructivist institutionalism. It regards actors as reflexive with regard to themselves, their norms, their ideas, and the existing institutions (Schmidt 2010). It also entails an important role that actors assume when fighting about which norms and scripts are to be deemed appropriate: they shape an understanding of culture as not merely one coherent set of rules and norms but rather as a pool of such factors that includes contradictory norms, values, symbols, and beliefs. Moreover, politics are characterized by the interpretation of the actors and their negotiations along with the struggle for the "right" set of institutions (March and Olsen 1989; Katzenstein 1996). This approach offers us a more refined understanding as to why actors follow the scripts and the "logic of appropriateness" (March and Olsen 1989, 160–62): this adherence is not the automatic result of cultural adherence but develops in accordance with their current beliefs about what is right or wrong, legitimate or illegitimate.

To sum up, for my study of the autocratic parliament, I make use of the constructivist approach within the framework of historical institutionalism, as it helps to "unpack the institutional black box" and to reveal how institutions not only constrain behavior but also arise from the behavior of strategic actors (Bell 2011, 892), as well as how they constrain and, at the same time, empower actors. I situate my understanding of constructivist historical institutionalism within a larger framework of constructivist comparative politics that generally understands the relation between agents and structures to be dialectic (Bell 2011), codetermined, or mutually constituted (Wendt 1987, 339). Constructivism stresses that these relations are intersubjectively constructed, which shifts the methodological approach to the *reconstruction of these perceptions* while still leaving room to theorize about how such relations shape politics. Constructivism is therefore regarded as "the true middle ground between rationalist and relativist interpretative approaches" (Adler 1997, 322). Daniel Green lays out the research agenda as follows: "The goal of investigation is causal *and* constitutive explanation *and* understanding, through thick description and analytic dissection of processes, and that CCP [constructivist comparative politics] should be sensitive to the possibility of more generalizable conclusions, beyond the specificities of case studies" (Green 2002, 47).

In my application of constructivist comparative politics, I use the constitutive explanation for autocratic parliaments shown in figure 1 based on the "set of relationships with other actors that define a social kind as such"

(Wendt 1998, 113). In the study of Egypt's 150 years of parliamentary history, I further develop this theoretical approach as I compare formal rights to actual practices and observe how the social meaning of parliament changed through actions and interactions. It is important to note that this study is not a return to the "old institutionalism" that explained parliaments by way of their historical development or the ideas and perceptions forwarded by actors as such (Rhodes 2006, 91). Nor is my interpretive analysis of parliamentary speeches and interaction—in the form of parliamentary minutes—a return to the behaviorism of the 1950s and 1960s, which studies individual parliamentarians and their attitudes alone (Martin, Saalfeld and Strøm 2014, 9). It is in the interactions between actors and structures that I see the point of entry for identifying and explaining characteristics of the autocratic parliament. Through a comparison of different authoritarian regime subtypes, I identify causal mechanisms underlying the development of mutually shaped relationships of parliament with the executive and the public.

A systematic study of parliamentary actions also provides an opportunity to observe incremental institutional changes and the agency possessed by the parliament as an institution. With regard to the constitutive relations of parliament, three fields of agency become visible. The first is discursive power, which emerges when parliamentarians claim to represent the public or a specific support group or channel public discontent into the political system. The second relates to the executive, namely, different means of holding the government to account and an expansion of the areas in which the consultation, approval, or legislative participation of the parliament is needed—most notably for budgetary and tax matters. The final field pertains to the development of the internal structure, rules, and practices of parliament, with regard to the time and duration of parliamentary sessions, committee structures, and internal procedures.

All of these elements contain power; however, actors need to put potential power into practice. Speeches and actions by individuals and groups in the assembly can have an impact in different ways: parliamentarians can criticize or justify governmental policies, they can form alliances within the assembly or with ministries, they can reach out to the public through the media or in direct cooperation with civil society actors, and they may use the rights and liberties that parliamentary membership grants them more frequently or creatively. They may do this for their individual interests or for group interests, or they may be responsive to the needs of the broader public. The members of the ruling elite and opposition members of parliament are at liberty to use these potential actions. Furthermore, the parliamentarians all develop their behavior based on past experience. As such, to explain the autocratic parliament it is necessary to study *how the potentialities of the autocratic parliament are put into practice* by actors. This includes a consideration of frictions and conflict among actors, along with miscalculations and unintended consequences.

The key to understanding these processes lies in the social meaning that actors attribute to policies, polities, institutional rules, the identities of other actors, and relations with the public. The exploration of social meaning is how the theoretical approach closely connects to a concise, empirically grounded concept of legitimacy. Following Weber (2010), I take legitimacy from the perspective of the belief in legitimacy (*Legitimitätsglaube*). The question of assessing legitimacy beliefs is, however, especially difficult in autocracies that suffer from a lack of democratic legitimacy (in terms of input or participatory legitimacy) and for which credible surveys are rare and freedom of speech is never fully granted. Compliance is not necessarily a sign of a regime's legitimacy: fear or apathy may well have the same result (Nullmeier and Nonhoff 2010). At the same time, contention does not have to mean that a legitimacy crisis has evolved, but it must be assessed based on the respective protest culture. Nullmeier and Nonhoff suggest conceptualizing legitimacy as the result of an evaluation process between legitimacy claims and legitimacy beliefs, framed as criticism or justification in regard to the political system as a whole. The problem that arises, however, is how to assess opinions of the system when this topic is generally taboo in most autocracies.

In order to overcome this issue, at least partially, I suggest starting from criticisms and justifications that can be encountered on the ground—in this case, in the autocratic parliament. In systematizing these evaluative beliefs, I differentiate among policies, political actors and institutions. One can identify norms on every level, and these are most commonly defined as "shared expectations about appropriate behavior held by a community of actors"

(Finnemore 1996, 22).[6] In this regard, norms, being evaluative beliefs, serve as the benchmark of appropriateness for the categories mentioned above. While a gap between claims and beliefs arises when actors disagree about the validity of a norm, actors can also differ in their interpretation of a norm and in their assessment of the extent to which a specific norm has actually been implemented (Reus-Smit 2007). Applying this concept of legitimacy to the autocratic parliament, it becomes clear why action within the assembly is important for scholars as well as for the authoritarian regime. Parliamentary speeches usually argue in favor of or against a particular issue, meaning that parliamentary discourse entails evaluations. The speeches are public and therefore relate to what the parliamentarians believe to be right for their group of supporters, constituency, or wider public. They relate to policies as well as to other institutions, such as the government. The parliament also directly interacts with the cabinet when parliamentary tools such as interpellations or questions are used. And, of course, interaction between parliamentarians reveals the composition of their own identities as well as that of their peers. When we compare these different actions and interactions, we can start to identify the degree and development of discord or unity among different groups. The topics, depth, and manner of criticism will certainly vary from case to case (Schuler and Malesky 2014); yet authoritarian regimes generally allow for some degree of criticism over time, as long as it does not pertain to the head of state or the question of the regime in itself.[7] Parliaments deal with central questions about topics such as social justice or the right economic order. As I will demonstrate, the substance of these ideas matters (Schmidt 2010), even within authoritarian regimes.

It is important to note that legitimacy beliefs in parliament first and foremost reflect the opinions held by parts of a broader coalition of the ruling elite. According to the authoritarian logic of representation, however, parliamentarians might also reflect the normative beliefs of their specific

6. Jepperson, Wendt, and Katzenstein similarly define norms as "collective expectations about proper behavior for a given entity" (1996, 54).

7. Even the authoritarian regime in Iraq under Saddam Husayn, usually treated as an extremely repressive dictatorship, allowed for some public criticism (Rohde 2010).

electorate and even of the public in general. In cases of oppositional members in the assembly, the spectrum of potentially conflicting opinions is broadened. This means that one should not regard legitimacy claims and beliefs raised in parliament as an assessment of regime legitimacy among the whole populace. Nor is parliament a representative sample of all relevant elite groups, as some groups might not play a central role in parliament at a given point in time, such as the army during the last years under Mubarak. Legitimacy claims and beliefs voiced in an autocratic parliament are representative of the networks that the parliamentarians stand for; they provide insights into the loyalty of the MPs who are relevant for the ruling elite and therefore constitute a crucial part of regime stability.

Identifying who holds which aims in parliament also allows us to investigate *the relational perspective of power*; that is, to observe power relations in their current constellation and further development. Although decision making mostly happens behind closed doors,[8] one can investigate the power distribution among different elite groups, especially in times of conflict, by comparing which group pursues what—and who ultimately wins the vote. Through this comparison, combined with the analysis of existent legitimacy claims and beliefs, one can ascertain whether the most influential parliamentarians are generally perceived as legitimate, if their decisions get approved, and how negative evaluations affect institutional legitimacy. If we identify negative evaluations of several dimensions of legitimacy, this may indicate that a general legitimacy crisis has evolved. In this sense, parliament is not only an actor but also an indicator of change in terms of power and legitimacy in an authoritarian regime.

Research Design and Methods

To further develop this model of autocratic parliaments and identify common patterns and trajectories, this book examines 150 years of parliamentary life in Egypt. This does not constitute a single case study but rather a

---

8. This lack of transparency is also found in democracies, for which it constitutes a greater challenge to the normative ideal (Loewenberg 2016).

diachronic comparative case study of parliamentary developments across different subtypes of authoritarian regimes,[9] first, in a monarchy (1866–1952) and in a republic (1952–2011). We uncover a trajectory that started out as a monarchy, shifted to a monarchy under British occupation, and finally became a constitutional monarchy (semi-independent from the British). Since the establishment of a republic, Egypt first had a single-party presidential system and then a semipresidential multiparty system. One could also argue that Egypt developed from a system of military rule (1950s) to a limited multiparty regime from the 1980s on. The Egyptian case also offers great potential for comparison, for example, regarding the party system: a one-party system (1956–76) versus a limited multiparty regime (1923–52; 1976–2011) versus a nonpartisan system (1866–1923).[10] Egypt exhibits long periods of stable (though never stagnant) authoritarian rule with incremental changes and sudden ruptures: mass uprisings (1919, 2011), a military coup (1952) and external intervention (1882). Table 1 provides an overview of all the regime subtypes, political systems, and parliamentary bodies from 1866 until today.

This diversity of institutional settings presents us with an opportunity to develop the concept of the autocratic parliament by applying a systematic analysis of the parliament's constitutive relationships within different political systems and their development during these historical stages, along with the opportunity to identify patterns of political dynamics across systems and regime subtypes.[11] Furthermore, I should emphasize

9. There are numerous typologies of authoritarian subtypes (for an overview, see Kailitz 2009). I use Hadenius and Teorell (2007), who build on the prominent typology of Geddes (1999). For a systematic overview of possible comparative research designs regarding regime types and subtypes, see Schedler (2013, 338).

10. Parties were established in the late nineteenth century but were not part of the political system until formal independence in 1923.

11. Covering this wide time span was only possible due to the wealth of literature about Egypt that has always been at the core of Middle East studies on account of its regional importance. Extensive research for every period was available, including data and observations on the parliament, its members, and their relations to the public and

Table 1

Overview of Regime Subtypes, Political Systems, and Parliamentary Bodies (1866–present)

Period	1866–82	1882–1923	1923–52	1953–2010	2011–today
Regime subtype	Monarchy	Monarchy under British occupation; protectorate (formally called sultanate, 1915–22)	Constitutional monarchy	Republic	Republic
Head of state	Isma'il (1863–79) Tawfiq (1879–92)	Tawfiq (1879–92) 'Abbas II (1892–1914) Husayn Kamil (1914–17) Fu'ad (1917–36) Informal: Lord Cromer (1883–1907) Eldon Gorst (1907–11) Herbert Kitchener (1911–14)	Fu'ad (1917–36) Faruq (1936–52)	Muhammad Najib (1953–54) Jamal 'Abd al-Nasir (1954–70) Anwar al-Sadat (1970–81) Husni Mubarak (1981–2011)	Supreme Council of the Armed Forces (Feb. 2011–June 2012) Muhammad Mursi (2012–13) 'Abd al-Fattah al-Sisi (since 2014)
Parliamentary system	Unicameral	Bicameral (1882–1912) Unicameral (1913–14)	Bicameral	Unicameral (1956–80) Bicameral (1980–2010)	Bicameral (2012–13), Unicameral (2016–today)
Formal title of parliament	1866–79: Majlis shura al-nuwwab (Consultative Chamber of Deputies) 1879–82: Majlis al-nuwwab (Chamber of Deputies)	1882–1912: Majlis shura al-qawanin (Legislative Council) and al-Jam'iyya al-'umumiyya (General Assembly) 1913–14: Jam'iyya tashrī'iyya (Legislative Assembly)	Majlis al-nuwwab (Chamber of Deputies) and Majlis al-shuyukh (Senate)	1956–71: Majlis al-umma (National Assembly) 1971–2010 Majlis al-sha'b (People's Assembly) 1980–2010: Majlis al-shura (Consultative Council)	2012: Majlis al-sha'b (People's Assembly) and Majlis al-shura (Consultative Council) Since 2016: Majlis al-nuwwab (Chamber of Deputies)

two points about the context for this study. First, the conceptual framework used here is built upon political institutional research, in general, and autocracies, in particular, without limitation to Egypt or the Middle East. Second, Egypt has often been included in cross-regional comparative case studies in authoritarian regime research and is never taken to be an outlier. This book should nevertheless be regarded as an invitation to further develop the concept in future comparative work. Diversity and change over time do not, of course, occur only in the political system but also in regard to "the other side" of the constitutive relations: for example, that which we might call "the public" also underwent transformations, such as through the introduction of a national press at the end of the nineteenth century, regional satellite channels and new independent newspapers during the 1990s, and the internet in the 2000s. From the very beginning, public protests recurrently affected the political system; contentious actors likewise developed in tandem, with labor and peasants becoming more organized (Beinin 2001) and spontaneous riots (recurrently food riots), marches, and demonstrations also occurring (1882, 1919–23, 1930s, 1952, 1970s, 2000s). Parliament's relation to the electorate remained complex, with selection and election mechanisms existing alongside one another; at the same time, strategies for vote rigging and vote buying were also constantly developing whenever new relevant actors appeared (Blaydes 2011). Both the public and the electorates faced periods of fewer or greater political rights and freedom.

To advance a systematic study of parliament in these diverse contexts, chapters 1 and 2 take a bird's-eye perspective of parliamentary development. By analyzing each political system since 1866, I systematically compare the formal rights that parliament had at the moment of institutionalization to how the parliamentarians made use of these rights and interacted with the public and the executive. The constitutive relations of an autocratic parliament illustrated in figure 1 provide the analytical framework. This study of long-term parliamentary development is

---

other political institutions. This was all used to draw conclusions about the concept of the autocratic parliament.

grounded in a comprehensive analysis of secondary literature. The causal mechanisms I identify in regard to the single constitutive relations of parliament serve as the basis for the five general characteristics that have shaped parliamentary development over the centuries.

Chapters 3, 4, and 5 present the results of a microanalysis of parliamentary action during the final five years of Mubarak's rule based on the interpretation of parliamentary debates with the aim of empirically assessing power relations, legitimacy claims, and beliefs. More specifically, I interpreted speeches and the interactions recorded in parliamentary minutes, which proved to be the best material available for accessing parliamentary actions, as I discuss below. The interpretive approach, which is to the best of my knowledge novel to the subject under investigation, had to fulfill the constructivist requirements of rigorous academic research: transparency, systematicity, and reflexivity. Transparency makes it possible for the reader to retrace and comprehend my interpretative steps, which follow a clear and systematic procedure. With regard to reflexivity, researchers must constantly reflect on their own position throughout the interpretative process (Schwartz-Shea and Yanow 2012). This not only applies to the way one deals with the sources under study but also involves the way the researcher has chosen and accessed the sources in the first place. I present a few notes from the field to address this last point.

In Egypt, parliamentary minutes are published in the official gazette (*al-Jarida al-rasmiyya*). In 2010, the first year of my research, all issues of the official gazette of the legislative period under study were available on the official homepage of the parliament. It was possible to save all issues as PDF documents and to use a search engine when looking for specific topics debated in the People's Assembly. During field research conducted in Cairo the same year, I also tried to gain access to the parliamentary archives that contained the official gazette to ensure a second source of access to the minutes in the event that the online archive became unavailable at some point. I went about this through official channels, writing emails to a contact address on the homepage and going to parliament myself to request access. I was handed a request form for permission to enter the archives. In the end, all of these attempts failed. My next course of action was to take the unofficial route, using my *wasta* (connections) from earlier research stays. It took nearly a month before I was granted permission to enter the archives—but, alas, without the possibility of making copies of the gazettes. At the time, this meant that access to the archives would not have allowed me to conduct the comprehensive analysis of minutes that was possible using my collection of electronic files.

I also found videos of parliamentary sessions on YouTube for the time period under study. Although there was no comprehensive collection of all sessions of a legislative period, I nevertheless found it helpful to actually *see* the interactions that I was studying in form of written texts. As I explain in more detail below, I could use this additional source to confirm the accurateness of the minutes. I also conducted interviews with members of parliament, albeit only with a small number. My research on the autocratic parliament started in 2010, and my original plan was to proceed with interviews the following year; however, my research subject was dissolved in 2011. I therefore chose not to make use of what little interview material I had collected.

Before continuing, I should make a few remarks about the advantages as well as the shortcomings of knowledge production based on interviews in this particular field. One great advantage was that the interviews were held at the MPs' offices, granting me access to the parliamentary building that was otherwise completely closed to the public. One fascinating observation was that the power asymmetry between the ruling party and the opposition was also expressed materially in the offices themselves: whereas an NDP deputy had a large office in the main building with luxurious furniture and oil paintings on the wall, the oppositional MPs I met had to make do in a container building with old, cheap desks and chairs. The interviews also allowed for participant observations. When spending time in the cafeteria of the People's Assembly, I could witness informal bargaining processes. One MP openly discussed his patronage potential in providing a job to a close relative (who later, not too gratefully, gave me an account of the corruption going on in his relative's constituency).

Second, the interviews themselves provided insights, albeit in very different ways. Whereas one NDP parliamentarian was completely frank about the clientelist relations that had brought him into the assembly, the next ruling party MP merely provided superficial accounts of the greatness of Egyptian democracy. An extremely active oppositional MP lamented the uselessness of parliamentary work and, just a moment later, handed me his various publications on his parliamentary activities, which he obviously deemed worthy of publishing. My experiences clearly demonstrate that information gained from interviews must be treated with a degree of caution, and not only because the researcher's positionality—in this case, as a European who is most likely prodemocratic—can have a significant impact on how the interviewee answers questions about the role of parliament, for instance.[12] Moreover, the authoritarian nature of the regime does, of course, affect what people say publicly. I could see the difference in 2011, when I again interviewed the NDP parliamentarian who had a positive outlook on Egyptian democracy: his account of what was occurring in the assembly was completely different from the one he had offered in 2010. I therefore chose not to conduct further interviews, as the aim of this study is to understand an authoritarian regime while it is operating, not after its dissolution (including attempts of interviewees to whitewash their own role in the regime).

This is not to say that we should dispense with interviewing MPs: over time, mutual trust can develop, and MPs share deeper insights into actual developments. Yet, from the institutionalist perspective that I work with here, the insights gained from interviews are merely an additional bonus. What really matters are the interactions among the MPs, which reveal their shared and contested norms regarding policies, political identities, and institutions—and not necessarily framed in a way that would be considered appropriate for an external observer. This is why I opted to analyze parliamentary minutes as the record of such interactions. There are, however, certainly several additional steps from the analysis of parliamentary minutes to the identification of norms that deserve scrutiny. The following

12. Because I am a scholar from a democratic country, there are also tensions in regard to research ethics that arise from my attempt to gain access to an actor's view about an authoritarian institution. For further critical reflections on this issue, see Weipert-Fenner (2018).

reflections demonstrate how I interpreted the minutes, the challenges that I faced, and the limitations that may result from this approach.

My approach to interpretation—sequential analysis—is derived from German sociologist Ulrich Oevermann and his methodological approach, which is referred to as objective hermeneutics. The analysis is "always primarily directed at the reconstruction of the latent sense structures or objective meaning structures of those expressive forms in which the object of investigation or the question under study is authentically embodied" (Oevermann 1996, 4; English translation quoted in Reichertz 2004, 290). Although most constructivist scholars, including myself, would disagree that sense or meaning are objective—that is, given and static—and would rather argue that they are socially constructed and thus renegotiated and under constant development, the method still proves helpful. The idea is to analyze individual contributions as choices in relation to a realm of alternatives; understanding these choices uncovers their specific significance. To compare what was done or said in relation to what was *not* done or said is the guiding technique of interpretation in sequential analysis (Oevermann 1991, 2000). Accordingly, the researcher analyzes the text in tiny, successive interpretive steps in regard to three questions: How might the text potentially continue (a question prompting the researcher to consider the realm of possibilities)? How did it continue, and what kinds of potentialities were actualized? And, how does this affect the ways in which the text would continue? Throughout the analysis, the researcher must identify both how actors perceive the specific situation within these relations and how they react to it through their actions or words. Analyzing the sequence of actions or words in parliamentary debates makes the social meaning of policies and polities and the role of parliamentarians visible and makes contestation over these topics comprehensible as well.

Before applying these questions to parliamentary speeches and conducting an interpretative analysis in the narrow sense, I would like to reflect on the two preparatory steps that converted the parliamentary interactions into the actual text I used for the analysis. These steps involved interpretations in a broader sense. The first interpretation of the parliamentary activity occurred when the speeches were written down by the recorder of the minutes. An analysis of these minutes indicated that this translation process from oral language to text is generally accurate. This is evident in the fact that the minutes notate the speeches in Modern Standard Arabic, the typical level of language used for official political statements and in the parliament. At the same time, however, the speaker's words in colloquial Egyptian are also recorded—seemingly as accurately as possible; these words are sometimes highlighted by quotation marks, sometimes in brackets, and sometimes not at all. The minutes are also accurate in cases when parts of a speech are later censored. One can find the original length of the deletion indicated as a line or an entire paragraph consisting a series of periods with a footnote informing the reader that this passage has been deleted with the approval of the People's Assembly. In most cases, one can guess at what the speaker has said because reactions to the censored words often repeat or paraphrase them. Or one can imagine what was said based on the reason given for the deletion. In most of the cases I observed, the censored statements were personal insults, frequently combined with name-calling and shaming. In some rare cases, the parliamentary minutes revealed a tendency to deal with personal attacks in a more relaxed manner.[13] As I discuss in chapters 3, 4, and 5, harsh criticism of policies and institutions was generally allowed. Whether censorship occurred but was not indicated in the text is difficult to prove, as I could not find any videos of these sessions on the internet. However, from the video footage I have seen of original sessions (on YouTube, for example) and from what I have gathered from the minutes, there was hardly any discrepancy between the minute texts and actual sessions in terms of style or vocabulary. Furthermore, each interference by the audience, such as applause or interjections, is indicated in the text. The minutes even indicate whether applause came from all members or only from the opposition. This is all to say that the first translation from an oral statement (and audience reactions to it) to text is relatively accurate, even though information about intonation and gestures is, of course, lost.

13. Egyptian Parliament, Official Gazette, *al-Jarida al-rasmiyya*, 2005, no. 21: 34–35, in comparison to 2009, no. 67: 9, 19, and 2009, no. 68: 14.

The second interpretative step was a translation from the Arabic text of the parliamentary minutes into English. I myself witnessed the extent to which a translation is also an interpretation, as my understanding and feel for the subject improved in the process of translation. I became more familiar with parliamentary procedures and traditions and aware of initial mistakes or misreadings that I have now (hopefully and mostly) eradicated.

From the reexamined English translation, I conducted an interpretative process in the stricter sense, in which I tried to understand the structure of the speeches and identify their social meaning. Here, sequential analysis as a part of objective hermeneutics was helpful for the reconstruction of social meaning, and it offered me the opportunity to expose the interpretation process to new perspectives. By reading the text sentence by sentence, or even phrase by phrase, scholars activate their own expectations by asking themselves how they would expect the text to continue. This question helps to increase the horizon of potentialities and evokes a reflection on the actual text from new angles. Another approach at this stage is to integrate other readers, who are not at all familiar with the context, into the process of interpretation. I did this for only a few speeches, as the process involved is extremely time consuming. Involving new readers definitely proved to be worth the effort, as presenting the text to colleagues generated completely new associations; while some of them struck me as completely odd, it broadened my perspective and helped me reflect on what I knew and what I took for granted.

For each single debate (held in one or several sessions), patterns of arguments were identified among the speakers and placed into relation to each other. Despite my attempt to stay as faithful to the text as possible, I am aware that purely inductive work is unrealistic since one automatically introduces issues or structures that were subconsciously expected or simply assumed. That is why scholars in favor of abduction claim that as hard as one might try to let the text speak for itself, interpreters will invariably be guided in part by what they already know. This is the way people typically manage their lives, and it is also part of academic research (Friedrichs and Kratochwil 2009). There is a great deal to be learned from one's own expectations and assumptions, especially when we are open to the idea that such expectations may not be met. Being surprised is a crucial moment in the interpretive process, as it offers new insights and raises further questions.

Like the translation process, interpretation of social meaning is not static but evolving. After analyzing the first parliamentary debate, the insights I gathered from it began to frame my expectations, thereby limiting my impartiality toward the text; but these insights also generated knowledge about the social meaning of the argument in relation to the broader discourse. For example, after some time, one recognizes whether a particular argument is an exceptional point or whether it is shared by the majority. When reflecting on one's expectations and the way they change, it is important to note that these are also affected by new theoretical insights one has gained or by developments within the context in which the study is embedded. In this case, the mass uprisings in several Middle Eastern and North African countries in 2010 and 2011 altered my view on words and meanings. To cite one example of many: In 2010 I read a parliamentarian's denouncement of the increase in suicides due to the socioeconomic crisis. The passage did not have the same meaning as when I read it again in 2011, following the self-immolation of Muhammad al-Buʿazizi, one of the triggers for the Tunisian revolt. Although interpretation is an infinite process, for pragmatic reasons one must stop the process at some point and provide a coherent interpretation, without forgetting that one is, in fact, just inventing another story of history.

In addition to being aware of their own limitations, scholars must be transparent about these limitations in order to provide the reader with an opportunity to retrace the conclusions of the interpretative process. This makes it necessary for the researcher to give a detailed account of the actual arguments, but it is also necessary to present the results in a readable manner. My compromise is to present the interpretations in a structured way according to the major topics debated in the parliamentary session I analyzed. For example, I give information about the speakers' political affiliations in the overview of lines of conflict and cooperation at the end of most sections. I specify party or organization only when I deemed this to be particularly relevant. This approach allowed me to focus on identifying which norms were employed to evaluate the policies, their relation to the public and other political institutions, and whether the parliamentarians believed these norms to have been implemented. At times, this way of presenting my results required me to employ a slightly narrative style that recapitulated speeches or interactions. If this presentation comes across as a bit lengthy, readers can always skip the reconstructed arguments and jump right into the summarized interpretation at the end of each section and chapter.

Overview of the Book's Structure

My theoretical approach to the study of autocratic parliaments uses Egypt's parliamentary history from 1866 to 2011 to uncover common trajectories and characteristics in parliamentary dynamics. For every political system during this period, I compare formal rights held by the parliament to the actions within parliament, as well as interactions with constituencies, the public, the government, and the head of state (see figure 1).

As monarchies are often thought to operate in a fundamentally different manner from republics, chapter 1 starts with a study of parliamentary dynamics under three different forms: absolute monarchy, monarchy under colonial rule, and constitutional monarchy. This chapter shows how the first national representative body in Egypt developed from a consultative chamber into a legislative body, benefiting from informal European imperialism that undermined the position of the monarch. The monarch granted concessions to wealthy landowners to ensure their support, and these landowners, in turn, slowly expanded parliamentary rights and attempted to safeguard them in a constitution. When the British replaced the monarch and extended their control over Egypt, the former parliamentarians built an alliance with Egyptian army officers with the aim of reinstituting a powerful parliament and Egypt's financial autonomy—safeguarded by a constitution. This alliance led to broader mobilization in the form of the famous 'Urabi Revolt, which was stopped only by the British occupation of Egypt. I demonstrate that even in a monarchy under formal colonial rule, parliamentarians can use their role as intermediaries to bargain and, with time, obtain more rights in terms of setting agendas and budgets, as well as greater legitimacy through elections rather than appointments. After achieving formal independence for Egypt, the popular Wafd Party actively used parliamentary means in a wide range of political fields. Constant interference by Britain and the Egyptian monarch, however, created the impression of an unstable and paralyzed system. Parliamentary performance contributed to this perception when the Wafd Party became less responsive to socioeconomic needs, resulting in mounting frustration and political polarization. This delegitimized the parliament and, ultimately, the entire political order, paving the way for the military coup of the Free Officers in 1952.

My analysis of the terms of office of the three Egyptian presidents (Jamal 'Abd al-Nasir, Anwar al-Sadat, and Husni Mubarak) in chapter 2 shows similar patterns compared with the three cases of monarchic rule. These leaders found it difficult to halt the incremental expansion of parliamentary rights or reverse concessions being granted on the part of the core elite to ensure the goodwill of the parliamentarians. When al-Sadat attempted to do so by dissolving a parliament that was strongly opposed to his economic and foreign policies, opposition parties in the newly elected parliament picked up where the old parliament had left off. 'Abd al-Nasir and Mubarak were more careful in balancing different elite groups, along with their norms, beliefs, and political institutions. The former used parliament as a counterweight to the strong single party, while the latter used an expanded parliamentary role in the economic reform process to disperse responsibility for changes that were likely to cause social discontent. I argue, however, that there were other unintended processes underway that reveal the agency of the autocratic parliament. Under 'Abd al-Nasir, for example, parliamentarians became increasingly critical of the government, especially over bread-and-butter issues. Being dominated by the right wing of the ruling elite, parliament also successfully lobbied for more moderate land reform policies and became active in supervising ministers. Under Mubarak, the opposition learned to use control tools and to report to the public on parliamentary affairs. Additionally, in times of no opposition, parliamentarians used greater involvement in economic legislation to respond to social fears associated with neoliberal reforms, to slow down their implementation, and to combine this legislation with their own agenda setting and a critical stance toward certain ministers. In the 2000s, however, the balance between those who backed and those who opposed these reforms was lost while economic restructuring accelerated.

The ways this imbalance affected parliamentary practices as well as legitimacy claims and beliefs are examined in chapters 3, 4, and 5, where I present an extended application of the constructivist approach for the study of autocracies. The Competition Protection Law (also referred to here as the antitrust law) was selected as a "most likely" case of parliamentary agency for an interpretative analysis of parliamentary debates in the last five years of the Mubarak regime. The law was introduced in 2005 without much criticism, and there were attempts to make it stricter in the middle of the socioeconomic crisis in 2008, although these were blocked, ostensibly by business oligarchs in parliament. This stirred a great deal of public attention, and the Competition Protection Law became the symbol of the private businessmen's control over politics. But the law was also used to hold government accountable in 2009, reflecting the development of interinstitutional relations in times of popular discontent.

Chapter 3 analyzes norms in regard to economic policies and the role of the state, showing that serious struggles can exist over fundamental political questions, such as that of the economic order. The study of the Competition Protection Law, a pillar of Egypt's economic restructuring, was initially passed with great expectations regarding its effect on price decreases, economic development, justice, and equality. In the face of price hikes and shortages of basic goods in 2008, the majority of MPs lost hope and trust in the free market economy and the capability of the state to protect the people from private business interests. Although divergent opinions favoring a weak state and complete freedom of the market had all but disappeared, they still won every vote in the assembly.

Chapter 4 looks into the development of the idea of representation over time and shows how identities—both of the represented as well as the representatives—became politicized. They were increasingly deployed as tools for delegitimization during conflicts that emerged in relation to the economy, the state, and growing social grievances. By 2009, Egypt was no longer seen as having good relations with the foreign countries that had been perceived as potential economic models in 2005; these former role models were later considered a threat because of their foreign companies and investors with mostly exploitative intentions. Within parliament, the identities of members themselves turned into contested issues: fellow parliamentarians tried to revoke the parliamentary rights of those MPs who happened to be well-known private businessmen and accused them of representing only their personal interests. Diminishing legislative responsiveness by the ruling party led the opposition to cast the ruling party's representativeness into doubt, which in turn incited heated debates and justifications. Chapter 4 also shows how parliamentarians reframed their main reference group in times of public discontent: instead of referring to "the consumer," parliamentarians began to speak of "the citizen" or even "the street."

Chapter 5 investigates how the parliamentarians made use of and interpreted parliamentary tools and how they evaluated different political institutions. Occasional comments relating to the regime clearly revealed that none of the members of parliament believed in the democratic façade. In contrast, although the liberal nature of interpellations and other parliamentary tools for holding the government accountable were taken very seriously, they repeatedly clashed with the autocratic nature of the regime. The ruling elite always justified the limitations of oversight rights by citing formal rules. Yet the more arbitrary these interpretations became, the more contention they caused. The same held true for one-sided decision making in favor of the business wing that led to a loss of trust in parliament as a whole. At the same time, my analysis shows how actual practices reflected autocratic regime logic: the president, for example, was presented as an independent institution, even by the opposition. In contrast, members of the ruling party expressed their mistrust toward the prime minister. Furthermore, the normative belief in serving a nonspecified conception of "the people's interests" was used by both opposition and ruling party members to delegitimize an actor or institution. Similar to the results from the processes depicted in chapter 4, this concept of general welfare brings to mind Rousseau's *volonté générale*, as it did not tolerate any form of pluralism, and it regarded the common good as preexisting rather than the result of a political process—a belief that also had a strong impact on post-2011 Egypt.

In chapter 6, I present a broader overall picture of the autocratic parliament and use the events of 2011 and after to draw conclusions about the autocratic parliament in the context of regime destabilization (2010–11) and reinstitutionalization processes (2011–13). To conclude, I present five general characteristics of the autocratic parliament that bring together all the results of the parliamentary analysis in regard to power, legitimacy, contention, stability, and regime type in itself, which are a promising theoretical framework for guiding future comparative studies.

1

Parliamentary Agency under Monarchic Rule, 1866–1952

This chapter investigates the autocratic parliament during different forms of monarchic rule: under absolutist and constitutional monarchy as well as under formal and informal imperial rule. Starting with the emergence of parliamentarianism in 1866, I show how, in less than twenty years in the context of power shifts and legitimacy crises, the Egyptian parliament was able to turn from an initially purely consultative body into a legislative assembly. This period is rich with institutional learning processes, power gambles, and (potentially) unintended consequences in institutional interactions. Although parliament's evolution toward a legislative function came to a halt upon British occupation in 1882, assemblies under British rule slowly but steady expanded their rights, and even succeeded in attaining budgetary prerogatives.

The periods before British occupation (1866–82) and under it (1882–1923) were both characterized by assemblies comprised of rural notables whose wealth was mainly based on large-scale land ownership. They were important taxpayers as well as intermediaries between the monarch and the rural population, and they ensured the implementation of political decisions made in the capital—most importantly tax collection. As such, these early parliaments resemble the origins of parliamentarianism in England in the context of feudalism.[1] Addressing the vast literature on

---

1. For a very brief overview see Payling's "Middle Ages: Parliament and Politics before 1509" (2018), part of the enormous research project *The History of Parliament*.

the history of parliaments in Europe would be beyond the scope of this study.[2] Yet a truly global parliamentary history remains desideratum for research that would help overcome the misconception that liberal or democratic institutions are a genuine European invention that can only be adopted by other regions such as the Middle East and North Africa. One result of this assumption is that it gives rise to the politicized debate about the complementarity of Islam and democracy. As I show in this chapter, there is no exceptionalism to be found. How parliament developed can be explained by its intermediary role between the public and the constituencies, on the one hand, and the head of state and the government, on the other. As in Europe, the intention of the core elite to politically integrate relevant actors in order to ensure their cooperation took on an institutional life of its own.

This understanding of the Egyptian parliament, including the important role of unintended consequences, is supported by the analysis of the third period under constitutional monarchy with informal British influence (1923–52). This period has long been called the "liberal experiment" and was taken as proof that Egypt was not (yet) capable of democratic rule. In contrast, I argue that this period should also be interpreted as an autocratic regime since the head of state was never subject to free and fair elections and had the prerogative to dissolve parliament at any time—and the king, supported by the British, did exactly this. The breakdown of this political order was not a failure on the part of democracy; rather, it was due in part to an autocracy in which parliament could not develop a balancing function because it was repeatedly dissolved or had its constitutional rights curtailed (1930–36). Top-down manipulation is just one factor that explains the growing public perception of the ineffectiveness and thus illegitimacy of the political order. In addition, the actors inside of parliament also contributed to this perception: the presence of parties in the assembly was a novelty for Egypt's parliamentary life, and its most important actor was the Wafd Party, which was extremely popular for its prominent role in

2. The latest conceptual approach to bringing these experiences together is found in Ihalainen, Ilie, and Palonen (2018).

the struggle for independence. Yet over the years the Wafd seemed more occupied with internal struggles and safeguarding its role in the political system than actually responding to social grievances. One result of this oversight was the rise of populist movements. This period therefore serves as an example of how the balancing function of parliament eroded over the years, eventually contributing to a full-fledged regime crisis that ended in a military coup.

The Context of Institutional Development: State-Economy Relations and External Actors

Three major challenges have shaped Egypt's state-economy and state-society relations for decades, if not centuries, and they have affected the constitutive relations of parliament as an intermediary institution. The first is the question of the role of the state; namely, whether it should be strong and centralist or a decentralized system that relies on local intermediaries. The second is the matter of which economic system is best suited to fight poverty and underdevelopment. The third is the issue of how to deal with external actors who have recurrently tried to control domestic economic structures. The continuity and interconnectedness of these challenges have affected peoples' lives for generations and have shaped the actors and institutions of Egypt since the nineteenth century.

"Modern" Egypt is usually associated with Napoleon's occupation of the country from 1798 until 1801 and his attempt to create a strong centralist state inspired by the French model. However, this perspective neglects the fact that, over the centuries, all the governors of Egypt had striven for this goal, from the reign of the Mamluks—Turco-Circassian military slaves who ruled Egypt during 1250–1517—to the reign of the Ottomans starting in 1525, when Sultan Sulayman tried to take over the central government with the *Qanunname-i Misr* (Philipp and Haarmann 1998). The struggle to obtain and uphold a power center that controlled the entire country remained practically the same: Would the dominant political group—whether a Mamluk household or an Ottoman Pasha—be strong enough to exercise control over tax collection? Or would it have to rely on intermediaries who would most likely divert a substantial portion of the collected taxes into their own pockets? This problem most often occurred in rural areas, far from the capital of Cairo where the rulers resided. The more central power depended on such intermediaries, the less tax revenue would actually reach the ruler. This led to the development of tax farming, a system in which the ruler granted tenancy rights for a plot of land to a so-called tax farmer, who could then levy taxes from a peasant who cultivated the land. The result was a higher tax burden for the peasants, since tax revenues were no longer just for the ruler but now included a surplus for the tax farmer (Baer 1962; Cuno 1992; Richards 1982).

Besides the situation faced by the rural poor, the so-called hydraulic nature of the country likewise justified strong, centralist rule. As Egypt had been dependent on the Nile floods for centuries, life was both literally and existentially centered along the river. To best utilize these floods, agriculture relied on an irrigation system to divert water onto the fields. Maintaining thousands of canals and dams required an enormous infrastructural effort that could only be achieved by a capable and centrally organized actor. In times when a strong, central state was able to invest in the irrigation system, agricultural output was high and Egypt experienced prosperity. Today, this logic, in its original meaning, holds true only in relation to maintaining dams and artificial lakes constructed in the mid-twentieth century, which have allowed for the Nile to be regulated. However, the argument that Egypt requires a strong, central governing power that is able to operate large-scale infrastructural projects continued to be used to justify autocratic rule.[3]

The second and third of Egypt's challenges—the role of external actors and the struggle for the appropriate economic policy—are especially entangled on account of Egypt's colonial past. As mentioned, Egypt became a part of the Ottoman Empire in the early sixteenth century; however, the Ottoman Pasha was most often merely one part of a power

---

3. Such as the Toshka project under Mubarak (see Bush 2007, 1610–12) or the return to mega-infrastructural projects under President al-Sisi since 2014 (e.g., the expansion of the Suez Canal).

structure among the Mamluk households. This changed with the ascendency of Muhammad 'Ali, an Albanian mercenary who assumed control of Egypt in 1805, initially in the name of the Ottoman Sultan but soon autonomously from the Sublime Porte. He is referred to as the modernizer of Egypt to this day, as his ambitious structural reforms granted him the centralized power his predecessors had always longed for. His primary aim of creating a strong army to achieve complete sovereignty depended on increased tax revenues, which he achieved by abolishing tax farming and introducing a centralist administration. He also directly intervened in the economy by selecting crops and determining prices. His strategy involved restructuring the agriculturally dominated economy through a shift from subsistence to cash crops, which, at the time, mainly comprised of long staple cotton. Besides this, Muhammad 'Ali also initiated industrialization projects (Baer 1962; Owen 1969; Rivlin 1961, 87–102). When he helped the Ottoman Sultan recapture the Hejaz from the House of Saud, the Ottomans welcomed his strength. However, he would become a threat to the Ottoman Empire upon taking over substantial parts of the Ottoman province of Greater Syria. Although the Sultan's power had become too weak to stop the ambitious ruler of Egypt, the "Great Game" between Britain and Russia was already at work. The British intervened and forced Muhammad 'Ali's forces to withdraw from Syria in an attempt to maintain the Ottoman Empire as a bulwark against Russia. Yet the British also put pressure on Muhammad 'Ali to open the markets and stop regulating prices. They pushed him to abandon monopolies and reduce tariffs, or, in essence, to cease protecting Egypt's newly developing industry. As a consequence, industrialization soon came to a halt (al-Sayyid Marsot 1984). The military loss paired with a dramatic fall in cotton prices together constituted the final blow against the strong centralist state. Muhammad 'Ali could no longer afford to continue state-controlled tax collection, and he reverted to using intermediaries. Rural notables leapt at the chance to expand their influence and wealth, thus setting the foundations for a wealthy feudal landowner class. Nevertheless, Muhammad 'Ali's family, whose dynasty did not end until 1952, amassed the largest share of land and wealth (Toledano 1990, 65).

When Saʻid (1854–63) assumed power, he implemented a crucial decision that had been debated for decades: the construction of a canal that would link the Red Sea with the Mediterranean. From an economic perspective, the canal was a brilliant idea in terms of generating revenue, especially in a time of burgeoning international trade. From a political perspective, however—and the reason why Muhammad ʻAli had refrained from starting construction—it made Egypt vitally important to the British as a sea route to India. Since the Great Game was already indirectly influencing Middle East politics, Muhammad ʻAli feared that the canal would cause Egypt's newly acquired autonomy from the Ottoman Empire to immediately be lost to the British. This concern was soon forgotten once his rule ended, and in the 1850s French engineer Ferdinand de Lesseps was awarded the concession to finally build the canal as an element of Saʻid's plan to modernize Egypt.

The monarch found the right approach to socioeconomically developing Egypt along the lines of the Western model of modernization, which is typically associated with large-scale infrastructural projects. Not only did the canal alter Egypt's geostrategic role, as Muhammad ʻAli had always feared, it also imposed a huge financial burden. As with many great infrastructural projects, costs exploded while the project was being carried out; when Saʻid became unable to fulfill the financial obligations, European banks were more than willing to grant lines of credit and loans. The British and the French were particularly engaged in the project. As the fiscal situation worsened during the reign of Khedive Ismaʻil (1863–79), European countries increased financial pressures and converted this into influence on domestic politics. Ismaʻil tried to create an alliance with rural notables, to whom he granted political influence in exchange for their support in maintaining financial independence. Despite these efforts, the Europeans were able to gradually encroach, until ultimately a British and a French representative became part of the government itself. This so-called Dual Control de facto only served the interests of European creditors (Hunter 1984; EzzelArab 2002). The European powers also ousted the resilient Ismaʻil and installed his son Tawfiq (1879–92) as a more cooperative ruler. As a puppet of foreign powers, Tawfiq lacked legitimacy from the very beginning. He proved unable to prevent the 'Urabi movement, an alliance of mainly military officers and rural notables. The latter aimed to reinstate the parliament and enact a reformed constitution meant to achieve a sovereign Egyptian state with financial autonomy (Weipert-Fenner 2011). The British would not tolerate this, and they sent a fleet to end it, marking the beginning of the British occupation of Egypt in 1882.

The British essentially held Egypt as a giant cotton farm, without any economic diversification. Large landowners adjusted to the British quite well and were also politically integrated in representative assemblies while, at the same time, the majority of the population suffered from poverty and diseases. Farmers in particular were susceptible to bilharzia, a parasite-induced disease, as a result of working in standing water on their fields. The educational system was kept underfunded, especially in the area of girls' education.[4] Industrialization was completely put on hold, and all existing companies and the financial sector were put in the hands of foreigner owners. The vulnerabilities that this economic system created recurrently surfaced and could no longer be ignored once the First World War erupted. Exports to countries fighting against the British were stopped, imports decreased, prices for basic goods soared, and wages remained low. At the same time, peasants and their livestock were deployed for a military campaign in Palestine (Tignor 1976, 42).

While the socioeconomic crisis mobilized the lower segments of society, occupation by a foreign power fueled educated Egyptians' discontent, which was exacerbated by Egypt being officially declared a protectorate in 1914. These resentments culminated in the 1919 Revolution, a countrywide and cross-class uprising that led to the unilateral declaration of Egypt's independence from the British in 1922 and the establishment of a constitutional monarchy in 1923. The political movement in the fight for independence was championed by the Wafd Party and its iconic leader, Sa'd Zaghlul. The party was strongly influenced by large landowners (as I will explicate below). At the same time, wealthy landed families also

---

4. For a very impressive description, see the autobiography of the intellectual Salama Musa (1958).

participated in attempts at building the institutions of nascent economic nationalism. The main aims were to diversify the economy to make it less vulnerable to floating prices for cotton on the world market and to develop an Egyptian industrial and financial sector to keep profits inside of the country. This led to the foundation of the Federation of Egyptian Industries and the Egyptian General Agricultural Syndicate, both of which lobbied for state assistance and for the protection of Egyptian producers (Tignor 1976). The most important innovation, however, was the establishment of Bank Misr in 1920, which sought to finance Egypt's industrialization. The bank also established companies, mostly related to ginning and transporting cotton, and lobbied for the state's active role in economic development. It became a region-wide symbol of the attempt to fight imperial economic dependence; ultimately, however, this failed as the bank went bankrupt in 1939 (Davis 1983).

While the wealthy landed elites dominated both political and economic nationalism along with all of the other parties of the time, the king and his family remained the largest landowners. Egypt's social structure did not substantially change during the period of constitutional monarchy. The call for social justice, which had been a driver of the 1919 Revolution, did not bring about wealth distribution. Socioeconomic reforms remained very limited, contributing to dissatisfaction among large portions of the growing population. Although industrialization started to develop, out of a population of thirteen million, only half a million worked in the industrial sector (Aglan 2003, 160). Frustration with unfulfilled expectations of life improvements fostered antiregime movements, such as the fascist group Young Egypt and the Islamist Muslim Brotherhood and paramilitary youth organizations. It also led to waves of public protests by students and workers starting in the mid-1940s. These developments partly paved the way for the military coup by the Free Officers in 1952. This group abolished monarchic rule in Egypt that had shaped and been shaped by parliamentary institutions since the early nineteenth century. No matter how radically opposed to a monarchy the design of an Egyptian republic was intended to be, it could not overcome the establishment and engrained dynamics of the autocratic parliament created under khedive and monarchical rule in Egypt.

Early Traits of Parliamentarianism in Egypt

In his search for the beginning of Egypt's parliamentary history, the Egyptian historian Muhammad Khalil Subhi finds early traits of parliamentarianism in the institution of the two diwans—consultative bodies introduced during the early Ottoman era in Cairo. As explicated earlier, parliament is here taken at its minimum qualification as a representative intermediary body. The extent to which these bodies can be regarded as parliamentary predecessors is, however, questionable, as they primarily consisted of officials while the administration was, at the time, mostly in Ottoman hands (Subhi 1939–47, 4:5). The focus, rather, was on recruiting experts for consultation and not representation, although some members such as the Islamic scholars ('ulama') and "prominent men" (Raymond 2000, 193) were also integrated. When the French occupied Egypt in 1798, Napoleon installed local councils called diwans, followed by the Grand Diwan in Cairo that comprised additional segments of society: urban notables, mainly merchants and Islamic scholars, along with rural representatives from the provinces, Copts, Syrians, and Ottoman officials (al-Jabarti 1994, 38). For many historians, the Napoleonic diwans constituted the beginning of parliamentarianism in Egypt. Abdel-Malek views them as "les germes de régime représentative" and their statutes as "la première constitution de l'Égypte moderne" (1975, 263).[5] Yet it might be an exaggeration to deem these councils to be the seeds of parliamentarianism, since some of them existed for merely a few months and the French occupation itself came to end after four years. Nevertheless, the very idea of Egyptians being represented by notables in a consultative body was a novelty for the country.[6]

5. In a similar vein, see Landau (1953, 7) and "Tarikh al-Sulta al-Tashri'iyya fi al-Hukuma al-Misriyya," al-Hilal, 1913, vol. 22, 83–91.

6. Albert Hourani ([1968] 1993) drew attention to the role of notables (in his case to urban notables) as intermediaries in the politics of the Ottoman Empire, although he did not focus on the relevant institutions that emerged from the politics of notables. In spite of later criticism, especially of the functionalism and structuralism in his concept (see Gelvin 2006), his work clearly inspires this study of parliament as an intermediary institution.

Muhammad 'Ali, the so-called modernizer of Egypt, introduced a representative body only after completing his administrative centralizing reforms described in the previous section. Even though we find different names for the body[7] along with differing founding years,[8] there is consensus among scholars that the body's high level of representation of rural notables was one of its remarkable characteristics. It consisted of ninety-nine traditional village leaders (*shuyukh al-balad*)—quite significant compared to the thirty-three members personally appointed by Muhammad 'Ali—as well as twenty-four district governors and four Islamic scholars. Al-Sayyid Marsot explains this overrepresentation of rural notables as Muhammad 'Ali's need to gain their support for his vast reform program, which mostly affected the rural population. These reforms included an agricultural transformation from subsistence to export-oriented farming, large-scale recruitment of peasants for infrastructural projects and the army, and the expansion of a centralized tax-collection system. All of these changes could very well have faced heavy opposition; but by including the village leaders in the political system and following their advice on several topics, Muhammad 'Ali won their support and could more effectively implement his reforms (al-Sayyid Marsot 1984, 108). Yet this institution was dissolved in 1837 and replaced by a diwan system of expertise instead of representation. This might have had to do with the decline in Muhammad 'Ali's power, especially once the British forced the free trade agreement upon him and with the Sublime Porte in 1838. As notables in the governorates outside of Cairo undermined the central planning of production, imports, and exports, Muhammad 'Ali might have lost faith in the idea that the integration of rural notables in the diwan would actually bolster his rule. Subsequent rulers 'Abbas I (1848–54) and Sa'id (1854–63) installed expert councils with consultative functions; Egypt's parliamentary history would not gain momentum until the reign of Isma'il.

---

7. *Majlis al-mashwara* (Landau 1953, 7), *Majlis al-mashura* (Abdel-Malek 1975, 263), *Majlis al-shura* (al-Sayyid Marsot 1984, 108), *al-Majlis al-'ali* (Subhi 1939–47, 4:12).

8. For example, 1818 ("Tarikh al-Sulta al-Tashri'iyya fi al-Hukuma al-Misriyya," *al-Hilal*, 1913, vol. 22, 87), 1824 (Subhi 1939–47, 4:7), 1829 (Landau 1953, 7).

Parliament Seizes the Moment:
From Consultation to Legislation, 1866–1882

In 1866, Khedive Isma'il[9] (1863–79) introduced the Majlis shura al-nuwwab (Consultative Chamber of Deputies), composed of seventy-five deputies from fourteen governorates. Only men with the means to pay a land tax of at least five hundred piasters were eligible to serve (Abul-Magd 2010). They were selected by electoral colleges that reflected the power structures in the governorates, and thus limited the pool of assembly members to provincial rural notables (a'yan al-rif) (EzzelArab 2009, 302). These notables, mainly from the Nile delta region, had benefited from the administrative and agricultural reforms under Muhammad 'Ali and particularly from increased demand for long staple cotton during the American Civil War. Close proximity to the European market allowed them—in contrast to cotton producers in Upper Egypt (Abul-Magd 2010, 696)—to amass a considerable amount of land and to reach mid-level positions in the bureaucratic apparatus of the provinces. These notables were distinct from the Turco-Circassian elite, the *dhawat*, remnants of the caste of military slaves, who were brought in from the Caucasus during Mamluk and Ottoman rule. During the nineteenth and early twentieth centuries, a process of assimilation with Egyptians could be observed; however, from 1860 to the 1880s, they exclusively held high positions in the army, in the administration, and on the khedive's private council (EzzelArab 2009, 302; al-Sayyid Marsot 1984, 131).

Scholars have suggested various reasons, both external and domestic, as to why the chamber was installed. The Egyptian historians al-Rafi'i and Subhi tend to assume that Isma'il was pursuing higher aims, such as progress and popular participation (al-Rafi'i 1982, 89; Subhi 1939–47, 4:15). Other historians have argued that power consolidation was the driving force behind this move. In regard to the chamber's composition, it is likely that Isma'il enacted the chamber for reasons similar to those of Muhammad 'Ali thirty years prior. Because of the construction of the Suez Canal

---

9. Isma'il achieved formal recognition of his title as "khedive" instead of "wali" in 1867, but for the sake of clarity I use his better-known title for the previous years as well.

under his predecessor, Saʿid, Ismaʿil faced heavy financial constraints on account of servicing debts to foreign financiers. Schölch argues that the creation of an institution that would constrain the khedive's power, at least pro forma, assuaged the worries of foreign creditors while increasing Egypt's creditworthiness (Schölch 1972, 27).[10] As these notables had been rising in wealth and administrative influence since the 1830s, it would have also been reasonable to win over the notables as important taxpayers and collectors for the khedive's cause. The notables, as representatives, could even legitimize higher taxes on the basis of their approval in the assembly (Hunter 1984, 53). Furthermore, Ismaʿil might have wanted to foster confidence in his reign and, by limiting his powers at a national level, create incentives for further investment in the country's economy and infrastructure, including irrigation systems (Cannon 1988, 31). Cole, however, proposes that the institution diverted attention to the rural notables and away from the royal family's land grab by granting the illusion of participation (1993, 30).

The degree to which these explanations resemble theoretical concepts for contemporary authoritarian institutions—parliaments, in particular—is remarkable. From increased legitimacy to improving the climate for investment (for foreign and domestic investors) by constraining institutions, we can find many of these arguments also present in current debates. With the notable exception of Egyptian historians, most authors infer that the chamber was never powerful and hence never played a role in Egypt's politics on account of its top-down creation (Cole 1993, 31; Schölch 1972, 30). As elaborated on in the critique of existing accounts, the following overview of the development of the Majlis shura al-nuwwab clearly demonstrates that motives for creating and even maintaining an institution, from the perspective of an autocratic ruler, might differ from how the parliament developed in reality. One can observe the changes in these institutional dynamics by looking at the parliamentarians' behavior as well as at the charters and constitutional texts.

---

10. Indeed, the European press was enthusiastic about the introduction of the chamber. See Landau (1953, 8) and Barakat (1977, 378).

From its founding until the time of the British occupation, this first parliamentary institution went through four stages.[11] During the first ten years, the chamber conformed to the role accorded to it by the formal framework, namely the two relevant charters (al-la'iha al-asasiyya and al-la'iha al-nizamiyya[12]) that limited the scope of the assembly to a consultative role in domestic affairs only. It did not even have the prerogative to set the agenda or initiate debates on its own initiative. Moreover, the time for assembly granted annually was limited to two months, and sessions were held behind closed doors. These limitations did not, however, prevent the deputies from quickly figuring out how to represent their interests. This can be observed in their parliamentary actions, such as demanding the termination of the existing tax farming system, the redistribution of unexploited land to potential investors (namely themselves, as wealthy landowners), and amendments to inheritance laws to protect their property against fragmentation (Abul-Magd 2010, 697–98; Barakat 1977, 380–81). The activities of the deputies never conflicted with the khedive in any significant way, making it difficult to gauge the chamber's real power vis-à-vis the monarch. The notables instead concentrated on cooperation with the khedive in ways that would also serve their own personal interests. For instance, they accepted one major reform, the so-called *muqabala* law, which guaranteed a 50 percent tax reduction on landed property for lump payments of six years' worth of taxes. Moreover, it established full property rights for land.[13] This was proposed on account of the khedive's desperate financial situation, with the members of parliament solely focusing on their own profit in exchange. The fact that this was completely ruinous for the country beyond the short-term was of little importance to the deputies, as was the lack of transparency regarding whether payments would actually reach the state coffers or go directly into the pockets of the khedive (Baer 1962, 10–11; Hunter 1984, 180–81).

---

11. For a comprehensive analysis of parliamentary development in Egypt between 1866 and 1882, see Weipert-Fenner (2011).

12. The original documents can be found in al-Rafi'i (1982, 314–24).

13. On the development of land property rights, see Weipert-Fenner (2011, 56–66).

The first stage seems to have prepared the deputies for more autonomous and even contentious parliamentary actions as they practiced parliamentary procedures such as carrying out committee work, giving speeches, and submitting proposals (Hunter 1984, 52–54). Furthermore, one might argue that spending two months together created a sense of coherence among the notables; they eventually came to discover that they shared interests and were in a position to develop common strategies to pursue them. This might explain how the MPs were able to assume a more active role as soon as the opportunity arose, as was made possible by the increasing influence of the European powers after 1875. The more it seemed that Egypt would be unable to service its foreign debts, the more the foreign powers tried to appease creditors by creating committees and dispatching delegations. This culminated in the creation of the Caisse de la Dette Publique in 1876, which directly channeled Egypt's revenues to the debt service. Any changes to the revenues would henceforth have to be negotiated in advance with the Caisse, thereby stripping the khedive of his budgetary power. However, as the European countries involved were unable to reach consensus when dealing with the khedive, the French and the British increased their influence on the political system and created the system of Dual Control. With this, the two countries agreed that a British inspector would control Egypt's financial affairs and a French counterpart would control public works, specifically the Suez Canal (Hunter 1984, 179; Mommsen 1961, 36–37). In 1878, Egypt's financial situation deteriorated even further, instigating a new initiative, the Commission of Inquiry, which demanded that the khedive's land be nationalized and made available as collateral for servicing the debt. Furthermore, it suggested that the two European inspectors be promoted to the position of ministers in a newly created executive organ, the Ministers' Council (Majlis al-wuzara'). It replaced the Private Council (al-Majlis al-khususi), which had been under the khedive's control and dominated by the long-established Turco-Circassian elite. The new cabinet was composed of Europeans and Egyptians deemed to be "collaborators." They proposed financial cuts and tax increases that would have directly hurt the rural notables (EzzelArab 2002, 46–48).

During this time (1876–78), the khedive increasingly integrated the Chamber of Deputies into the political debates, most likely because the assembly members were as hostile toward European intrusion as he was. He convened the chamber for special sessions and granted it an unprecedented amount of information on budgetary affairs. The MPs were also able to discuss matters of taxation and land property in detail. In exchange, the chamber supported the khedive and directed criticism at the institutions dominated by Europeans, which had brought Egypt's sovereignty into a deep crisis. Although it is true that the chamber might have been used by the khedive as an instrument for consolidating his power (Schölch 1972, 81), it is certainly too early to speak of the chamber as a constitutional counterweight to the khedive, as al-Rafi'i claims (1982, 173–77). At the same time, one could very well imagine that the new privilege of discussing budgetary and tax affairs was very attractive to wealthy landowners in the assembly (Hunter 1984, 211). The desire to not only discuss these issues but also have a say in them might very well have sprouted here.

In 1879, opposition to the European powers and the politics they pursued intensified (Harrison 1995, 55). Army officers protested for better working conditions and higher salaries; meanwhile, ever harsher methods of tax collection further alienated the population from the government (Hunter 1984, 203–5, 213–16). In this heated atmosphere, the deputies in the chamber demanded a greater say in tax affairs and rejected the dissolution of parliament by the cabinet. Instead, they insisted on prolonging the legislative period, and they articulated a new attitude in their speeches. Some of the deputies began to speak of the chamber as the foundation of "civilization and justice," and the idea of representing the Egyptian people was brought up. Although the MPs made use of interpellations against ministers, they did not possess the means to enforce this tool of holding the government accountable (al-Rafi'i 1982, 178). In the context of this new confrontational spirit, and also pushed by the European powers, the prime minster issued a decree that allowed the cabinet to restructure financial legislation. This included a repeal of the *muqabala* law without involving the Chamber of Deputies in the process. As a consequence, cooperation intensified between parliament and the khedive, culminating in a broader elite alliance that issued the so-called National Program (al-la'iha al-wataniyya). This constituted an alternative to the cabinet's attempt to redefine the legal framework of financial affairs. The idea behind the National Program was to safeguard Egypt's budgetary and overall sovereignty and, at the same time, create a trustworthy financial and political system that would calm worried creditors in Europe (EzzelArab 2009). While the role of the British and the French in Egypt would have been limited to financial control, as had been exercised during the years of Dual Control, European power would nonetheless have remained in the system. In addition, the financial obligations to the Ottoman Sultan and European financiers would have remained out of the reach of parliamentary control (EzzelArab 2002, 56, 69–71; al-Rafi'i 1982, 203; Schölch 1972, 91–92). An important element in the National Program was to keep the *muqabala* law in place, including the invested sums and property rights of the rural notables (EzzelArab 2009, 311).

The central feature of the political reforms was promoting the chamber to a parliament with full legislative rights. This change was symbolized in an amendment to the official name of the institution: the term *shura* was eliminated, thereby overcoming its limitation to a consultative role (EzzelArab 2002, 72–73, 75). These wide-ranging modifications made new regulation of the chamber necessary, leading to the constitutional draft of 1879.[14] Among its forty-nine articles, most important were provisions giving parliament the right to approve taxes as well as state expenses for the first time (Articles 45 and 46). Parliamentarians gained immunity, a salary, and more time for their work (three months instead of two for a legislative session, and a legislative period of three years). Internally, the speaker of the parliament was now elected by the assembly members rather than appointed by the khedive from among the Turco-Circassian elite. The assembly received the right to grant itself rules of procedure. Legislation was divided among the cabinet, which had the power of legislative initiative; the parliament, which had the right to discuss, modify, and reject the draft law; and the khedive, who could approve or reject the

---

14. The following analysis is based on the draft text printed in al-Rafi'i (1982, 214–20). Al-Rafi'i's source is *al-Ahram*, 1879, no. 12.

draft law. In case of an unresolved dispute, the monarch could dissolve parliament; if the newly elected assembly supported the opinion of its predecessor, its decision was binding.

Views on this constitutional draft differ greatly among scholars. Schölch regards it as a paper tiger, without real power in relation to the monarch (1972, 179). EzzelArab, in contrast, argues that the power of the khedive was already evaporating. This means that the provisions in the constitution could have provided real influence to the rural notables in parliament (EzzelArab 2004, 562–67). However, the draft text would never be implemented, as several European countries protested against the new order from the outset. Their very serious opposition led the alliance around the khedive to fall apart and brought Isma'il's reign to an end. He was succeeded by his son Tawfiq, whom the European powers considered easier to manipulate. This power transition resulted in the installment of a new cabinet, and the Chamber of Deputies was dissolved.

It would take the former deputies nearly two years to take up political action once again and join forces with a group of army officers. Rallying behind the charismatic officer Ahmad 'Urabi, they made three demands of Khedive Tawfiq during the famous demonstration of the army in front of 'Abdin Palace. First, the army called for an increase in the number of soldiers to 18,000. The purpose of this increase was to create more senior posts and thereby increase the opportunity for native Egyptians to make a career in an army that had, until then, been dominated by the Turco-Circassian elite. The two other demands were to reinstate the Chamber of Deputies and to write a new constitution. The pressure created by the unruly officers led Tawfiq to make some concessions, including new elections for the Chamber of Deputies in November 1881. At first, parliamentary life was marked by self-restraint on the part of all participating actors (Schölch 1972, 140–47, 176–77). Work on a new constitution continued in the assembly; its committees and the deputies even proposed regulations that would have decreased their own decision-making power. Yet the overall goal was clear: safeguarding Egypt's autonomy vis-à-vis European powers and eliminating reasons for them to further penetrate the Egyptian system and occupy the country. The French occupation of Tunisia in 1881 amplified the latter fear.

Ultimately, these attempts at moderate reforms did not prove success-ful. In a joint diplomatic note, Great Britain and France declared uncon-ditional solidarity with the khedive, which the members of parliament perceived to be an indirect threat of intervention. After this, the deputies abandoned their self-restraint, and—in cooperation with a new cabinet that included 'Urabi himself and additional allies—they designed and enacted a new constitution and electoral law in the following month.[15] The constitution granted the parliament broad powers, including the right to authorize taxes and budgetary oversight (Article 30–38), embedded in a system of checks and balances among the cabinet, government, and par-liament. The budget, for instance, had to be approved by a special com-mittee of which half the members were representatives of the ministers' council. Moreover, financial obligations to foreign countries were explic-itly excluded from parliamentary budget oversight (Article 34). The con-stitution of 1882 also included the 1879 rights of immunity, a fixed salary, and longer legislative periods (of up to five years). All committees were still to be formed on an ad hoc basis, except for the budget committee. The interpellation of ministers and holding them accountable for the work of their ministries put restraints on executive power (Article 19–22).

Even though the deputies attempted not to encroach on the vital inter-ests of foreign creditors, the European powers did not tolerate this autono-mous development. After a failed attempt to assassinate Ahmad 'Urabi, tensions mounted. The British "men on the spot" began to report home about the 'Urabi alliance, calling it a xenophobic, Islamist, and militaristic movement that manipulated parliament for its own ends (Harrison 1995, 89–91).[16] The portrayal of Egypt at the brink of chaos made Great Britain and France send two fleets to Alexandria, where violent clashes led to the city's bombardment in July 1882 (Galbraith and al-Sayyid Marsot 1978; Chamberlain 1977). The military struggle for independence was short

15. The following analysis is based on the draft text printed in al-Rafi'i (1982, 220–25). Al-Rafi'i's source is *al-Waqa'i' al-Misriyya*, no. 9, Feb. 1982. For an English transla-tion see Blunt (1922).

16. Mayer (1988) presents the very different interpretations of the 'Urabi movement that Egyptian historiography has produced over the decades.

and fruitless; the British occupied Egypt that year. Formally, however, the British assumed only administrative control of Egypt, with Evelyn Baring (later Lord Cromer) as general consul of Egypt; it was not until 1915 that Egypt was declared a British protectorate.

In sum, the first parliament of Egypt exhibited considerable development, from a formally consultative body to a chamber with decisive powers over budgetary and tax affairs and the means to hold the government accountable. This progress started when the actors within the institution first learned how to use the assembly for their own ends (1866–76). The khedive then promoted the chamber to counter the encroachment of the European powers into the political system (1876–79). The rural notables, as deputies, started to initiate the constitutionalization of vital parliamentary rights, most importantly taxation and budgetary oversight, initially cooperating with the khedive (1879). Once the British and French replaced the monarch with his son, Tawfiq, the MPs once again attempted to preserve their institutional rights in 1882, this time in an alliance with revolting officers under Ahmad 'Urabi—a development that ended with the British occupation of Egypt.

The example of Egypt's first parliament resembles a condensed version of the development of European feudal assemblies, which gradually gained more rights and continually constrained monarchic power over the course of centuries (Loewenberg 2016, 10). The growing weakness of Khedive Isma'il through informal European imperialism seems to have accelerated the process, as the monarch tried to create a strong alliance against the foreign powers and their local collaborators. However, the logic of imperialist rule would not tolerate the autonomy that the parliamentarians tried to gain. At the same time, one should not misinterpret this development as a quest for democracy, since the parliamentarians clearly pursued the interests they shared as large landowners and cotton producers, without any intention of further power sharing or participation.

Parliament under Occupation:
Pressure against the British, 1882–1914

Under British rule, a bicameral system was installed that existed until 1912. It consisted of the Consultative Legislative Council (Majlis shura al-qawanin) with thirty members, fourteen of whom were appointed by the khedive and the government on a permanent basis, and sixteen of whom were elected every six years by provincial councils. Even though this council had only a consultative role on budgetary matters and legislation, the government had to justify its decisions to the council, which convened five times a year. For almost two decades, this institution was dominated by the old Turco-Circassian elites, who were experienced in political affairs and hostile toward the British. Their influence decreased with the steady rise of new, educated Egyptian elites. The second chamber, the General Assembly (al-Jam'iyya al-'umumiyya) had eighty-two members; it included the members of the legislative council as well as all of the ministers on the khedive's council. Forty-six of the deputies were elected every six years by electors from all of Egypt.[17] An amended electoral law raised the required minimum amount of land tax that the candidates had to pay to 5,000 piasters, resulting in the continued dominance of the same large landowner families (Abul-Magd 2010, 699). The General Assembly met at least once a year, significantly less often than the Consultative Legislative Council, but with broader prerogatives. Any new tax had to be approved by the assembly, and its opinion had to be taken into account on a broad range of issues, including infrastructural projects, land classification, and public debts. Again, the main challenge for the executive was to justify its decisions to the assembly members in case they rejected a government proposition. Although the assembly did not have the right to propose legislative initiatives, it was allowed to place issues on the agenda and discuss them on its own behalf. The deputies also received considerable financial compensation, ensuring that they could focus on parliamentary work. They were certainly not completely free, however, as the president of the Consultative Legislative Council, appointed by the khedive, also presided over the General Assembly (Goldschmidt 2013, 314; Landau 1953, 41–45).

17. In 1883, 903,395 electors voted on behalf of a population of around 6.8 million people. This means that only 13 percent of the Egyptians actually had the right to vote (Landau 1953, 45).

In the council's first years, some suggestions by the deputies were adopted, but most members remained silent throughout the sessions. Beginning in 1892, when the new khedive, 'Abbas Hilmi II, succeeded his father to the throne, the deputies used their acquired experience to assume a more active and even contentious role, primarily against the British. The nascent Egyptian national press along with French newspapers contributed to hostility against the British (Tollefson 1990, 551). Following the khedive's confrontational course against the occupation in the early years of his rule, the Consultative Legislative Council rejected the 1893 budget on the grounds that it was presented to them on too short notice.[18] Even though the budget was released in spite of the assembly's protest, it marked the beginning of further criticism within the chamber aimed at the British. Not only did the deputies blame the British for the huge costs of the occupation that Egypt had to bear, but they also pushed forward with their own issues, such as expanding education (Landau 1953, 45–48). The legislative council also took a supportive, though moderate, stance toward the khedive's attempts to limit the British personnel and influence on the Egyptian police and army (Tollefson 1990, 551–52).

Outside of the parliamentary bodies, two major nationalist parties developed during this period. The more influential one was al-Hizb al-watani, founded in 1897 and led by Mustafa Kamil. The other was the Hizb al-umma, established in 1907 and headed by Ahmad Lutfi al-Sayyid. Although growing popularity allowed Kamil to establish ties with the parliament and even with the powerful president of the Consultative Legislative Council, Isma'il Muhammad Pasha (1899–1902), Kamil's party did not make a direct entry into the assemblies. On the other hand, Hizb al-umma members, mainly comprising wealthy landed elites, were granted access to the representative institutions but were not permitted to voice party politics in the chamber. If they attempted to do so, the speaker of the assembly would abruptly stop them (Rizq 2000).[19]

18. Khedive 'Abbas Hilmi II changed his position toward the British and the growing nationalist movement several times (Goldschmidt 2013, 23–24).

19. For an overview of the development of all relevant parties, see Long (2004, 204–6).

The increasingly nationalistic public discourse was also felt in the most important decision-making process in which the two assemblies were involved at that time: the attempt to extend the Suez Canal Concession in 1909. Pressure from the Egyptian public and the national press had increased to such an extent that the executive was eager to attain the assembly's support on this issue. Yet this calculation proved wrong: the members of the General Assembly used their room to maneuver and spent two months intensively debating the issue. Landau talks of "passionate speeches" (1953, 52) held against the extension of the concession, pointing to an awareness on the part of the deputies about the effects of rhetoric not only on their colleagues in parliament but on the public in general. Ultimately, the protest by the General Assembly curbed the plans of the khedive and the British (Abi-Hamad 2012, 8). For Eldon Gorst, serving Consul General of Egypt, the representative institutions now presented a threat to his rule. He despised them as representatives "of a class of wealthy Beys and Pashas," agitated by "few interested parties" (quote in Hunter 2007, 235).

Growing confidence among the assembly members also manifested in demands for further institutional rights. Starting in 1905, appeals were made to the khedive and the British to introduce purely representative institutions of elected members only. The new British Consul General, Herbert Kitchener, heeded these calls and introduced a new institutional body, the Legislative Assembly (al-Jamʻiyya al-tashriʻiyya). It consisted of sixty-six elected and seventeen nominated deputies and members of the cabinet (Binder 1978, 124). In contrast to the previous nomination system, the appointments ensured representation of various communities and professions. Accordingly, the assembly consisted of four Copts, three Bedouins, two merchants, two doctors, one engineer, two members of educational professions, and one municipal representative (Landau 1953, 55). The other two appointed members were the president and the vice president. Every two years, one third of the sixty-six were elected for a six-year term. Now, every law had to be debated in parliament. The Legislative Assembly was entitled to discuss any governmental act and to introduce proposals of its own; it also had a veto right on budgetary matters. Nevertheless, as in the years before the occupation, all financial obligations to a foreign power, be it the Ottoman Sultan or British financiers, were excluded from parliamentary control.

Following this increase in parliamentary rights, the elections of 1913 had a higher turnout than previous ones. However, it did not manage to exceed 20 percent in rural areas and remained under 5 percent in urban centers, resulting in a high percentage of landowners in the assembly (74 percent). Along with increased participation, these elections also marked the beginning of electoral programs propagated by candidates, among them Sa'd Zaghlul. This popular broker between the nationalistic movement and the British had previously been minister for education (1906–8) and minister of justice (1910–12). In his new role as member of parliament and vice president of the assembly, he used his political experience to take a critical stance toward the government and fought for parliamentary rights (Landau 1953, 55–57). However, World War I would begin only one year later; parliament was dissolved, and Egypt officially became a British protectorate. Parliamentary life in Egypt was not revived until the official declaration of independence and the installment of a new political system.

In drawing lessons from these observations, it is striking to note that, even under occupation, the weak formal framework of parliamentary institutions was increasingly brought to life and used as a foundation for further institutional empowerment. The deputies developed the parliamentary bodies during a time when a new force was arising through the formation of a national press and nationalist parties: nascent public opinion. Additionally, and similar to the 1870s, growing parliamentary activism coincided with the anti-British position of the khedive following his accession, but also autonomously developed afterward when 'Abbas Hilmi II took a more cooperative stance with the British. The assembly members assumed the nationalist cause, though generally in more moderate ways, at the same time pursuing their personal and group interests. The Turco-Circassian elite tried to reestablish the autonomy of the army and police through the Legislative Council while the Egyptian landed elites in the General Assembly decided on infrastructure projects such as irrigation systems and railway expansion for their agricultural industry, which favored the north over the south of Egypt (Abul-Magd 2010, 699).

This means that even during British occupation, the autocratic parliament was driven by balancing pressure from outside of the political arena as well as by the aim of bargaining with the executive regarding the respective social groups' interests.

The Constitutional Monarchy:
Parliament and Party Politics Meet, 1923–1952

After the end of the war, members of the Legislative Assembly formed a committee that tried to negotiate Egypt's independence with the British high commissioner, albeit without much success. Frustrated, the committee gathered signatures for a public mandate, hoping to form a delegation for the Paris Peace Conference in 1919 that would demand Egypt's independence from Great Britain. Sa'd Zaghlul, who had been vice president during the last parliament under British occupation, headed the delegates and was accompanied by former fellow parliamentarians (Badrawi 2000, 134–35). As such, past MPs were the founders of the Wafd Party, Egypt's new nationalist movement and most important political party from 1923 on.

The period starting with Egypt's formal independence was once labeled the "liberal experiment" (al-Sayyid Marsot 1977). The constitution of 1923 followed the Belgian model of a constitutional monarchy and encompassed major elements of liberal democracy, such as individual liberties, equality before the law, and the protection of property rights. At the same time, power was greatly concentrated in the hands of the monarch. He not only led the executive branch but also participated in legislation with the two chambers—the Senate and the Chamber of Deputies. The king could veto any law passed by the parliamentarians, whereas only a two-thirds majority could overrule the king's decision. Decrees enacted by the executive branch at times when the parliament was not convened had to be later ratified by the chambers. Whereas members of the Chamber of Deputies were each indirectly elected by electors for a five-year term, only three-fifths of Senate members had to compete in elections. The other two-fifths of the Senate, as well as its president, were appointed by the king. The king also had the power to dissolve parliament (Botman 1991, 30–32; Maghraoui 2006, 130–31).

When the Egyptians were called upon to cast their vote for the first time after obtaining formal independence, the Egyptian historian Yunan Labib Rizq describes an "election fever" that swept through broad segments of society, leading to the high level of voter turnout of around 80 percent. The results were clear and unsurprising: the nationalist Wafd Party, which was mainly responsible for formal independence, won 192 out of 214 seats. The Liberal Constitutional Party (Hizb al-ahrar al-dusturiyyin), which had split off from the Wafd, won nine seats, and the National Party (al-Hizb al-watani) four (Rizq 2000). For the first time in Egypt's history, parliamentary life was now attached to party politics. From this time until the end of the constitutional monarchy, Egyptians would freely cast their votes, and the free elections usually resulted in a Wafd-dominated parliament.[20] The party profited from its leading role in the struggle for independence, while its conservative wing of large landowners could also count on the votes from the peasants on their estates (Thornhill 2010, 283).

The first years of parliamentary life (1924–27) started off with a great number of issues under debate. The parliamentarians fought for independence not only from Great Britain but also from Turkey, which had taken over the imperial obligations of Egypt to the Sublime Porte. Furthermore, they developed the political institutional system and amended the electoral law to abolish indirect voting and property and wealth requirements (Landau 1953, 67–68). Badrawi considers parliament to have fulfilled a "fiscal watchdog function" until the death of Sa'd Zaghlul in 1927, when, for the first time, members of parliament openly criticized the high expenditures of the palace and called for the equal treatment of royal and public employees (2005, 108). From 1939 on, members of parliament recurrently brought up cases of corruption and misappropriation of state funds (Youssef 1983, 31–32). The parliamentarians did not even shy away from conflict with Islamic scholars, accusing a congress at al-Azhar University of having been heavily financed by the ministry of religious endowments

---

20. Two exceptions are the heavily manipulated elections in the early 1930s, when the king seized absolute power until 1935, and the elections of 1945, which the Wafd Party boycotted.

(Badrawi 2005, 98–102)—a matter that was connected to the very sensitive issue of religious legitimacy. The king attempted to legitimate his rule by reinstalling the caliphate in Cairo after the dissolution of the Ottoman caliphate in 1923. The debate about the relation of religion and politics was fueled by 'Ali 'Abd al-Raziq's concept of Islam without a caliphate, published in 1925 in his book *al-Islam wa-Usul al-Hukm*.[21] Though vastly differing views on the topic existed outside of parliament, in the press, and among the public, it was a matter of course for the parliamentarians that the legislature should be the institution to decide on whether Egypt would be made into a caliphate or not (Gershoni and Jankowski 1987, 63–65). Misako Ikeda—focusing not only on the control function of the parliament—shows that the educational reforms of this period, including the introduction of tuition-free schools and a primary school curriculum, were not top-down decisions. Instead, the parliamentarians adopted public demands and directed them into the political system (Ikeda 2005, 234). The same applies to labor demands: in 1926, the Wafd-dominated parliament allowed labor spokesmen to voice the grievances and demands of a growing workers' movement, such as the recognition of trade unions and syndicates and unemployment compensation. Ten years later, when the Wafd was again in power, several of these demands were even put into law (Deeb 1979b, 193, 200).

Despite these achievements, mainly during the 1920s, parliament's reputation still deteriorated, and the entire system destabilized in the 1930s and 1940s. Scholars have long argued that the "liberal experiment" failed because Egypt was incapable of appropriating the Western concept of political liberalism: Egyptians either lacked the intellectual capacity to comprehend liberal ideas (Safran 1961) or they were unable to leave partisan politics aside and join forces for the sake of constitutional development (Vatikiotis 1969). Colonialism, however, has been excluded from these accounts. French scholars tend to ascribe the failure to British imperial politics, with a clear preference for the French approach to colonialism

---

21. For more information on this debate, see Finianos (2002, 163–76) and Binder (1988, 128–69).

(Colombe 1951). Maghraoui rightly points out that even authors such as al-Sayyid Marsot, who try to defend the Egyptians against these accusations, fall into the trap of colonialism by apologetically claiming that Egypt was able, by all means, to transform itself and adapt to the requirements of the foreign political systems. In fact, they deny the role of their own identity and wholly submit to the idea of Western states as models to be emulated. Moreover, Maghraoui offers a complex picture of liberal intellectuals who made use of European concepts of citizenship and nationalism and therewith forced Egyptians to either accept foreign concepts and the alienation from their communal identity or reject the concept of liberalism altogether. He also finds these contradictions and tensions in the constitutional text that framed the struggle for influence among political groups (Maghraoui 2006, 141–45).

Another common explanation focuses on the power constellation of the regime as a whole, which essentially precluded successful parliamentary rule. In what has been described as a triangle of political forces, each corner pulled in a different direction and thus prevented effective stabilization within the new system (Deeb 1979a; Whidden 2013, 101–30). One of the corners was represented by King Fu'ad (1922–36), who had been installed by the British because he was the only pro-British heir of the Muhammad 'Ali dynasty. He was succeeded by his son Faruq (1936–52), whose accession to the throne was carefully managed by the British behind the scenes. Despite this, Thornhill described the early period of Faruq's rule as a "patriotic Egyptian royal house with its own nationalist agenda" before he turned into a "playboy monarch" (2010, 282, 280). Although both kings were, in many ways, dependent on the British, they constantly tried to expand their power through political maneuvering vis-à-vis the representatives of the ailing British Empire. However, the British, as the second major player in Egypt, maintained control of many parts of the administration and the army and could therefore still credibly threaten the political local actors with another military intervention. The rationale of informal British rule was to balance the nationalist movement of the Wafd with the palace. This divide-and-rule strategy was embedded in tumultuous regional and international developments: for example, the British integrated the Wafd within political decision making during critical periods, such as with the formalization of British military control of the Suez Canal in the Anglo-Egyptian defense treaty of 1936 (Thornhill 2010). The British even delegitimized King Faruq in 1942 by using the British military to force the monarch to appoint a Wafd leader as prime minister. In the years when the Axis powers sought control of the Middle East, a nationalistic yet strong Egypt was more favorable to British interests than a weak monarchic and collaborative government. Once this threat disappeared, so too did British support for the nationalistic party. The Wafd Party was the third major force, and it dominated the parliament, so every time the palace or the British wanted to weaken the Wafd, they would dissolve the Chamber of Deputies. Consequently, in spite of the five-year mandate, elections of the chamber took place much more frequently—the average duration of a legislative period was 2.8 years.[22] However, the Wafd learned their lesson and became a more cooperative bargaining partner (Thornhill 2010), abandoning the fight against the monarchy to safeguard their political positions, and thereby damaging their fundamental legitimacy as a nationalist movement (Reid 1980, 734; Gordon 1989, 208).

In both arguments—drawing either on the constitutional setting or on power relations—democracy seems to be the underlying benchmark for evaluating the constitutional monarchy. It is questionable, however, whether this period should be regarded as the failure of democracy or rather as the collapse of autocracy (Zaki 1995, 11). Votes for parliament might have been cast freely most times, but the position of the powerful head of state was never up for a vote, nor was British rule, which was applied by informal means and backed by military presence. Ultimately, the king could dissolve parliament at any time. I argue that an analysis of political institutions and parliament, in particular, from the perspective of an authoritarian regime provides another explanation for the breakdown of the constitutional monarchy.

22. Election years for the Chamber of Deputies were 1924, 1925, 1926, 1929, 1931, 1936, 1938, 1942, 1945, and 1950 (Binder 1978, 125). For the members of parliament and the duration of legislative sessions until 1935, see Subhi (1939–47, vol. 6).

A closer look at the parliamentary activities reveals not only that parliament reflected broader political changes but that changes within the assembly were also significant for the whole regime. First of all, internal splits occurred when many dedicated Wafd members, especially members of the urban intelligentsia, left the party after being alienated by the leadership style of Zaghlul's successor, Mustafa al-Nahhas (Badrawi 2005, 108). Starting in the late 1930s, the Wafd resorted to censorship to curb the growing anti-Wafd press and also—within the new cooperative atmosphere toward the king between 1950 and 1952—to prevent negative reporting about the palace (Gordon 1989, 199). Concurrently, corruption scandals hit the party, revealing how top leaders had enriched themselves, relatives, and friends by making use of their powerful positions (Reid 1980, 727–35). Frustration with the party's leadership led to fragmentation within the organization and to groups splintering from the party entirely.[23] Changes within the Wafd likewise affected the way the majority party behaved toward other parties in parliament. Opponents of the Wafd even spoke of the party as exercising a parliamentary dictatorship, especially under Zaghlul's successor, al-Nahhas. This accusation was based on the latter's use of the Wafd's supremacy without any willingness to compromise with oppositional forces (Badrawi 2005, 108; Deeb 1979a). Smaller parties were thereby motivated to use their potential to tip the scale when there was deadlock between the most powerful actors. The Liberal Constitutionalists, for instance, ignored their key political positions and opted for an alliance with the king in 1930, when the party decided to participate in a government by decree. This "Government of the Iron Grip" introduced a new, illiberal constitution that remained in force until 1936, when the former one was reinstituted (Maghraoui 2006, 128–29).

The constitutional text of 1930 was a clear expansion of the king's prerogatives and constituted a loss of power for the parliament. The monarch had the right to veto any legislation and to nominate the majority of

---

23. Among them were Ahmad Muhammad and Mahmud al-Nuqrashi, who led a group that split off in 1938, and al-Kutla al-wafdiyya, led by Makram 'Ubayd in 1942 (Maghraoui 2006, 134–35).

senators, rather than only two-fifths as before. In addition, the Chamber of Deputies lost its right to make legislative initiatives in financial matters (al-Sayyid Marsot 1977, 143). The constitution of 1930 did not enjoy any popular support, nor did the repressive style of the prime ministers during that period sit well with the public. In 1935, Egypt experienced labor and student protests, which rallied for a return to the 1923 constitution together with the major parties (al-Sayyid Marsot 1977, 175–76). However, it was only after protests had started that the Wafd took an active position against the new constitutional order, abandoned its cooperative approach to dealing with the government in place, and joined an alliance with other parties, the "patriotic front" (Jankowski 1970, 78–80). To appease the Egyptian populace, the British and the palace agreed to reinstall the original text of 1923.

Changes within the Wafd caused both internal criticism and critical activism in parliament to vanish; in the 1940s, power was left to the conservative class of large landowners, who dominated the other political parties of the time as well. The result was a decrease in the number of socioeconomic reform activities in parliament, which occurred during a time of a growing socioeconomic discontent. The Great Depression would also hit Egypt: inflation increased, wages stagnated, and unemployment soared (Farah 2009, 70; Reid 1980, 733). In spite of growing public protests, the Wafd leadership did not show any intention of increasing participation in social activism, but used their appeal among the masses to strengthen their bargaining position with the king and the British (Botman 1991, 33–34). The other parties also participated in the political game during these years, lacking a broader political agenda and motivated merely by a quest for power. In 1950, when the Wafd was back in power in both parliament and government, the prevailing nationalist public discourse at the time led Prime Minister Mustafa al-Nahhas to use the practice of speech from the throne in parliament to threaten Britain with a unilateral annulment of the Anglo-Egyptian defense treaty.[24] Without a plan

---

24. The speech from the throne is a tradition dating back to the beginnings of parliamentarianism in Egypt, when the khedive would open a session with a speech to which the deputies had the right to respond. See al-Sayyid and Mahran (1984, 11).

for implementation, the Wafdists could not shake this promise, and they attempted to appease the public by pushing a number of social reforms. At the same time, however, they stayed true to their old patronage politics and covert negotiations with the palace and the British (Gordon 1989).

Patience with the new political system in general vanished on account of this prolonged period of low responsiveness and the meager number of concessions made too late. Frustration with the parliamentary system grew, and alternatives to the existing political order developed, leading to a rejection of the multiparty system due to its tendency to bring about disunity. The most influential groups were the Islamist Muslim Brotherhood (al-Ikhwan al-Muslimun)[25] and the radical, nationalist Young Egypt (Misr al-fatat). The 1940s were marked by an increasingly violent atmosphere, and various groups, including the Wafd and the Muslim Brothers along with youth organizations that supported the palace, had secret military wings (Jankowski 1970). Political violence in the 1950s—assassinations of top politicians, the outbreak of riots, and urban unrest—paved the way for the coup of the Free Officers in 1952.

In sum, under the constitutional monarchy, parliament as an institution failed not only when regarded as part of a "liberal experiment" but also from an authoritarian regime perspective. The repeated early dissolutions of parliament and the cutback of parliamentary rights in the constitution of 1930 (until 1936) impeded incremental institutional development, as had been experienced in the 1870s and the 1900s. This, in turn, diminished the political results that parliament could achieve as an intermediary. Moreover, after the revolution of 1919 and the enactment of the constitution of 1923, a new order that included parliamentary rule had been imbued with hopes of social justice and national independence. Responsiveness on the part of parliamentarians to growing socioeconomic grievances, however, decreased considerably. As such, expectations remained unfulfilled, and the gap widened between legitimacy claims made by political actors and legitimacy beliefs held by an ever more mobilized public.

---

25. For the beginnings of the Muslim Brotherhood, see Mitchell (1993) and Lia (1998).

As parliamentary life and party politics merged, the growing aversion to parties and their seemingly endless struggle for power made it relatively easy for the representative chambers to be abolished after the coup of the Free Officers. The next chapter begins with a reintroduction of the representative assembly, which was consciously dissociated from party pluralism. This single party was never actually termed a party but rather presented as a mass organization—referred to as a "union" or "rally" in official rhetoric. Twenty years would pass before the multiparty system was reinstated and party politics fused with parliamentary life once again.

2

Parliamentary Contention and Innovation in the Egyptian Republic, 1952–2010

When considering autocratic parliaments under various forms of monarchic rule, we can see that parliamentarians have taken advantage of their share of power and have attempted to enlarge it. Their success has depended on the broader configuration of elites: a monarch defending his autonomy against imperial influence would strengthen parliament as a potential ally, for instance, while a monarch dependent on imperial support to remain in power would see parliament as a threat and try to reduce its rights. The latter case has often caused contention among parliamentarians, who have not wanted to part with any privileges. Despite these different constellations, the way parliamentarians have acted is significant in terms of the general perception of the institution and relative to the given context—one that includes specific norms regarding policies and political institutions. The successful balancing of parliament as an intermediary has the potential to boost regime stability while a negative perception of parliament can contribute to a crisis.

This chapter shows that similar dynamics can be observed when we look at Egypt as a republic. Under 'Abd al-Nasir, an intra-elite rivalry developed between a right-wing-dominated parliament and an increasingly leftist single-party. Playing this important role as a counterweight, parliament was able to expand its consultative and legislative roles as well as its government oversight rights. In particular, after Egypt's defeat in the Six-Day War of 1967, the president was weakened and sought the support of parliamentarians and their associated networks, one reason that 'Abd al-Nasir abandoned socialist policies in 1970.

In his first years as president, Anwar al-Sadat continued to strengthen parliament as a pillar of support, leading the assembly to become more and more active. Once al-Sadat felt more powerful after the strategic victory of 1973 and initiated his controversial *infitah* reforms, he realized that he could not control the institution as he wanted. His relationship with the parliament turned contentious, particularly after the 1977 bread riots. Public pressure against specific policies was then channeled into parliament, leading al-Sadat to enact interinstitutional modifications designed to weaken it. As the conflict was still ongoing when al-Sadat was assassinated in October 1981, it is difficult to judge whether the initial empowering reforms of parliament would have had the unintended consequence of actually undermining al-Sadat's legitimacy and ultimately bringing down his regime.

Nevertheless, his successor, Mubarak, had learned the lesson from his predecessor, and he restored a balance between different elite factions inside of parliament while also enacting modest and gradual reforms that would not constitute a harsh break with widely held norms on policies. The presence of oppositional parties in the 1980s, in contrast to the 1990s, did not alter much in this regard. It was only with the slow rise of private businessmen to the most powerful group of actors within the ruling party over a period of decades that this balance was once again lost during the 2000s. Opposition MPs increasingly used parliamentary tools and different media channels to direct growing public discontent with the country's socioeconomic situation toward the assembly, thereby bringing this imbalance to the fore. This is yet another example of an autocratic parliament proving to be not so easily controlled by the core elite. A closer analysis of the years 2005–10 in chapters 3, 4, and 5 will show how this growing legitimacy crisis could be observed in parliament, and how the loss of parliament's balancing function became one of the catalysts for the 2011 uprising.

State-Economy Relations from 'Abd al-Nasir to al-Sadat and Mubarak

Until the eve of the January 25th Revolution in 2011, the mainstream narrative about the history of Egypt's economy stated that after the failure of the socialist experiment of 'Abd al-Nasir's reign, his successor, al-Sadat, took a historic step by opening the economy. However, due to persistent corruption and inefficiency, Egypt remained economically stagnant. These obstacles were finally overcome in 1991 through the Economic Reform and Structural Adjustment Program formulated by the International Monetary Fund (IMF) and the World Bank. In the 2000s, a group of technocrats and private businessmen allied with one of the sons of President Mubarak gained political influence and accelerated the process of privatization and liberalization initiated by these international financial institutions. Such efforts received global praise; for instance, Egypt was recognized as Top Reformer of the Year 2008 by the World Bank. However, this is a one-sided and rather distanced view of these developments. The following overview, from 'Abd al-Nasir to Mubarak, examines the challenges and responses that shaped the state's role in the economy and the part played by external actors. The resemblance to aspects of the monarchic period highlights the importance of structural issues particular to Egypt and the logic of authoritarian rule that shaped parliamentary dynamics.

Egyptian economist Jalal Amin argues that, during the constitutional monarchy (1923–52), the informal influence of the British, in cooperation with a still-dominant feudal regime founded on agriculture-based wealth, prevented Egypt from embarking on a more ambitious program of industrialization (Amin 2011, 45–48). This changed once the Free Army Officers seized power in 1952. President Jamal 'Abd al-Nasir (1954–70) reformed the agricultural sector and ushered in a new process of industrialization. In terms of agrarian reform, he made use of the old idea of eliminating the intermediary level of cooperatives and replacing wealthy landlords with state officials (Bush 2007, 1601). Through several laws introduced between 1952 and 1969, he redistributed 12 percent of the nation's land to landless families. Nevertheless, private property continued to persist legally, as did large estates of up to 300 feddan per family (1 feddan = 0.42 hectares), which was also a result of recurrent backlashes by landowner families within the ruling elite against complete communalization (Springborg 1979).

Here again, the solution to development was found in the state-led economy, which simultaneously aimed for independence from foreign actors. However, 'Abd al-Nasir's ideal of a strong state was authoritarian in nature, and it relied on a social contract that sacrificed political rights for social welfare. Repression and a lack of opportunities for participation became acceptable for many Egyptians, who benefited from heavy state investment in various sectors. For instance, the educational system was expanded to such an extent that, between 1952 and 1966, the number of pupils enrolled in primary schools rose from 1.3 million to 3.4 million (Bush 2007, 1603). The national output increased by 6 percent, and per capita income rose 3.2 percent annually. Inflation was low, and rents, controlled by the state, were kept at a moderate level (Amin 2011, 50–51). The state became a major creator of jobs, with 'Abd al-Nasir pursuing an import-substitution approach to economic development. The president, however, was wary of allowing peasants and workers to join forces, and he tried to prevent any strong alliances from forming against his rule. He also created corporatist organizations, such as the Egyptian Trade Union Federation, meant to control the workers and curb any independent action.

To give his authoritarian rule a unifying identity, 'Abd al-Nasir rallied the masses around the idea of Pan-Arabism, with himself as the "voice of the Arabs" (*sawt al-'arab*), and mobilized them against foreign interference. His greatest success on this front was nationalizing the Suez Canal in 1956. The combination of his welfare efforts and assertive nationalism provided a foundation for populist state-corporatism. But this form of authoritarian rule was unfeasible after the defeat in the Six-Day War in 1967, which brought with it a huge financial burden. The war led to a 600 percent increase in military expenditures—in other words, it absorbed 25 percent of GDP and decreased the finances available for further investment and poverty reduction (Amin 2011). It also marked the end of large sources of external funding from both the United States and the Soviet Union, which were attracted by Egypt's neutrality in the Cold War. Despite the rhetoric, 'Abd al-Nasir's model of development also relied on foreign money, not in the form of debts but as food aid from the United States or support for such infrastructural projects as the High Dam from the Soviets. In yet another echo of Muhammad 'Ali's experience, the means to maintain a strong state were no longer available after the military defeat. This led 'Abd al-Nasir to partially withdraw from the economy and pursue a foreign policy reorientation toward the United States in the Rogers Plan of 1969. After 'Abd al-Nasir's sudden death in 1970, it was his successor, Anwar al-Sadat, who would actually implement this political and economic turn and bring it further, which became famous as the *infitah*.

Infitah means opening, and the initial plan aimed to open the Egyptian economy to foreign investment. Statistics from this period indeed point to positive development: between 1975 and 1985, the economy grew by 8 percent and per capita income increased by 5 percent. However, these numbers hide the fact that growth was based on unsustainable sources originating from the oil boom of the 1970s. After reconquering Sinai from Israel in the October War of 1973, the oil fields on the peninsula were revived and the Suez Canal was reopened, generating massive revenue in a time of increasing trade. Moreover, the Arab Gulf states needed guest workers, which led to a huge migration of Egyptians to Saudi Arabia, the United Arab Emirates, Kuwait, and Iraq. Not only did this ease the job situation in Egypt, but workers also sent substantial remittances to their families at home, which enabled the poor and middle classes to cope with increasing prices and inflation.

On the other hand, these developments concealed the fact that the radical opening of the Egyptian economy, free of protections, harmed the national manufacturing and agricultural sectors. Expectations tied to foreign investors proved misguided: instead of investing in sustainable industrial or agricultural projects, the sectors that attracted capital—and hence boomed during that period—were construction, contracting, and trade, mainly in the import sector. This, in turn, led to a massive increase in food imports and a dramatic decline in agricultural productivity, which undermined poverty reduction in the countryside. Wheat was—and still is—a crucial crop in Egypt, and its consumption increased by 9 percent due to massive population growth from the 1960s on, while productivity stagnated at around 2 percent (Bush 2007, 1603). The sensitivity of the wheat issue became evident in 1977, when President al-Sadat planned to cut subsidies for bread. This caused the so-called bread riots, public protests across the country that quickly led the president to capitulate. Until 2011, the subsidized bread price was kept constant—although there was scarcity and manipulation in the quality and weight of bread. Because of the gap between demand and domestic supply, wheat was imported from the United States, financed by US loans.

The new model for the overall economy was built on cash-intensive, export-led agriculture. It was based on private ownership and provided incentives for growing high-value, low-nutrition foodstuffs and cut flowers. Once again, as the strong state withdrew, the time came for the intermediaries, and not the broader populace, to profit. A class of nouveaux riches with close contacts to the president emerged, while the general populace increasingly had to struggle for life (el Tarouty 2015). While large landowners, capable of investing huge sums of money to meet the demands of international markets, reappeared on the scene, Egypt had to import half of its food in the mid-1980s (Bush 2007, 1603).

The government at the time also borrowed heavily from foreign banks and investors. The extent to which this was necessary remains in doubt: when 'Abd al-Nasir died, Egypt had a foreign debt burden of 5 billion US dollars, and after the end of al-Sadat's reign the burden grew sixfold to around 30 billion US dollars in just ten years. The first instance of Egypt facing difficulties getting additional loans occurred after the Egyptian-Israeli Peace Accord in 1979, at which point all Arab creditors stopped further business with Egypt. The other blow came from international markets: the oil boom in the 1970s led to a massive capital surplus in the West, which was reinvested in the third world at exorbitant interest rates. When oil prices began to drop in the mid-1980s, creditors' willingness to borrow fell dramatically. This means that although Mubarak's foreign policy turn toward a cold peace with Israel had again brought Egypt closer to the Arab world—including the oil-rich Gulf states—access to new money began to shrink and nearly dried out. In spite of this, Mubarak continued to rely on heavy borrowing in the fashion of his predecessor. The debt level reached 45 billion US dollars, almost 150 percent of the GDP, and debt servicing cost Egypt 50 percent of its total exports. It was at this point that international financial institutions entered the scene. In 1987, the IMF offered Egypt an extension of the repayment period for its debts, after a debt restructuring and prolongation of payments; but this was conditioned on the implementation of an austerity program. The structural adjustment program mainly required the Egyptian state to reduce expenditures and its active role in the economy, and to lessen welfare benefits such as subsidies for essential goods and services (Moench 1988; Amin 2011).

Egypt also experienced the well-known vicious circle of reducing public investment in the economy to improve the state budget, which ends in an economic downturn. GDP growth fell to 4 percent, per capita income fell to 2 percent, unemployment increased, and wages did not grow in tandem with price development despite sinking inflation rates (Amin 2011, 61). The actual relief of Egypt's debt situation coincided with the Iraqi occupation of Kuwait in 1990. Egypt's support for the US intervention against Saddam Husayn proved to be of such strategic importance that the Gulf states and the Paris Club gradually reduced Egypt's debt by half up until 1994. Of course, this financial assistance did not come for free, nor was it offered "only" in exchange for a vital, yet noncrucial, foreign policy move. In fact, new structural adjustment programs (SAPs) were introduced in May 1991 by the IMF, and in November 1991 by the World Bank, based on the concepts of privatization, liberalization, and the reduction of state expenditures. In the 1990s, the ruling elite around Mubarak tried to buy time by pointing out the potential dangers to Egypt's stability if reforms came too abruptly, so provisions were implemented reluctantly and slowly. The gradual, balanced approach was not only symbolic but also built on satisfying the two camps within the ruling elite coalition: those in favor of expanding the private sector, and advocates of the public sector. Although the interests of different powerful actors were satisfied, al-Sayyid claims that the beneficiaries were mainly public sector managers and provincial elites. The latter profited from the sale of public assets and enterprises on a local level (1990, 59). This means that, yet again, intermediaries profited and expanded their local influence as the state withdrew its economic control due to financial restraints.

In spite of its cautiousness, the Mubarak regime embarked on macroeconomic stabilization efforts, such as the liberalization of the interest rate on the Egyptian pound and of the foreign exchange market. Egypt became a member of the World Trade Organization and the Greater Arab Free Trade Agreement between 1991 and 1998. By the end of the decade, the attention had shifted toward trade and institutions. Up until 2004, laws were introduced to promote exports; special economic zones were installed and the exchange rate was liberalized. A number of trade agreements were negotiated with the European Union, the Common Market for Eastern and South Africa (COMESA), and Jordan, Morocco, and Tunisia (Agadir Free Trade Agreement) (Alissa 2007, 5–6). A major shift in government policies took place when business elites themselves took over powerful positions within the ruling party and political institutions. From 2004 on, the new prime minister, Ahmad Nazif, and his ministers dramatically accelerated the privatization process, and they sold off more state companies (in terms of total asset value) in one year than during the previous ten years combined. The pace of privatization was accelerated for agricultural land as well.

However, the Egyptian economy remained marked by a high concentration of wealth in the hands of the few, the only difference being that these entrepreneurs now belonged to the private sector. The linkage between the political and the economic systems played a major role in the privatization process, and it gave preferential access to proxies of the ruling elite. State institutions for protecting the market economy were weak, and competition policies were often not a focus for the elites. As a result, a class of big business–owners developed that owned large shares of the industrial and service sectors (el Tarouty 2015). Agricultural capitalism also flourished, leading to greater inequality in land distribution than even before 'Abd al-Nasir's land reform in the 1950s (Bush 2007, 1612). In addition, continued state interventions challenged the characterization of Egypt's economy as liberalized and free. Especially in regard to determining prices, costs for food and energy were mainly regulated by subsidies, though often to the advantage of large companies rather than the poor. Furthermore, the informal economy in Egypt expanded, with estimates claiming it represented up to 40 percent of Egypt's economic activities. Informal workers did not receive state compensation for the negative effects of the economic restructuring.

While the private sector experienced annual growth rates of up to 8 percent, state expenditures in the educational sector declined from 5.2 to 4.0 percent of GDP (United Nations Development Programme and Institute of National Planning 2008, 297). The health sector remained underfunded, with privately financed health costs growing from 63 to 70 percent

(Egyptian Initiative for Personal Rights 2009, 28). Furthermore, the social buffer against the negative effects of the privatization process was weakened, as illustrated by the government's handling of surplus workers. One of the biggest problems inherited from the corporatist policies of 'Abd al-Nasir's reign was the employment of unnecessary labor. For example, around 25 percent of workers in the textile sector were superfluous, but the social effects of mass layoffs would have been unpredictable. To avoid instability while selling off public sector companies, laws were enacted that forbade layoffs or decreases in wages after privatization.[1] To keep investment in Egyptian companies attractive, the government relied on early retirement schemes to motivate workers to leave their jobs in exchange for compensation. These amounts, between 40,000 and 50,000 Egyptian pounds, enabled people to start a new life as a taxi driver or as an owner of a grocery store, earning roughly the same income they would have in the textile mills. In 2004, this compensation scheme was reduced at the same moment that privatization increased under the cabinet of Ahmad Nazif.

All of these policy changes coincided with price increases, mainly for food and basic goods. Although subsidies shielded against some of these hikes, the cost of living was rising dramatically for low and medium-income Egyptians. Social unrest grew, and workers increasingly started wildcat strikes, most often with company-specific demands such as the payment of promised wage increases and bonuses. A nationwide campaign for a national minimum wage of 1,200 Egyptian pounds emerged, initiated by a group of politicized workers together with labor-related non-governmental organizations. Local and national protests culminated in the largest wave of labor protests in Egypt since 1946 (Beinin 2010, 12–15; El-Mahdi 2010, 389–95). During the global financial crisis, when food speculation increased and pushed prices to record highs on the world market, the effects were felt all around the globe, including in Egypt. As rice and beans reached exorbitant prices, consumption shifted to the reliably subsidized 'aysh baladi, a low-quality bread. This caused bread to become

---

1. "Historian Joel Beinin on the Egyptian Labor Crisis," *The Human Experience*, Feb. 4, 2011, http://humanexperience.stanford.edu/beininegypt (site discontinued).

scarce, and people had to wait in long lines in front of bakeries. Spontaneous riots broke out, invoking the collective memory of the bread riots of 1977. With the situation growing ever more sensitive, the army intervened and distributed bread on the streets produced in military factories.[2]

These economic reforms and social consequences are the point of departure for chapters 3, 4, and 5, which analyze the debates around the antitrust laws, which represented a milestone in Egypt's transition from a state-led to a free market economy. They are likewise part of a development spanning centuries, demonstrating the ups and downs of state control in the economy, which varied according to the relative strength or weakness of the central state. Here we see that parliament and its members are embedded in a socioeconomic context marked by various degrees of external influence in domestic affairs, the existence of poverty and social inequality (along with attempts to overcome them), and the winners and losers of reforms among the ruling elite.

Gamal Abdel 'Abd al-Nasir's Single-Party Regime: From Intra-Elite Struggle to Interinstitutional Conflict, 1952–1970

After the coup of the Free Officers in 1952, it proved simple to abolish the parliamentary and party structure created by the monarchy, as it had become a symbol of a failed, corrupt, and fragmented political system. As early as the 1940s, the founder of the Muslim Brotherhood, Hasan al-Banna, had disparagingly called the multiparty system "*hizbiyya*," stating that parties lead to disunity and represent only special interests rather than the common good (Awadi 2004, 82). In a similar vein, after the coup, Jamal 'Abd al-Nasir, who assumed the presidency in 1954, delegitimized the constitutional monarchy as only having been an instrument of large landowners and capitalists. To him, parties represented a system utilized by foreign powers, one that Egypt should not copy. Instead, 'Abd al-Nasir declared mass movements to be a more suitable form of political organization for

---

2. "Egypt and Food Security," *Al-Ahram Weekly*, Oct. 23–29, 2008, no. 919; "Egypt's Army to Tackle Bread Crisis," *BBC News*, Mar. 17, 2008, http://news.bbc.co.uk/2/hi/middle _east/7300899.stm.

Egypt, as they granted everyone the opportunity to participate regardless of social and economic background, especially considering that parties under the monarchy had been dominated by wealthy landowner families. As al-Banna before him had done, 'Abd al-Nasir avoided the term "party," instead opting for "rally" or "union" (Harik 1973, 84–85).

The constitutional setting remained preliminary throughout 'Abd al-Nasir's reign. It built on the 1923 constitution and, besides establishing a republic and a single-party system, weakened the legislative power of parliament by giving presidential decrees law-like status (Brown 2002, 79). As a de facto single-party system, the mass organization created by 'Abd al-Nasir dominated the National Assembly—the parliament that had been reinstated with the constitution of 1956 and newly elected in 1957. It was dissolved when Egypt and Syria formed the United Arab Republic (UAR) between 1958 and 1961. In 1960, the UAR National Assembly convened for the first time, comprising four hundred Egyptian and two hundred Syrian members. It was abolished upon the breakup of the UAR one year later.[3] The National Assembly was then newly elected in 1964 with the enactment of a new provisional constitution, and again in 1969, the last election before 'Abd al-Nasir's death.

The development of parliament during 'Abd al-Nasir's reign was closely connected to that of the single-party. Yet, as will become evident, the national leadership of the party did not determine the makeup of the parliament; during times of power struggle among the elite, the two institutions were, in fact, rivals. During 'Abd al-Nasir's reign, three successive mass organizations were formed (see table 2): the Liberation Rally (1953–56), the National Union (1957–61), and the Arab Socialist Union (ASU) (1962–76). In contrast to many other post-colonial, single-party regimes, 'Abd al-Nasir's mass organization was not the same grassroots movement that had earlier led the anticolonial struggle. As discussed in the previous section, the Wafd Party had fought for independence but lost its credibility during the constitutional monarchy (Binder 1978, 41), which explains its limited relevance as a mass organization at the beginning of 'Abd al-Nasir's

---

3. For more information on the United Arab Republic, see Jankowski (2001).

Table 2

Development of the Single Party under 'Abd al-Nasir

Liberation Rally 1953–56	National Union 1957–61	Arab Socialist Union 1962–76
• Broad social base • Eclectic ideology • Party organization loose, incomplete, lack of discipline • Autonomy for local level (elections of basic unit)		
		Restructuring Phase 1963–67 • Professionalization • Stricter hierarchy: nomination instead of election • Youth organization

reign. Accordingly, the Liberation Rally was formed to organize support for 'Abd al-Nasir, who at the time was about to consolidate his power. This entailed integrating student and labor unions within the mobilization and organizational structures of the Liberation Rally (Vatikiotis 1969, 83; Waterbury 1983, 312). Similarly, the National Union, headed by future president Anwar al-Sadat as its secretary general, was also supposed to bind influential persons to the regime and to prevent opposition. Despite being renamed the Arab Socialist Union, the organization's main principles remained the same until 1963; namely, creating a broad social base subordinated to executive power and led by an eclectic ideology to attract diverse groups (Harik 1973, 86). The party's organization remained loose and incomplete, and it lacked discipline.

A gap also remained between the national and provincial level and the district and village level. The first was organized hierarchically, with members of its high party committees and the government selected by the leadership. The latter, in contrast, was composed through relatively free elections, reflecting the local distribution of influence, including shifts in power distribution. In rural areas, this meant that village mayors and well-off farmers dominated the party; in provincial towns, these local elites comprised notables, civil servants, professionals, and teachers

(Harik 1973, 87–88). The great losers within this power distribution were large landowners, who had lost economic power due to the land reform and, as a consequence, also lost much of their political influence. As Harik argues, the local level retained its autonomy, for it never threatened the concentration of national power in the president. Party cadres at the lower levels did not have much of an effect on policy implementation, as this was reserved for the civil bureaucracy (1973, 89).

From 1963 to 1967, the leadership initiated a reform of the ASU to increase political participation at all levels. Pressure to do so came from the absence of an institution that could ease the adoption of socioeconomic reforms at the local level. Moreover, cooperation with the Soviet Union put enormous pressure on 'Abd al-Nasir to release communists from jail. Although they were not allowed to establish a communist party, their political activism led to a leftist turn in the regime (Pawelka 1985, 78). 'Abd al-Nasir's solution was to transform the ASU into a cadre party (Waterbury 1983). The restructuring was effectively implemented by 'Ali Sabri, who served as prime minister between 1964 and 1965 and as the party's secretary general from 1965 to 1971. The restructuring rested on professionalization and a stricter hierarchy accompanied by the elimination of elections at the local level. Party cadres would be appointed from above and received intensive training in the newly founded institutes. A major push for a more active ASU was spearheaded through the creation of a party youth organization. As it turned out, reforms to revitalize the mass movement toward purposes of political participation failed—not because they lacked effectiveness but rather because they were too effective. Conflict arose between the old party elites and the new, active, well-trained cadre. The power concentration in the hands of the bureaucrat 'Ali Sabri, in particular, provoked countermeasures to block his penetration into all power structures. Officers personally subordinated to 'Abd al-Nasir were installed in the ASU leadership, and the army—under the control of another ambitious officer, 'Abd al-Hakim 'Amir—attempted to stall the empowerment of the ASU. Moreover, the parliament developed into the right-wing counterpart of the increasingly left-oriented ASU. The final turning point in the restructuring of the ASU came with Egypt's dramatic defeat in the 1967 war with Israel. Instead of a party that alienated

large segments of its former allies, the regime could no longer afford ene-
mies from within its own ranks, and it opted again for an expansive yet
superficial umbrella organization. Owing to the disastrous economic situation, the regime was particularly in need of the support from the wealthy
and upper classes, which stood in contrast to the socialist model of the
cadre party. Turning away from a state-led economy was presented to the
broader public as a logical means of ending state-controlled mass organization and ushering in a new era of pluralism (Pawelka 1985, 79–80); the
election of party cadres at the top national level was introduced in 1968
for this purpose.

With this short overview of the development of the mass organizations
in Egypt under 'Abd al-Nasir, we now turn to the role and functioning of
the parliament at that time. The National Assembly was, in fact, limited to
representatives from a single party. Potential candidates required approval
from the party before the electoral race, which automatically excluded
oppositional forces. Nevertheless, the parliament under 'Abd al-Nasir
was a place of public criticism and certain observations on parliamentary
activity can be made.

In the years under 'Abd al-Nasir, the parliament consisted of 360
members, ten of whom were appointed by the president. Each of the 175
electoral districts (*markaz*) sent two deputies to the National Assembly
in Cairo. The creation of districts was originally based on police districts
but developed independently afterward. Candidates for the parliamentary elections had to be approved either by the executive committee of
the National Union or by the party secretariat of the Arab Socialist Union
(Harik 1973, 86–87). In 1962, a provision was endorsed that 50 percent of
the parliament had to either be workers or peasants—a stipulation derived
from the National Charter, in which 'Abd al-Nasir proclaimed the alliance of the working forces. Even though "workers" were in fact primarily state officials or public sector employees and peasants were "enmeshed
in governmental rural patronage networks" (Baaklini, Denoeux, and
Springborg 1999, 224), representation of the lower classes increased. Poor
candidates received funding from the government for their electoral campaigns (Binder 1978, 313); thus, the percentage of wealthy businessmen,
lawyers, senior officials, officers, and landowners sank between 1960–61

(the election year for the UAR parliament) and 1964, when the Egyptian chamber was newly elected (Dekmejian 1968, 361). Still, local and regional networks and ties existed among certain families. Their influence translated into offices in the National Union as well as into seats in the National Assembly (Binder 1978, 119). The elections were characterized first by a strong preselection of candidates. In 1964, for example, only 1,748 out of the 3,570 nominated candidates were ultimately able to run in the elections (Binder 1978, 311–13). Second, an average of five candidates would run for office in a single district, also indicating a high degree of intra-elite competition. As the party itself was never strongly rooted in society, elections reflected local power structures that were related to landownership in rural areas. This explains why parliament, in a single-party system, could develop relatively independent of the Arab Socialist Union and eventually turn into its antagonist.

The assessment of parliamentary activity in the years under 'Abd al-Nasir would appear to be a question of the glass being half empty or half full. Pawelka points to the fact that only a small number of legislative initiatives ever achieved their targets. In the late 1950s, not a single draft law made by the parliament came into force. At the end of the 1960s, around 7 percent of parliamentary proposals were accepted. Furthermore, issues of foreign policy, national defense, and the government's program were mostly left untouched in the debates. Instead, room for articulation and criticism seemed to exist only in the realm of social policies, infrastructure, agriculture, and regional and local issues (Pawelka 1985, 95–97). But are such observations actually an argument against the significance of the parliament? Institutional developments take time, but they did, in fact, happen; an example is the increase of parliamentary proposals, which is quite reasonable considering that MPs could articulate and lobby for their causes from 1964 on. This also matches patterns found under monarchic rule, in which the National Assembly dealt with social and economic issues first, on account of the backgrounds of many parliamentarians and the needs of their constituencies. Socioeconomic issues in a developing country are of great importance; this was especially the case for 'Abd al-Nasir, whose legitimacy rested on the promise of socioeconomic prosperity for the broad population.

These general trends are supported by more detailed accounts of parliamentary life. Dekmejian observed that, following growing public discontent, bread and butter issues were increasingly expressed about supply shortages for food and consumer goods as well as their rising prices. He states that the intensity of criticism increased from year to year and finds that the parliamentarians actually "carve[d] out an area of action in the Egyptian political process" (1971, 160). For example, the National Assembly achieved a redrafting of the budget in 1964; even on the highly sensitive issue of the Yemen War that Egypt was fighting at the time, the MPs pushed the head of the military, 'Amir, to make some of the information about the war public (Dekmejian 1971, 158). Parliamentary life was even more active on topics with which the MPs were more familiar and which supported their interests. In 1957, for instance, members of parliament with an agronomist background prevented one of 'Abd al-Nasir's protégés from pushing for more radical reforms of collective property tenure policies.[4] In the late 1960s, conservative landowners reversed communalization reforms when the left wing was weak once again (Springborg 1979, 55, 61). MPs also held the government to account for cases of the mismanagement of state authorities within their constituencies (Dekmejian 1968, 363).

The parliament's internal structure likewise developed, such as in the area of committees—generally regarded as positive indicators of parliamentary power and expertise. Public hearings took place, and committee heads and members gained in importance, among them the committee of reply (*lajnat al-radd*). Here, the MPs prepared a response to the prime minister's report at the beginning of every parliamentary session (Dekmejian 1971, 160).[5] These developments took place in the mid-1960s at a time when the 'Abd al-Nasir regime faced mounting pressure. As mentioned above, the left wing had become stronger and dominated the single party. Thus, some scholars argue that empowering parliament appeared opportune for 'Abd al-Nasir for a number of reasons. In general, it can be

---

4. For perceptions of 'Abd al-Nasir's reform policies in rural areas, see Harik (1974).

5. This is a reinterpretation of the parliamentary tradition of the speech from the throne, discussed in chapter 1 and in al-Sayyid and Mahran (1984, 11).

regarded as an attempt to increase legitimacy by granting more political freedom. Baaklini, Denoeux, and Springborg suggest that granting space for criticism meant that critical voices would be channeled into parliament and kept under control at the same time. This appears to be the same "safety-valve" argument discussed in the introduction. Here again, it is unclear where the line should be drawn between a safety valve and a magnifying glass—which brings the executive to take the MPs' considerations into account and adapt policies accordingly. Another purpose of the stronger parliament was to allow deputies critical of the government to help keep ministers in check and provide an excuse for eliminating certain ministers when needed (Baaklini, Denoeux, and Springborg 1999, 225).

All of these effects—which 'Abd al-Nasir may have intended when parliament was reelected in 1957 or from which he simply profited when they occurred—should not be mistaken as the only outcome of parliamentary development from that time. In fact, parliament used its room for maneuvering, including a greater say on specific policies, when the regime was weakened after the 1967 war in particular. The members of parliament increasingly learned how to represent issues of public interest, such as the food supply, but also to achieve more moderate versions of socioeconomic reforms, including land reforms. Through this, they developed the institution by activating and defining parliamentary procedures and mechanisms anew. Headed by Anwar al-Sadat as the assembly's speaker, along with his deputy, Sayyid Mar'i, parliament defended and even extended its rights after the 1967 war, when ASU supervision of the nomination of candidates was circumvented. As Baaklini, Denoeux, and Springborg write, the right wing even seized the opportunity to expand their representation in the chamber (1999, 225–26). From this perspective, the post-1967 abandonment of socialist policies initiated by 'Abd al-Nasir in 1970 appears to be a victory for parliament, as does the succession of the assembly's speaker to the presidency after 'Abd al-Nasir's death.

Multiparty Politics and Parliamentary Contention
toward President al-Sadat, 1970–1981

When al-Sadat assumed power, he claimed that one of his major goals was to "build a state of institutions" (Springborg 1979, 52). The first step

Table 3

**Development of the Parliamentary and Party System
in the Egyptian Republic, 1953–2011**

Parliamentary Body		National Assembly (1956–58)	United Arab Republic National Assembly (1960–61)	National Assembly (1964–71)	People's Assembly (1971–2011)	
Party System		Single-party system (1953–75)			Three-party system (1976–78)	Multiparty system (1978–2011)
Ruling Party	Liberation Rally (1953–56)	National Union (1957–61)	Arab Socialist Union (1962–76)		Arab Socialist Party (Egypt Party) (1976–78)	National Democratic Party (1978–2011)

of institutional reform was to rename the parliament to People's Assembly (Majlis al-sha'b) in 1971, leaving the ASU party structure as it was (Beattie 2000, 82). Instead, al-Sadat focused first on the individual level and imprisoned the strong man of the ASU, 'Ali Sabri, and other top elites under 'Abd al-Nasir (Springborg 1979, 62). A profound reform of the party system only occurred once al-Sadat consolidated his presidency after his success in the October War of 1973.[6] As table 3 shows, after the monarchy was abolished, the party's reorganization coincided with a reform of the legislature only once. This highlights how parliament is part of a complex polity and is not a coherent set of institutions simply designed by the head of state and calculated for the purpose of stabilizing the regime. Some institutions are inherited, some reformed, and some created anew, which leads to an ongoing reconfiguration of the polity. Actors adapt to new institutions and changes in interinstitutional relations; the al-Sadat era is

---

6. It would be an exaggeration to speak of a military victory, as Sadat rather achieved a stalemate with Israel through his surprise attack. Nevertheless, the October War was a great success for Sadat, as he gained enough diplomatic weight to win back the Sinai Peninsula in negotiations.

a good example of the agency of co-opted actors, of how they try to utilize changes for their purposes, and of the gap between the ruler's intentions for institutional reforms and actual developments.

The transition from a single-party system—which was never referred to as such because 'Abd al-Nasir wanted to avoid using the term "party"—to a multiparty system occurred in an intermediary step. Before completely liberalizing the political arena, the Arab Socialist Union discussed its division into platforms (*manabir*) along the major political lines. An agreement on four platforms was reached in December 1975: the left, the Nasserist, the right, and the center. The decision was not, however, based on a broad agreement: the initiative to split up the mass organization actually came from the right wing, which opted for more political liberties in contrast to the left, which still followed the idea of a strong, unified mass organization with a vanguard. In 1976, an agreement was reached to call the various factions organizations (*tanzimat*) instead of platforms, and to divide the ASU into three parts, joining the two leftist groups into one. This further weakened the left, as very heterogeneous actors had to find common ground. The right rallied for the economic opening of Egypt and the revitalization of the private sector. The center was called Arab Socialist Egypt—widely known as the Egypt Party (Waterbury 1983, 365–66)—and was bound to al-Sadat. From the very beginning, open and fair competition between the organizations did not exist. Instead, it was clear that the Egypt Party was absorbing the ASU's resources, their members, and their claim to legitimacy for representing all of socialist Egypt (Cooper 1982, 192).

In 1977, the political arena was opened one step further when permission to establish political parties was granted and, accordingly, all the organizations officially transformed into parties. Al-Sadat's Egypt Party was renamed the National Democratic Party (al-Hizb al-watani al-dimuqrati) in 1978, and the more leftist faction within the ASU founded the Nationalist Unionist Progressive Party (Hizb al-tajammu' al-watani al-taqaddumi al-wahdawi, usually known as Tagammu), while the right wing gathered within the Socialist Liberal Party (*Hizb al-ahrar al-ishtirakiyyin*, usually known as *Ahrar* (Liberals). When the Tagammu Party became too critical of al-Sadat's economic liberalization policies, it was heavily repressed and marginalized in the political arena. The Socialist Labor

Table 4

Composition of the Pluralist Legislature under al-Sadat

	1976–79	1979–84
Arab Socialist Party/ National Democratic Party	280	330
Socialist Liberal Party	12	3
Nationalist Unionist Progressive Party	2	—
Socialist Labor Party	—	29
Independents	48	10
Appointed	10	10

Adapted from Waterbury 1983, 366, 371. Number of independents from Rizq 1991, 66.

Party was to be held in check by al-Sadat's brother-in-law, Mahmud Abu Wafiya (Fahmy 2002, 72–75). All the other newly founded parties were also headed by former members of the ruling elite under 'Abd al-Nasir and al-Sadat (Albrecht 2013, 39–42). The Wafd, the former popular nationalist party, reestablished itself as the New Wafd (al-Wafd al-jadid) in an attempt to reenter the party system, only to be dissolved by a referendum a few months later (Makram-Ebeid 1989, 425–30).

The introduction of the multiparty system should not be mistaken for democratic liberalization; the dominance of the president's party continued, and only opposition parties that did not question the regime as such were tolerated. The fact that the president supported the foundation of these new oppositional forces clearly indicates that the ruling elite must have expected a stabilizing effect from it.[7] Another move toward liberalization was to allow independent candidates to run in the 1976 elections, in which they actually attained 14 percent of the seats. Among them were two members of the Muslim Brotherhood, marking the first time that the Islamist organization, though still legally banned and therefore operating informally, had made it into a representative assembly (see table 4).

7. For an elaborated version of a functionalist perspective on the Egyptian opposition that also conceptually integrates the agency of oppositional parties, mainly as influence on the public discourse, see Albrecht (2013).

After 1978, however, al-Sadat reverted almost immediately to political deliberalization, which indicates that liberties had led to unexpected consequences that ran counter to al-Sadat's desire for stable rule. The emergence of outright criticism of the president inside parliament demonstrates the ultimate difficulty in managing critical voices in the political institution. To better grasp these processes, my focus will now turn to the ten years of rule under al-Sadat, including three different parliamentary settings: the People's Assembly under the single-party rule of the ASU (1971–75), two years of parliamentary life with the three organizations (*tanzimat*) (1976–77), and the beginning of the multiparty system in parliament in 1978 up to the assassination of al-Sadat in 1981.

One particularly noteworthy novelty for the parliament was that, for the first time in the constitutional history of Egypt, the Islamic shari'a was declared to be "a main source of legislation" (Article 2) in 1971, and then subsequently changed to "the main source of legislation" in the constitutional amendment of 1980. This did not, however, have any further repercussions on formal power relations established in the constitution of 1971, according to which the government, assembly, and presidency were to be interconnected in terms of their competences and responsibilities. Parliament exercised legislative power and had the right to approve the budget (Article 86); it shared the right to initiate laws only with the president (Article 109). Although the cabinet had to approve any modifications that the parliament suggested on the state budget (Article 115), the government was very much dependent on the president, who appointed all ministers, including the prime minister (Article 144). Parliament had the right to question, interpellate, and withdraw confidence from ministers, while the president's consent was needed to dismiss the prime minister (Articles 124–27).

The first session of the renamed and newly elected People's Assembly in 1971–72 was a moment of high parliamentary activity. Here again, we find the pattern of a weak executive relying on the legislature for support and legitimacy. Al-Sadat struggled with power rivalries among the ruling elite, especially 'Abd al-Nasir's allies, as well as with a weak economy and desolate army. Although the assembly of 1971 generally supported al-Sadat, the MPs were aware of the president's weakness and used it as a chance to increase parliamentary activity for legislation and oversight (Cooper 1982, 175–76). This resulted in the expansion of the internal organization of the People's Assembly; new leadership positions were created, the number of committees increased along with their degree of specialization, and a power hierarchy among the members of parliament became visible. Among the most influential posts were the speaker of the assembly and the committee heads, particularly those for economic and legislative affairs.[8] Legislative and supervisory parliamentary activities were expanded in an unprecedented way, especially in blocking presidential decrees (10 percent) and governmental proposals (28 percent). The number of passed laws initiated by the assembly rose to 18 percent (Cooper 1982, 162–63). At the same time, the MPs seized the moment to sharpen the contrast between themselves and ordinary members of the ASU; making reference to their elected status, they stressed that parliament was "the symbol of the return to a more democratic and liberal style" (Waterbury 1983, 365).

Yet al-Sadat strove to keep a degree of control over parliament by appointing his close ally Sayyid Mar'i as assembly speaker while also instigating interinstitutional conflicts between the assembly and the ASU to keep them both in check (Springborg 1979, 52). Al-Sadat accumulated power by assuming the office of the prime minister (1973–74); by way of his symbolic rather than military victory in the October War, he became strong enough to block activities by the People's Assembly. This specifically meant that parliament was no longer able to stop presidential decrees while the cabinet members became less willing to respond to parliament's questions and complaints. Compared to the legislative period from 1969 to 1971, however, the number of questions, requests for information, and complaints remained high (Cooper 1982, 163–65), as shown in figure 2. In return, the MPs received more budgetary insight in 1973. In 1976, the newly created Central Auditing Organization (CAO) was subordinated to parliament (Waterbury 1983, 365).[9] As the following analysis reveals,

---

8. The outstanding role of these parliamentarians remained an important characteristic until the end of the Mubarak regime in January 2011.

9. See also chapter 3.

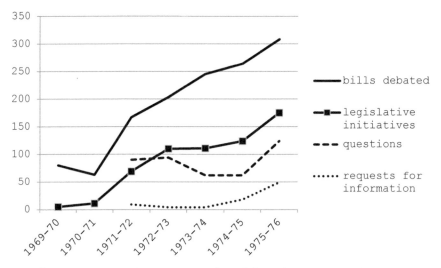

2. Parliamentary activities, 1969–76. Adapted from Cooper 1982, 164–65.

activities in parliament exhibited different trajectories that were far from simply being desired top-down outcomes.

Throughout this period, parliament remained an institution of what Hinnebusch refers to as the sub-elite, within which he identifies local notables, civil servants, representatives from the public sector and the military, and leaders of syndicates and chambers of commerce (1981, 447). An examination of parliament's activities suggests it continued to be an institution in which different groups could acquire or protect privileges. Landowners, for example, managed to fight against a tax on agricultural products. After this measure was enacted in the middle of the budget crisis in 1978, the members of parliament once again managed to eliminate the tax in 1981 (Waterbury 1983, 293). Landowner interests were also safe-guarded in the struggle against state farms that had started under 'Abd al-Nasir. In cooperation with agricultural engineers, who were repeatedly invited to committee hearings as experts, the assembly members fought for a competitive agricultural market (Springborg 1979, 62). The MPs with a background in trade who profited from al-Sadat's economic opening successfully deterred the imposition of a fixed profit margin on imported goods (Waterbury 1983, 178).

However, pressure from specific constituencies could not counterbalance the ever-growing pressure from a public that struggled with inflation and stagnating wages as a consequence of the deteriorating socioeconomic situation. This is likely the reason why members of parliament changed their behavior in regard to the *infitah* reforms: initially, in 1974, the legislature issued laws that simply formalized al-Sadat's plans for an economic restructuring of Egypt. As public protests against the government's policy arose, the MPs changed their attitude and turned critical (el-Sawi, el-Sawi, Shuman, and el-Mikawy 2002, 37). Attacks on al-Sadat's economic policy increased from the leftist Tagammu Party, and from the high number of independent members of parliament. As a newly constructed opposition, the former members of the ruling party took their role very seriously, as did the almost fifty independent candidates who were allowed to enter parliament for the first time in the Egyptian republic. Among them were MPs with ties to the New Wafd Party, as well as those with leanings toward the Muslim Brothers. One independent member of parliament received backing from the militant Islamist organization al-Jama'a al-Islamiyya, and other prominent figures who had fallen from grace under 'Abd al-Nasir also reappeared in the assembly (Beattie 2000, 199–200). All of these MPs used the platform to further attack the executive. Even in retrospect, one of the independent deputies, 'Adil 'Id, portrayed their role from 1976 to 1979 as the first instance of real opposition to the government since the revolution of 1952 ('Id 1984, 3).

Indeed, with the bread riots of 1977, contentious behavior within the People's Assembly intensified and the parliamentarians became a curse rather than a cure for the president's attempt to consolidate power. Whereas the cabinet members at first tried to appease the MPs by addressing numerous questions and interpellations, by 1978 the government's mood changed and the parliamentarians were accused of hampering the ministers' activities (Reinich 1977, 80–81). Additionally, criticism arose within parliament toward al-Sadat's negotiations with Israel. Both strands of public contention served as a justification for deliberalization. New laws banned parties that did not embrace the goals of the 1952 revolution. This was used against the New Wafd, leading to its dissolution less than four months after its reinstitutionalization. Another law was aimed at inhibiting criticism against al-Sadat's policy toward Israel and prohibited all parties that opposed the Camp David Accords (Baaklini, Denoeux, and Springborg 1999, 228). Another example of conflict between parliament and the presidency was the reform of the personal status law, which aimed to broaden women's rights in marriage and divorce. The draft law failed three times in parliament in the years 1971, 1975, and 1977; al-Sadat finally managed to push it through in 1979 (Sonneveld 2006). In some instances, he even managed to withdraw immunity from a number of resilient MPs. In 1979, parliament was dissolved and voices critical of Camp David were shut out of the subsequent elections; only unabashed and massive vote rigging ensured this result. The new Socialist Labor Party, which had been created top-down in an effort to replace the contentious Tagammu Party on the left side of the political spectrum, ran counter to the intentions of its originators, criticizing al-Sadat where its predecessor had left off (Fahmy 2002, 74–75).

As contentious as some parliamentarians might have been, however, one should not mistake parliament for a democratic institution attempting to act as a counterweight to the autocratic president: the representative institution ultimately always approved even the major reform policies. It passed the Camp David Accord with Israel and the *infitah* economic reforms. It passed the repressive laws against public protests and the press after the bread riots of 1977 and the infamous Law of Shame in 1980, which essentially criminalized all forms of public criticism (Kienle 2001, 19–20). Parliament remained as autocratic as its constituent relations. As the examples above highlight, parts of the elite bargained for specific privileges and expressed grievances on behalf of the wider public. As intermediaries, they achieved adjustments, not a reversal of policies.

In regard to foreign and domestic issues, the large discrepancy that existed between the general legitimacy claims made by the executive and the legitimacy beliefs held by parts of the public as well as MPs became visible in parliament. The People's Assembly proved to be more disruptive than the president had likely assumed. In another attempt to stall parliamentary contention, al-Sadat once again took over the position of prime minister from May 1980 until his assassination. He opted for broader institutional reforms in the constitutional amendments of 1980:

he introduced a second chamber, the Consultative Council—or Majlis al-shura—the membership of which he kept under tight control (Beattie 2000, 263). Moreover, he lifted the limitation of two presidential terms (Article 77) and tightened the conditions for the freedom of press. In order to bring stability back to his rule, al-Sadat also tried to appease the public by giving the multiparty system constitutional protection (Article 5) and strengthening the role of Islamic shari'a as the main source of legislation (Article 2). He also imbued his economic liberalization with constitutional protection by reducing the socialist character of the constitution and eliminating Article 4's claim of suppressing class distinctions. The amended text only aimed at "narrowing the gap between incomes, protecting legitimate earnings and guaranteeing the equity of the distribution of public duties and responsibilities."[10] Despite attempts at appeasement, growing dissatisfaction persisted with al-Sadat's foreign policy as well as with the worsening socioeconomic situation and with corrupt state officials (Hinnebusch 1985, 76). In spite of the reduced number of oppositional politicians, discontent continued to be channeled into parliament. Those who had managed to be elected into parliament used any means available to monitor the executive and even rejected laws. Major criticism was raised in relation to prices and the supply of goods (Altman 1981, 349).

Whether the attempts to stabilize his rule would have proven successful remains unknown—President al-Sadat was assassinated by a militant Islamist on October 6, 1981. It is hard to say whether dissent within and outside of parliament could have significantly changed the regime. In any case, the al-Sadat era once more demonstrated how difficult it can be to curtail parliamentary criticism without resorting to overt repression or substantial compromise. Interinstitutional relations thus always retain a delicate balance among the institutions involved, resulting in a constant struggle for influence. Moreover, actors within parliament played a crucial role in developing the legislature. In fact, this is true for all three variations of parliament under President al-Sadat. Within the single-party,

---

10. For a translation and further details on the amendments, see Abdel Fattah (2008, 77).

three-party, and multiparty legislative system, decisions made by the executive came under attack, especially during times when the president and his government were weak due to the military defeat of 1967, public protests against social grievances, and the new foreign policy toward Israel. This also once more proves that parliament, as an institution, inherently reflects the concerns of the public in any party system. The executive's lack of responsiveness ended up heating parliamentary debates. It is difficult to estimate how parliament might have developed further, or whether al-Sadat would have been able to restore order, had he not been assassinated. In any case, the new man at the pinnacle of leadership in Egypt, Husni Mubarak, opted for another, more balanced, approach in respect to the parliament, and successfully did so for nearly three decades.

Mubarak: Intra-Elite Rivalry, Rapprochement of Parliament, and Public Protest, 1980–2011

Husni Mubarak, the vice president under al-Sadat, had also served as secretary general of the National Democratic Party and therefore had strong ties to the ruling party. When he assumed the presidency of the republic, he simultaneously became the party chairman. He had to cope with a parliament that had a tarnished reputation on account of manipulation by al-Sadat in the elections of 1979. In a familiar move of opening and closing the realm for potential participation, Mubarak opted for a limited degree of openness in order to increase legitimacy in the 1984 and 1987 elections. In the 1990s, however, there were hardly any oppositional forces to be found in the People's Assembly, and the ruling party mostly managed parliamentary affairs on its own. The 2000s, by contrast, saw a pluralist parliament once again in terms of party and organizational representation. At first glance, the Mubarak era appears to present a simple pattern of parliamentary framework development: the 1980s were characterized by a pluralistic parliament, the 1990s by an NDP-dominated parliament, and in the 2000s parliament was again pluralistic. Throughout these thirty years, the electoral system was constantly altered, meaning that voters faced modified electoral rules every time they went to cast their vote. Additionally, the formal rights of the People's Assembly were modified by constitutional amendments several times. For the sake of clarity, we will present a decade-by-decade analysis, which includes the electoral framework, the resulting composition of the assembly, and its activities in each phase. Observations about the 2000s will also serve as the background for the interpretive study of parliamentary debates, as this is the period under investigation in chapters 3, 4, and 5.

Parliamentary Activities in the 1980s

Following a request from opposition forces, the electoral system was changed from a majority, individual-candidate voting system into a proportional system. The idea behind this move was to dispose of a voting system based on the principle of "winner takes all" and enlarge the representation of various political forces (Baaklini, Denoeux, and Springborg 1999, 229). Yet Mubarak added stipulations that ran counter to the original intent of the proposal, including a minimum threshold of 8 percent for a party to enter parliament. Moreover, a new system of counting votes was introduced that favored the ruling party. Additionally, all seats that would otherwise have been granted to parties with less than 8 percent of the vote were allotted to the largest party. Districts were geographically enlarged and, correspondingly, reduced from 175 to 48. The total number of seats in the People's Assembly increased from 350 to 448; as such, the seating capacity of the assembly's plenary hall was exceeded, as its maximum was just 390 (El-Sawi, Ghoneim, and Kamel 2005, 18).[11]

These stipulations clearly favored the ruling party and led to the exclusion of many minor opposition forces. Yet the (most likely) unintended consequence of this move was the alliance among the strongest opposition forces—the New Wafd, which had been allowed to resume its activities in 1983, and the Muslim Brotherhood, which was still tolerated but not registered formally as an organization or a party; this alliance enabled them to overcome the 8 percent barrier (for an overview of electoral results see

---

11. I am not certain whether this was intended as in the case of the British House of Commons: when the Commons was rebuilt after the Second World War, Churchill decided to keep its original size, despite its being too small for the 635 MPs, to ensure that the plenary never appeared empty, as not all assembly members were always present (Loewenberg 2016).

Table 5

Composition of the People's Assembly in the 1980s

	1979–84	*1984–87*	*1987–90*
NDP	320 (88%)	390 (87%)	300 (70%)
Socialist Liberal Party	3	None	56 (17%) for the Islamic Alliance (38 Muslim Brotherhood)
Socialist Labor Party	29	(4 appointed)	
Muslim Brotherhood	None	58 (13%) for the alliance (50 New Wafd, 8 Muslim Brotherhood)	
New Wafd	None		35 (10.9%)
Tagammu	None	None	None
Independents	10	None	48
Appointed by president	10	10	10

Adapted from Ranko 2015, 77, 116.

table 5). The New Wafd was clearly the larger partner in the alliance, with 50 MPs, whereas the Muslim Brotherhood held only 8 seats in parliament. This modest number of seats for the well-known and popular Muslim Brotherhood reflected the limitations of Mubarak's promises of pluralism (Al-Awadi 2004, 80–81). The electoral success of the New Wafd likely owed to its newcomer status as a new opposition force with uncontested credibility in the republican era. The party, of course, also drew legitimacy from its historical legacy as the nationalist anticolonial power in the first half of the twentieth century.

The opposition parties also joined forces in another judicial move against the regime, taking the electoral law to court for discriminating against independent candidates. Their grievances were approved by the Supreme Constitutional Court, which ruled that independent candidates should be allowed to run for at least one seat per district. This led to a maximum number of forty-eight seats for independents in the 1987 elections, whereas four hundred seats were reserved for party candidates. However, officially running as an independent did not necessarily mean that the candidate lacked a party affiliation. The electoral results showed that forty of the elected independent candidates were directly backed by the NDP, five were affiliated with the party though not directly supported, and the remaining three were won by Muslim Brothers. According to the logic of authoritarian elections, the important thing is that actors relevant to the regime are integrated into parliament. The success of independent candidates also testifies to their power and relevance to the regime, based on their financial means to buy off votes or their social capital in form of support of the electorate, local notables, or functional groups. It also granted more autonomy and bargaining capital to the independent MPs, as they demonstrated that they did not require the party in order to succeed. This phenomenon of the "NDPendents" increased dramatically over the decades; candidates who were known to belong to the NDP ran as independents but later joined the NDP parliamentary group. They became a bane for parts of the ruling elite, whose power rested in the dominant party, particularly in the 2000s (Koehler 2008, 984).

Another amendment to the electoral law in 1987 removed the stipulation that redistributed all seats from parties that were under the 8 percent threshold to the largest party, a framework that produced two winners within the opposition camp. On the one hand, the only party to surpass the threshold on its own was the New Wafd. On the other hand, the Muslim Brotherhood achieved the greatest increase in seats, from eight seats in 1984 to thirty-eight in 1987. As opposed to cooperating with the New Wafd, as they had done previously, the Muslim Brothers now became the leaders of the new alliance with the Labor Party and the Liberal Party; however, the initiative to build an "Islamic Alliance" originated with Ibrahim Shukri, head of the Labor Party, who intended to turn his party into a more Islamic-oriented organization (Al-Awadi 2004, 136). It is worth reemphasizing that both parties had been established as a kind of "fabricated" opposition: wings of the former single party, the Arab Socialist Union, with influential members handpicked by former President al-Sadat to control the parties. Ten years later, these parties had attained autonomy and joined forces with a powerful, outlawed Islamist organization, becoming the largest oppositional force since the establishment of the republic.

Makram-Ebeid attributes the Muslim Brothers' electoral success to the "substantial financial resources" that enabled an "impressive deployment of posters and banners blanketing the walls of cities and villages throughout the provinces" (Makram-Ebeid 1989, 433–34). However, the electoral campaign seemed to actually be the result of the Brotherhood's real strength—analyzed by Mohamed Fahmy Menza (2013) in detail—which rested on their provision of services through a vast network of Islamic charity organizations that had developed since the 1970s. When al-Sadat allowed the Islamists to develop their organization as a counterweight to leftists and Nasserists, Islamic charities also assisted in delivering welfare services formerly provided by the state. With their locally rooted organizations, parliamentary candidates from the Muslim Brotherhood were able to compete with NDP candidates for the support of lesser notables who served as local intermediaries between the voters of a constituency and MPs. From this perspective, the success of the Muslim Brothers follows the logic of electoral authoritarianism based on clientelism. Being in control of the repressive security apparatus, the ruling elite would never allow completely free elections, and the Islamists' share of parliamentary seats therefore did not reflect their real support; as such, the Brotherhood complained of large-scale vote rigging (Al-Awadi 2004, 114).

From a very high level in the first parliamentary session of the fourth legislative period (1984–85), the total amount of activities significantly dropped in the following session (1985–86), and even further in the third session (1986–87) (see figure 3). This was, of course, a result of the early dissolution of the People's Assembly before the end of the regular term, but it also corresponds to a general trend, as demonstrated by the numbers from the fifth legislative period (1987–90). Although the numbers from the 1987–88 session increased in absolute terms, the amount of questions and requests for information never again reached their initial levels.

In explaining the decrease in parliamentary activity, Springborg refers to the exceptional role of the speaker of the assembly. In an alleged attempt to pacify the legislature, Mubarak appointed Rif'at al-Mahjub to this post, a candidate who had already held high positions under President al-Sadat. Al-Mahjub ruled over the assembly in a rather dictatorial manner; not only did the oppositional MPs protest his behavior (even walking out of

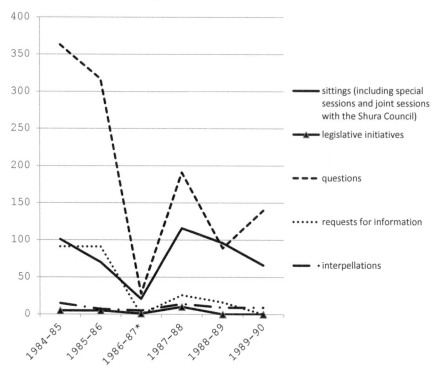

3. Parliamentary activities, 1984–90. Adapted from 'Awad and Tawfiq 1996, 191, 361–95. * Dissolved before end of term.

the assembly several times), but he also lost the support of several NDP members in parliament. Among his arbitrary manipulations, al-Mahjub suddenly and unexpectedly dissolved the assembly in 1986. He also did not convene the parliament on time after the elections in 1987—the parliament was finally officially reconvened only after the opposition was on the verge of protesting this delay publicly (Springborg 1989, 191–92).

Another explanation is that Mubarak's less controversial and more balanced approach to foreign and economic policies, in comparison to his predecessor, helped to placate the deputies (Shehata 2010, 118–25). Shifting to a Cold War with Israel and rapprochement with the Arab world directly addressed outright criticism within parliament in regard to the Camp David Accords of 1979. Mubarak did not reverse the economic reforms already in place but managed to diminish polarized opinion against them in various ways. First, he initiated a national dialogue that included the opposition in deliberating the policies. Mubarak postponed an IMF austerity program and also invested in Egypt's industry. He also symbolically fought against corruption by prosecuting the most well-known corrupt figures among the new business elite. Responding to major criticism against al-Sadat, Mubarak's more balanced approach ended the legitimacy crisis that had become visible in parliament. El-Mikawy describes the 1980s debates in parliament as negotiations about policy preferences that took place in a general atmosphere of bargaining and compromise (1999, 124–25). Analyzing parliamentary debates about the privatization process in Egypt, al-Sayyid found that there was a general consensus in favor of the transition to a free market economy; the only defectors were from the left-wing opposition parties. Apart from general approval, some disagreement between NDP members working in the public sector and those engaged in private business was still present, as the former continued to oppose "ultra-liberalization" and supported gradual change (al-Sayyid 1996, 322–25).[12] Another example of dissent within the ruling party was criticism aimed at the extension of the emergency law, which even three NDP members of parliament refused to vote for (Baaklini, Denoeux, and Springborg 1999, 232).

Apart from the studies mentioned here, scholars have generally focused more heavily on the phenomenon of opposition MPs than on ruling party members of the assembly. Given that the majority of parliamentary activities were, in fact, performed by NDP members, we are still left with a biased and incomplete picture of the People's Assembly, requiring further analysis of the parliamentary debates themselves.[13] However,

12. Al-Sayyid's (1996) study is part of the book *Privatization in Egypt: The Debate in the People's Assembly*, edited by Abd-El Elah, Badran, and Wahby, which corresponds to the major theme of this book and covers the years 1984–95. Yet its various articles remain more general and thus highlight very broad developments. Other available studies on this period tend to be more descriptive than analytical; see, for example, al-Tawil (1992) and Yasin (2005).

13. For instance, out of 767 discussions about committee reports between 1984 and 1987, only 19 were carried out by Muslim Brotherhood MPs, the most active part of the opposition bloc ('Awad and Tawfiq 1996, 193).

looking into the opposition within the People's Assembly in the 1980s, two different constellations have to be considered when analyzing the opposition's performance in the 1980s: the alliance between the Wafd Party and the Muslim Brotherhood from 1984 to 1987, and the alliance between the Brothers, the Labor Party, and the Liberals. 'Awad and Tawfiq found that the first alliance between the New Wafd and the Muslim Brotherhood (1984–87) was characterized by cooperation on many issues, such as education, social developments, media, and shari'a. They also coordinated their activities in debates regarding current events. However, both groups had their own focal points: whereas the New Wafd brought up environmental pollution, the Egyptian nuclear program, external relations with Israel, and reforms to the political system and to the agriculture sector, the Brothers raised topics related to Islamic law. The Muslim Brotherhood accused the government of violating the shari'a by doing business with banks that granted interest (*riba*), by producing and selling alcohol, and by allowing gambling. It is remarkable that the politically liberal Wafd joined the ranks of the Brotherhood in demanding that the media be bound to moral and religious values. The Muslim Brothers also emphasized violations of the rule of law, arbitrary imprisonment, and torture ('Awad and Tawfiq 1996, 215–17). Yet in spite of the fundamental ideological differences, Elshobaki regards the performance and language of the Brothers in parliament as being similar to those of their secular peers (2009, 150).

When considering the very small percentage of MPs who were Muslim Brothers (around 1.7 percent), it is astonishing how active these deputies were, especially in regard to interpellations. Throughout the entire legislative period, 18.5 percent of the interpellations were brought forward by Muslim Brotherhood MPs. However, in regard to other tools of parliamentary control, their share of interpellations was just slightly above their degree of representation, and never exceeded 3 percent ('Awad and Tawfiq 1996, 194–95). In debates about committee reports, their participation was marginal, even relative to their percentage of seats, dropping below 0.5 percent ('Awad and Tawfiq 1996, 207).

Leaving behind their former ally, the New Wafd ran on their own in the 1987 elections. They completely abandoned their demand for implementing the shari'a. Islamist influence could now be felt among the Muslim

Table 6

Parliamentary Activities of the Major Opposition Forces in the Fifth Legislative Period (1987–90)

	New Wafd	Muslim Brotherhood
Questions	25	57
Interpellations	4	8
Requests for information	5	10

Adapted from 'Awad and Tawfiq 1996, 398.

Brotherhood's new partners, the Labor Party and the Liberals. A comparison of the respective performance of the Brothers and the Wafdists after the dissolution of their alliance proves interesting: now finding themselves in an equal power constellation, the Muslim Brothers exhibited roughly twice the amount of engagement in control tools compared to the New Wafd (table 6). In the interinstitutional relations of that time, it is remarkable that the Islamic Alliance voted in favor of President Husni Mubarak's nomination for a second term (al-Awadi 2004, 113), at the same time demanding that the president resign his position as chairman of the ruling party during debates ('Awad and Tawfiq 1996, 366). This demonstrates both the outstanding role that the president had as well as the way in which the Brothers dealt with this role: rather than directly fighting the head of the system, they tried to divide him from the ruling party.[14]

The 1990s: Opposition Reduced, Balance Preserved

The opposition challenged the existing electoral law of 1987 regarding the prevailing discrimination against independents. In May 1990, the Supreme Constitutional Court declared the electoral law and the sitting parliament

14. See also Al-Awadi (2004, 14–16), who cites prominent Muslim Brotherhood leaders' claims that obedience even to the tyrant was a *darura* (a necessity) and was still better than the risk of anarchy or upheaval against the ruler, an element of classic Sunni political thought.

to be unconstitutional. Mubarak took advantage of the situation by holding a referendum that led to the dissolution of the 1987 parliament and to the introduction of a new electoral system. The major change was a return to the individual candidacy system that had been abolished in 1983. Kassem speculates that the strong alliances between oppositional parties were obstacles to the regime, and that by letting candidates run independently of parties the reform would weaken cooperation among them (Kassem 1999, 101). What happened instead was a boycott of the 1990 elections by most opposition parties in an attempt to push for the fulfillment of two major demands. First, they called for judicial supervision of polling stations and vote counting—up until that point, the ministry of interior had headed the electoral organization and controlled these aspects of the elections. Second, they demanded that the state of emergency be lifted to ensure broader participation and mobilization. Many factors might have contributed to the opposition forces overestimating their actual bargaining power vis-à-vis the regime. Anticipating the next presidential referendum in 1993, they may have speculated that Mubarak would have sought a legitimacy-bolstering nomination through a pluralistic assembly. Moreover, wide support for the regime's Gulf War policy was seen as crucial. Hence, opposition leaders might have thought that alienating the formal opposition forces would be intolerable to the regime.

The reality was quite different, though. The presidential entourage made only minor attempts to persuade the oppositional parties to participate in the elections. The main trump card in the hands of the regime was recruiting the Tagammu Party. The latter participated in the elections, breaking their alliance with the other parties and groups.[15] As a result, the People's Assembly included five elected Tagammu members and one appointed member. This appointment was a novelty, as Tagammu members had always refused to accept appointments in previous elections, regarding them as symbols of loyalty to the regime. Remarkably, all other individuals appointed to offices by the president were immediately

---

15. Kassem explains the dropout mainly as a result of personal rivalries among the party leaders of Tagammu and Wafd (1999, 103–5).

excluded from their parties (Kassem 1999, 107). As such, dissident voices in the legislature amounted to no more than twenty-nine, consisting mainly of Nasserists[16] and leftists who did not obey their parties' decision to boycott the elections. However, this was a dramatic drop from the ninety-one seats in the previous legislative period. Ultimately, the boycott resulted in rendering the opposition irrelevant. Outside of parliament, the opposition faced difficulty expressing criticism and mobilizing new supporters. The only means left at their disposal were the parties' own newspapers, which had limited readership. This enabled the government to pass a wide array of illiberal laws unopposed, which served the regime in its crackdown on the Islamists starting in 1992.

After this strategic miscalculation by the major oppositional parties and organizations in their electoral boycott of 1990, these parties all decided to participate in the electoral race in 1995. The New Wafd and the Liberals took different approaches in this context. The Liberals changed their behavior and switched to a more regime-friendly approach, similar to the Tagammu Party after 1990. Remarkably, the goodwill that the core elite offered to parties distancing themselves from the moderate Islamists of the Brotherhood had its intended effect: the New Wafd and the Liberals, former allies of the Brotherhood, avoided any leanings toward the formally outlawed, yet tolerated, Islamist organization (Kassem 1999, 109–15). The Labor Party, for its part, kept the Islamic references in spite of the elite's anti-Islamist stance. Beyond this strategy of divide and rule, the core elite used other tactics to keep the opposition in check. First, the electoral system was finalized too close to the ballot date and thus did not allow the oppositional parties sufficient opportunity to adopt a strategy; this would have been necessary since the number of electoral districts increased from 48 to 222. Second, repression, mainly against the Muslim Brothers, prevented more than 80 leading members from running—security forces even shut down the headquarters of the organization (Baaklini, Denoeux, and Springborg 1999, 233). Furthermore, large-scale manipulations on

---

16. Ideological Nasserists founded their own party, the Arab Democratic Nasserist Party, in 1992. Prior to that, they were members of the Labor Party or Tagammu.

election day and during vote counting ensured that only 14 members of the opposition were elected into the People's Assembly in 1995, with only one MP, a Muslim Brother, coming from outside of the "loyal opposition" camp. The largest opposition party ended up being the New Wafd, with six seats.

Another remarkable development was the dramatic increase in independent MPs that was due to the individual electoral system. In 1990, the NDP directly won 347 out of 444 seats but was ensured a wide majority by the 60 independent MPs who joined the NDP parliamentary group directly after the elections. In 1995, their number rose from 60 to 90, a development that would continue in the 2000s. Moreover, these independent candidates were not opportunistic newcomers to the political scene but former members of the NDP. The party became increasingly unpopular on account of its failing ability to channel services to its constituencies (Baaklini, Denoeux, and Springborg 1999, 236). This failure was related to a change within the NDP cadres: the rise of a new capitalist class enabled the nouveaux riches to run on their own without the party's support (Rizq 1991, 68). The rise of the profiteers from the economic liberalization was likewise visible in the general increase of private businessmen during the legislative period from 1995 to 2000: out of fifty candidates, thirty-six attained a parliamentary seat (Fahmy 2002, 172). This trend continued in the 2000s, gaining even greater importance. The growing fragmentation among the ruling elite in the 1990s was reflected in intra-elite conflicts within the assembly regarding posts and influence (Baaklini, Denoeux, and Springborg 1999, 236).

An examination of its activities in the 1990s reveals that parliament reflected the major national issue—the fight against militant Islamists—which was carried out by state security forces in crackdowns on all Islamists, including the Muslim Brothers. Parliament responded by passing a number of deliberalizing laws during these years, some of which led to heated debates in parliament (Ayalon 1995, 369; 1996, 270) while others were passed hastily without opposition (Ayalon 1997, 257). From the mid-1990s on, the majority of legislative activities concentrated on the economic infrastructure needed for the ongoing transition to a market economy. A comprehensive study of the role of parliament in the economic legislation process during the 1990s (El-Mikawy and Handoussa 2002) found that, although crucial laws were issued in the People's Assembly, the executive continued to be the main driver of these reforms. The legislative process remained weak because the parliament rushed drafts and passed "express laws," as they were called in the press. Furthermore, interventions in draft law debates focused on modifications that did not reflect the broader legal framework. As a result, many laws exhibited inconsistencies and imprecise formulations, and subsequently led to numerous amendments. Only half of the members of parliament actually took part in debates, with around 30 percent participating on a regular basis. However, the MPs who actively discussed economic reform laws constituted the parliamentary elite, especially chairmen and members of the central committees, such as the planning and budget committee and the economic committee (El-Mikawy 2002, 30–32). Although parliament did not play a decisive role in the economic legislation process, it influenced the government's pace for the ongoing reform program mainly by stressing the social impacts arising from these reforms (El-Sawi et al. 2002). Parliamentarians continued to raise issues that were neglected in the rush of economic restructuring, including education and environmental pollution). In contrast to the 1980s, when opposition MPs had provided a balanced view on the effects of economic liberalization, NDP deputies expressed these views in the 1990s, even in relation to members of the cabinet (El-Sawi et al. 2002, 38).

Parliament continued to play the role of articulator and defender of the social "consciousness." This is also highlighted by the fact that the parliamentarians with a business background did not use their mandate for political purposes, despite growing intra-elite competition for parliamentary seats that favored private businessmen. In a study of their activities, Amr Hashem and Noha El-Mikawy reveal that parliamentarians did not take a particularly active role or present specific opinions on macroeconomic issues, even though these MPs were evidently dealing with matters relevant to the private sector in general on an increasing basis. Moreover, their private sector advocacy within the assembly met with growing acceptance in parliament; it constituted a counterperspective to a public sector that had determined, or at least heavily influenced, the opinions of MPs up to that point (Hashem and El-Mikawy 2002, 56–58).

At the end of the 1990s, tools like questions or interpellations were used more frequently in the context of parliament's oversight function. Criticism of the government was justified on the basis of national issues rather than the needs of local constituencies as before. Calls were even made to reshuffle the cabinet, which the government occasionally heeded (El-Sawi et al. 2002, 38). Independent candidates were among those who contributed most to the critical stance toward the government. More important, MPs engaged in forms of parliamentary work that served to enhance their expertise, such as fact-finding committees. Deputies from the ruling party would even take a stand against their own government when their newly acquired expertise was contrary to the cabinet's official point of view. In general, the idea of publicly attacking ministers became more attractive in the 1990s, as the media placed greater attention on parliamentary activities (El-Mikawy 2002, 32–33). This may relate to a diversification of the media, which became more pluralistic through the development of independent Egyptian newspapers, such as *al-Masry al-Youm* and privately owned satellite channels.

In sum, the parliament reflected social concerns and public fears but retained its centrist position in regard to the governmental reform plan. Even with a low percentage of oppositional forces, the parliamentarians increasingly engaged in debates and did so with high degrees of expertise. Moreover, the private sector became more integrated in the political system, though without playing an active role—a constellation that laid the groundwork for future conflict. The government pressured parliament to pass many laws that were part of economic restructuring. Until then, although MPs could raise social concerns, such remarks merely entailed amendments to the reforms rather than opposition to them. In terms of parliament's overall role in the 1990s, the integration of parliament into lawmaking is apparent. The executive increasingly consulted with the legislature rather than ruling by decree, presumably in an attempt to legitimize support for these reforms by the People's Assembly. Social concerns and compromise on the part of the government increased this responsiveness. Yet this balance was precarious when groups with conflicting interests, such as the former public sector and the increasingly influential private sector, met in the assembly. As would become evident in the 2000s, as soon as one group became more powerful in parliament, decision making was no longer a result of compromise. At the same time, stronger opposition made up for the lack of responsiveness, and the parliament's role transformed from a mirror that reflected social fears to a magnifying glass, highlighting the negative side effects of the reforms.

Parliamentary Developments in the 2000s

Before the parliamentary elections in 2000, the Supreme Constitutional Court had declared the existing electoral law unconstitutional. This time, the court adopted one of the opposition's major claims that had contributed to the decision to boycott the 1990 election. It ruled that supervision of the polling stations by civil servants, as prescribed by the existing electoral law, violated Article 88 of the constitution, which assigned this role to Egyptian judges. Although the verdict was implemented in all three stages of the 2000 elections, electoral fraud simply shifted from inside the polling stations to their forecourt rather than leading to free and fair elections. Voters who did not support the NDP were denied entry to polling stations; security forces even used violence to keep oppositional voters in check, while plainclothes police roused trouble among the voters, instigating further uses of force (Kassem 2004, 63–67). Violence previously directed at candidates now turned against the voters. Not only was voting manipulated, but direct repression and violence caused widespread disillusionment and even voter hatred toward the state (Kassem 2004, 75–76).

One striking result of these elections was the decreasing success of NDP official party candidates, whose numbers sank to 175 seats out of 454. The number of elected independents who were either NDP members running independently or real independents who simply joined the NDP parliamentary group totaled 213. Altogether, the NDP bloc reached 388 MPs, easily regaining the two-thirds majority necessary to amend the constitution. The other outcome of the 2000 elections was a clear victory for the Muslim Brotherhood as the strongest opposition force, as they gained seventeen seats despite running as independents because of the official ban on the organization. Although the Brotherhood had been successful in elections during the 1980s, this was the first time the group clearly won more seats than the New Wafd, which only obtained seven (Thabet 2006, 17). The total number of Brotherhood MPs was even greater than the sixteen combined members of parliament of all the other licensed opposition parties.[17]

These major trends continued into the 2005 elections. First, the Muslim Brotherhood gained additional seats: with eighty-eight, it was now the largest opposition group since the abolishment of the single-party system. This result was all the more astonishing considering the dramatic increase in violence around the polling stations in the second and third round of voting, which prevented voters from entering. In contrast, the number of deputies affiliated with licensed opposition parties sank to just nine.[18]

The second trend was the continued decline in the number of seats held by official NDP candidates, which corresponded to the increased importance of independents joining the party ranks in parliament, even attaining a majority. The "NDPendents" now won 161 seats, compared to the 146 "real" NDP members.[19] Remarkably, the situation for the NDP did not improve despite the reforms initiated in 2002, which included the introduction of electoral colleges aimed at integrating the local level into the party's candidate selection process. The caucus was able to choose a number of potential candidates, but the final decision would be made by a central committee. As the party leadership would eventually come to learn, this process did not improve party cohesion, as frustrated party members who were not selected to be the official candidate often went on to run independently (Collombier 2007, 101–3). Following the logic of autocratic parliaments, intra-elite competition both within and outside of the ruling party selects and integrates the most relevant actors into the political institution (Blaydes 2011). But the system of clientelism and patronage was no longer sufficient to keep the elite in power, as violence continued to shape the outcome of elections, particularly in the second and third stages.

---

17. "Procedure and Polarization," *Al-Ahram Weekly*, Dec. 15–21, 2005, no. 773.

18. "Procedure and Polarization," *Al-Ahram Weekly*, Dec. 15–21, 2005, no. 773.

19. "The NDP Crisis," *Egypt Independent*, Dec. 25, 2010, http://www.egyptindependent.com/opinion/ndp-crisis.

Shukrallah (2005) summarized these elections as the worst since 1976 in terms of vote rigging and violence by state security forces.

Another key element to understanding the Egyptian parliament in the 2000s relates to the development of two major camps within the NDP. Observers have often described these camps as defined by a generational conflict between the old and new guard—or between conservatives and reformers—but the lines of conflict were more complex and included personal rivalries (Arafat 2009; Stacher 2012, 106). Generally speaking, the reformist wing primarily consisted of private businessmen who actively pushed for the acceleration of the Egypt's economic restructuring. The rise of this new guard first became politically relevant in 1999, when rumors spread that the reform wing would split off from the NDP and form a new party called the Future Party (*Hizb al-mustaqbal*). To forestall this move and preserve party cohesion, this wing was integrated more strongly into existing party structures as well as into new party organs specifically created for this purpose (Brownlee 2007). This became publicly visible upon the promotion of one of the key reform-minded politicians, Gamal Mubarak, a son of President Mubarak who had worked as an investment banker in London for several years. In 1999, his father appointed him and a number of his allies to the party's general secretariat. In 2002, Gamal Mubarak became the head of the newly formed policies secretariat (*amanat al-siyasat*), which included several other business elites.[20] Seven of them became members of the newly formed cabinet under Prime Minister Ahmad Nazif in 2004. The reformers succeeded the stalwarts from the old guard within the general secretariat, replacing 50 percent of them and their allies on the district and governorate levels (Collombier 2007, 108–9). Although he toured the countryside to win over the local level of the party for himself, Gamal Mubarak's harsh measures for restructuring the party were met with a high degree of criticism, not only for the policy

20. It is noteworthy that owners of small and medium enterprises did not have a say in the business reforms. Alissa relates this to the lack of participation in the process itself and the lack of representation of owners of small and medium-sized enterprises in the People's Assembly compared to the "significant representation of the business elite" (2007, 10).

changes but also for the new wing's political style. The vocabulary they used, the way they dressed, and the world they embodied was deemed appropriate for the business community but not for politics (Collombier 2007, 119). During the elections, these changes became apparent in a major shift in clientelist relations, mainly among urban constituencies. Obtaining a parliamentary seat increasingly depended on a candidate's financial resources, which could be used for vote buying or sponsoring the NDP; for example, by financing the president's electoral campaign or the party headquarters (el Tarouty 2015, 65–66). Long-term patronage relations became less important as the wealthy candidates paid out of their own pockets for services given to citizens rather than channeling state resources to their constituencies (Blaydes 2011, 106–8).

Besides changes within the broader ruling elite that affected the composition of parliament, the constitutional rights of the People's Assembly were modified as well. In the 2000s, the constitution was amended twice. The first amendment was in 2005, and it only targeted a single article that regulated presidential elections. Instead of having the People's Assembly choose a candidate to be voted on in a referendum, the president would now be elected by a direct public ballot. This allowed for multiple candidates; however, several eligibility restrictions were introduced that, at least for the 2005 elections, ensured victory for NDP candidate Husni Mubarak. The broader constitutional change happened in 2007, when thirty-four articles were amended. First, several socialist references were erased from the document, likely to give constitutional legitimacy to the reality of the capitalist economy that caused ever greater contention outside and within parliament. Regarding the political system, although the balance of powers was increased, new loopholes to the rule of law were introduced. This mainly pertained to the introduction of an antiterror article that would have allowed for the same sort of massive restrictions to political rights as the much-criticized state of emergency that had been in place since the assassination of President al-Sadat in 1981.[21] Positive developments were mainly in the realm of parliamentary powers: most

---

21. The state of emergency was not lifted until 2012.

important, the People's Assembly could now withdraw confidence from the government without a public referendum (Article 127). It also received the right to reject the government's program, presented to the parliament annually. Furthermore, Article 115 was amended and now permitted the legislature to propose amendments to the annual budget; the time allotted for studying the budget proposal was also extended. The second chamber, the Shura Council, received broader powers beyond a mere consultative function. Now it would have to give its consent for constitutional amendments and laws complementary to the constitution as well as for international treatises on peace and alliances (Bernard-Maugiron 2008, 402–4).

Though most commentators viewed these amendments essentially as lip service, it is notable that from a long-term perspective the scope of action for the both chambers was increased considerably. Decision-making power over the budget and the prime minister's dependence on the parliament constitute the most crucial parliamentary rights of all, and the elevation of the Shura Council to a legislative body was meaningful as well.

This once again raises the question of why the ruling elite would expand the parliament's role in the political system. The paper-tiger argument would say that granting these rights would have no real effect on power relations but would only foster a democratic image to appease an increasingly agitated public. Drawing lessons from the historical review, one could suspect there might be two different reasons for upgrading the parliament. The first would have to do with a growing private sector and the increasing relevance of private business elites in the eyes of the core elite. The increase of parliamentary power would create incentives for businessmen to cooperate and would ensure that private investment was respected and protected by the state; here, an eradication of the last remnants of the socialist system comes into play. Moreover, greater transparency and power division on budgetary matters as well as greater accountability of the government would be in the interest of the private sector. From this perspective, granting new rights to the parliament would be even more logical, as important businessmen were themselves present in the assembly and, as such, in control of budget and government planning. The second reason for granting more influence to parliament—even if just formally for the time being—might relate to maintaining cooperation with the regime at a time when growing frustration with the economic and social situation could have alienated other parts of the ruling elite who relied on channeling services to their constituencies. According to clientelist logic, these MPs needed to ensure their influence on distributional matters in the country, especially in the face of growing collective action and socioeconomic grievances.

Parliamentary powers may have been bolstered with these calculations in mind, and such accounts of the intention behind these amendments might explain the expansion of parliamentary rights. I argue, however, that these interpretations do not elucidate who would make use of such powers, for what ends, and how other groups might react. The observations that follow present existing broad and preliminary insights into parliamentary dynamics in the 2000s. Chapters 3 through 5 put forth an analysis of new material that provides a fresh look into the final years of parliament under Mubarak.

Resistance to change within the party was met with public discontent, as the socioeconomic situation was increasingly associated with the neoliberal reforms brought about by the NDP's new wing. As mentioned earlier, members of the NDP parliamentary group publicly spoke out against these reforms. Compared to the 1990s, when the parliamentarians could simply remind the government of its social responsibility, the worsening situation made it more and more difficult to provide critiques while simultaneously praising the government for its "modernizing" program. The following interpretative analysis of parliamentary debates will focus on exactly this point, thereby also uncovering how MPs dealt with this dilemma and how the new wing reacted to it.

One novelty of the last legislative period prior to the revolution was that public discontent increased all across the country and also directly in front of the parliament building. Commencing with foreign policy matters, such as the Palestinian intifada in 2000 and the Iraq War in 2003, public protests targeted domestic issues from 2004 on. Political protests against the rumored succession of Husni Mubarak by his son Gamal triggered the Kifaya Movement, followed by judges marching for judicial independence. Parliament became a place for and target of protests following a sit-in by property tax collectors in front of the council of ministers' building (around the corner from the People's Assembly) in 2007. From then on, workers from all across Egypt discovered that the government district, and particularly the street of the People's Assembly in downtown Cairo, were the perfect place to stage protests.[22] Here they received much more attention than in their often remote hometowns: journalists who had offices just around the corner would cover such labor activities, even those of small companies. Workers received support from neighborhood residents, including food and drink, and did not leave until their demands were met. But of course, this was also a symbolic place, representing the connection between the political system and the people. From 2008 on, protests near the doorstep of the People's Assembly became an everyday occurrence, with up to five different demonstrations taking place at the same time. Soon other marginalized groups used this area for public activism, including people with disabilities, who fought for jobs and housing, and urban residents, who protested against plans by state authorities to dismantle their homes.[23]

As the public got closer to the parliament, the parliament—at least the opposition—approached the public. The greatest bloc was the Muslim Brotherhood: they made use of parliamentary tools to criticize the government in an unprecedented manner, especially as the social crisis intensified, and they presented themselves as the parliamentary mouthpiece of the protest movement (Ranko 2015, 169). They also approached the public through the media by making use of the parliamentary space to express criticism. During the avian influenza crisis, when the government ordered all affected birds exterminated without offering compensation to those who earned their living from them, Muslim Brotherhood MPs protested the measure by eating chicken sandwiches on the doorstep of the parliament building—after notifying the media, of course (Shehata and Stacher 2006). The Brotherhood MPs also made heavy use of the internet

22. "Not Backing Down," *Al-Ahram Weekly*, Dec. 6–12, 2007, no. 874.

23. "Teachers, Physically Disabled Protest," *Egypt Independent*, Mar. 1, 2010, http://www.egyptindependent.com/news/teachers-physically-disabled-protest; Mustafa Ali, "Egypt's Brewing Revolt, Part 2: The Rising Class Struggle," *SocialistWorker.org*, June 8, 2010, http://socialistworker.org/2010/06/08/rising-class-struggle.

to spread information about their parliamentary activity. Practically every deputy had their own homepage, with information on the speeches and parliamentary tools the assembly member had used, along with press articles that covered the MP. The MPs' websites also presented pictures and information that showed their relationship to their constituencies, including attendance at conferences or such public events as *iftar* dinners during Ramadan. Moreover, the parliamentary group intensely reported about its work on ikhwanonline.com and a special magazine called *akhbar al-kutla*. In contrast, NDP parliamentarians did not begin presenting themselves online on any broad scale until 2009. Although difficult to prove, it seems that the NDP was reacting to the publicity garnered by the Brotherhood MPs; such publicity affected their expectations of how and the extent to which members of parliament should present themselves publicly.

The Muslim Brotherhood also published studies on their parliamentary work. *Al-Ikhwan fi Barlaman 2000* (Markaz al-Umma li-l-Dirasat wa-l-Tanmiya and al-Markaz al-Dawli li-l-I'lam 2005), for example, reported on the legislative period of 2000 to 2005. These were marked by a narrative style and featured summaries of speeches by Brotherhood MPs on themes such as general parliamentary functions, government oversight, legislation, or torture. It is interesting to note that this descriptive style can also be found in publications by independent deputies unaffiliated with any party or organization. For example, MP Jamal Zahran, a very active member of parliament from 2005 to 2010, published a book on his parliamentary activities (Muhsin 2008) that included long lists informing the reader about when he had delivered which sort of speech (question, interpellation, etc.) and whom he addressed, along with a summary of the speech. He also reprinted some speeches in their entirety and included photocopies of newspaper articles about himself. This is astonishing considering that Zahran is a political science professor who could certainly have written about his activities and the policies debated in a more analytical way. The implication here is that it was more about presenting *how much* one did rather than lobbying for a specific cause or addressing a particular audience.

Opposition members of parliament, particularly Muslim Brothers in cooperation with truly independent MPs, were very active within the assembly. They made use of control tools and had a high rate of attendance in the plenary (International Crisis Group 2008, 7). However, focusing only on the active opposition does not provide us with a comprehensive understanding of the issues at stake. An examination of the larger picture, taking NDP MPs into account as well, shows that fights across party lines revolved around debates over the economic policies. Representation, as one core function of the parliamentarians, became an explicitly contested issue. Moreover, the relations among parliament, government, and the president proved much more complex and dynamic, involving divisions within the ruling party.

Conclusion: The Parliament in the Egyptian Republic

For the sixty years during which Egypt was ruled by presidents rather than monarchs, parliamentary trajectories were similar to those that had existed before, with certain characteristics discernible across all political systems. First, working as part of an intermediary institution, the MPs expanded their rights by slowly but steady using their relative weight to bargain on behalf of the groups and localities they represented or belonged to. Aggravations of socioeconomic problems—including inflation, price increases, stagnating wages, and supply gaps—always found their way into parliamentary speeches. Second, under 'Abd al-Nasir and Mubarak, parliamentary rights were granted in a top-down manner to keep the MPs close to the regime in times of crisis, such as after the 1967 war and when the government accelerated the increasingly unpopular economic restructuring starting in the 1980s. As long as the core elite managed to achieve a balance between differing interests or to play them against each other, members of parliament were only able to expand institutional powers incrementally by making use of and developing existing tools. Third, in cases when compromise could not be achieved or part of the ruling elite opted to force its decisions through, the president or the government found it difficult to repress critical voices, as alienated parts of the broader ruling elite coalition used parliamentary means to defend their preferences; examples of this include al-Sadat's economic and foreign policies and the last decade of Mubarak's reign.

These general patterns were found in both a single-party and multi-party system. In the latter case, MPs of the ruling party were more contentious toward the government and more responsive to public discontent during times when there were lower percentages of opposition representation. Conflicts could take place in very different institutional constellations: between parliament and government, between parliament and the single party, or even within parliament. Furthermore, parliament's relation to the public developed over time: large-scale public protests were always picked up by the assembly and intensified existing intra-elite conflicts. A final incremental development that took place in the 2000s was the opposition MPs' active engagement with both the media and local constituencies and the pressure they placed on NDP members to at least partially follow through on new parliamentary practices, such as reporting about parliamentary activities on their personal web pages.

3

Fighting over Economic Policies and the Role of the State

All examples of the autocratic parliament presented in the previous chapters—under both a monarchy and a republic—highlight that successful balance and intermediation are closely related to actual processes of political decision making, particularly in the socioeconomic realm. Policies matter, not only in a democracy but also in an autocracy, where they can be subject to diverging interests and disputes. My access to parliamentary debates (via parliamentary minutes) allowed me to analyze shared as well as contested norms in a broad range of policy fields and to explore how these norms developed over time. This chapter focuses on the very general debate over the best economic model for Egypt and the appropriate role of the state within it—two major elements of state-society and state-economy relations. The chapter also presents the lines of conflict that emerged in this struggle. Strikingly, the divide between the ruling party and oppositional parliamentarians did not prove to be the decisive factor. The struggle over economic policies revealed a loss of hope regarding the benefits of the free market economy and led to the call for a strong state to protect society from the private sector. Although these calls appeared across parties, they were never translated into politics. Powerful actors behind the scenes apparently made sure that, in the end, parliamentary votes always opted for keeping the state weak as a market regulator. At the same time, while they were winning these votes, business elites within the ruling party defended their position less and less.

As observed in chapters 1 and 2, a growing sense of socioeconomic discontent was channeled into parliament. However, parliamentary decisions did not take this discontent into account or try to find a balance between different interests. What was seen as legitimate for a public parliamentary discourse—a strong economic role for the state—did not have much impact on the actual decisions being made.

Finally, before delving into debates themselves, I should mention that parliament's debates about the economic order and the role of the state were, of course, intertwined with a number of other important topics. Parliamentary interaction contained a wealth of material on many more issues that would be worth studying in depth, such as specific social policies or economic institutions like the Egyptian Central Bank. Furthermore, the debate transcripts included a great deal of information about the behavior of the Muslim Brotherhood MPs, their political aims, and their use of Islamic references. To present a clear and concise picture of the economic order and the role of the state, I have included illustrative examples and interesting details in the footnotes.

Introducing the Case: The Antitrust Law in Parliament

There are several reasons why I chose as a case study the legislative process involving the Law on Protection of Competition and Prohibition of Monopolistic Practices (qanun himayat al-munafasa wa-man' al-mumarasat al-ihtikariyya; Law No. 3 of 2005), referred to here as the Competition Protection Law. First, the law itself was initially considered a milestone in the economic restructuring of Egypt. Second, the expectations tied to the law clashed with a growing sense of socioeconomic discontent expressed over years through public protests. Finally, this law can be regarded as one of the most prominent cases in the last decade in which parliamentary practices came under close scrutiny by the Egyptian public. For many, it symbolized how private business interests had gained such a great degree of political weight that businessmen could manipulate laws according to their preferences. In this specific case, business tycoons in parliament kept the Competition Protection Law as weak as possible to further enrich themselves at a time when prices were increasing, inflation was growing, and wages were stagnating. El Tarouty describes how Ahmad 'Izz, the infamous business oligarch, lobbied behind the scenes against attempts by the old guard of the ruling party to strengthen the law, including through direct meetings with the president (2015, 67). Due to such blunt abuses of power by a segment of the ruling elite, the antitrust law (as it was called by the English press in Egypt) became a huge scandal, still referred to as one of the most obvious offenses against the rule of law under the Mubarak regime.[1] How a legislative process in an alleged rubber-stamp institution could turn into a contested topic becomes comprehensible when looking at how such manipulations violated shared economic and political norms.

The Competition Protection Law actually traces back to the very first antitrust guidelines that were created in 1985—ten years later, the first draft was discussed by the government. A number of versions were produced, and in 2001 a new initiative by Yusuf Butrus Ghali, the minister of economy and external trade, led to a debate of the eleventh draft within the cabinet. It was supposed to be passed to the People's Assembly the next year,[2] but in the end the draft law was not dealt with by the relevant committees until 2004. Considered one of the pillars of Egypt's transformation from a state-led to a free market economy, the antitrust law was finally debated and put to vote in early 2005, almost thirty years after al-Sadat had initiated the economic opening.

The parliamentary minutes analyzed here begin with a general discussion of the draft law as proposed by a joint committee composed of members of the committee for economic affairs and the committee of constitutional and legislative affairs in 2005 (referred to here as the "joint committee").[3] They reveal the expectations tied to the law as well as the fears and hopes attached to economic reforms. The antitrust law was next formally debated by parliament in 2008, with the first attempt to strengthen the law. This failed, and the press ascribed the failure to a blockade by business elites within the assembly. However, action and

1. See, for example, Eldakak (2012).

2. "Setting Competition Free," *Al-Ahram Weekly*, Feb. 1–7, 2001, no. 519.

3. The minutes were published in the Egyptian parliament's Official Gazette, *al-Jarida al-rasmiyya*, and are cited in footnotes by year and the number of the parliamentary session, with each page range that follows referring to an individual speaker. See the bibliography for further explanation and specific dates of cited sessions.

interactions within parliament were more complex than this, and a closer reading reveals much more, including a cross-party alliance in favor of stronger regulations against monopolies along with a counter-action by business elites a few weeks after the amendment was stopped. Both camps had to legitimize their actions and did so by employing different concepts of the economy and the state. The third time that the antitrust law came under discussion was in 2009, under the umbrella of the parliamentary control function; numerous questions, interpellations, requests for information, and calls for general debates were raised at this time. Following extreme price increases for basic goods in 2008, the antitrust law was used to hold the government to account by showing how ministers did not fulfill established norms concerning the role of the state, as set out by the law for protecting people from monopolies and price manipulations. Truly critical voices from within the ruling party could no longer be found, although NDP members and even private businessmen also made use of control instruments.

In regard to all of the public and parliamentary criticism toward the law, it might be surprising that, among legal scholars, the Egyptian antitrust law was not regarded as a complete failure—quite the contrary when compared to international standards and experiences in other developing countries. As in other emerging markets, the fundamental question behind Egypt's economic transition was whether to emulate elaborate and complex laws found in industrialized nations, such as those in the United States or European countries, or whether it would be more appropriate to gradually introduce and develop such laws domestically. In the complex case of competition protection, the latter option was seen as preferable for Egypt (el Dean and Mohieldin 2001). This entailed maintaining simple and easily comprehendible regulations in the form of per se rules and bans, in contrast to a "rule of reason" approach. The latter builds on the assumption that no action necessarily hurts the competitive market, and each action must be deliberated separately with regard to its effects. However, this approach requires a great deal of resources and effort on the part of authorities and judicial staff. Eggert (2011) claims that, especially in a country like Egypt, where judges are rarely educated in both law and economics, per se rules could help instill a transparent and simple regulative system. Considering this challenge, she comes to the conclusion that Egypt introduced an antitrust law that may be regarded as a simplified version of the US and EU competition protection laws. However, some articles entailed a rule of reason approach that stood in contrast to several per se regulations found in the law. This mix of approaches imparted a degree of insecurity. In addition, the elements of the rule of reason enlarged the workload required during the implementation process.

Aside from this, Eggert positively assesses that the law entailed the possibility of excluding the provision for basic needs from the rules of free competition. For an economy in transition, this serves as a buffer against negative effects on the lower strata. Yet Eggert criticizes the law for failing to name excessive pricing as a criminal offense. Even though providing solid evidence by way of prices is complex and costly, it is also one of the key aspects of competition protection. In regard to the scare-off effects of the law, Eggert claims that when the potential for imposing sanctions was raised in 2008, the law managed to create an effective deterrent. Furthermore, the leniency policy that was at least partially introduced and the possibility of state intervention through fixing prices are suitable means for gradually introducing an antitrust law (2011, 184–85).

The real obstacles to effective competition protection lay in implementing these policies, especially through the role of the watchdog organization, the Competition Protection Authority (CPA), established in 2006. Although formally and geographically separated from the government, the CPA remained under the supervision of the minister for trade and industry. Furthermore, the minister decided whether to bring complaints raised by the CPA to the public prosecutor and also decided on the pay grade of CPA employees. This opened the door for exercising political influence on the authority's decisions and did not reflect the ideal of an independent authority. The composition of the CPA's managing board also reflected the dominance of the ruling party, since nine of the fourteen members of the board belonged to the NDP. Apart from its leaders, the CPA consisted of fifty-four employers, many of whom were highly qualified but inexperienced young graduates. Further diminishing the CPA's independence, they had to rely on ministries and chambers of commerce to conduct market studies and other investigations. Although the

CPA was far from perfect on paper or in its implementation, Eggert still acknowledges that it constituted a valuable starting point for competition protection, bringing some cases to court or at least to the public's attention. When it failed to convict a company of monopolistic practices due to a political entanglement, it learned from this failure and tried to use other means to strengthen competition in the relevant sector. Furthermore, the CPA cooperated with authorities in other countries to learn from their experiences and tried to raise awareness of competition in Egypt (Eggert 2011, 188–93).

This very short overview shows that there were a number of shortcomings from an external-legal perspective; nevertheless, the law did establish a serious basis for competition protection. Interestingly, the issues that legal analysts have raised only partially correlate to questions relevant for the MPs. This underlines that disputes over the law were more than mere window dressing, but represented serious political debates that should be understood and analyzed.

The Transition to the Free Market Economy

The Competition Protection Law was regarded as one major pillar of Egypt's economic restructuring. As such, debates reveal not only what the parliamentarians thought of the law itself but also how they viewed the economic transformation as a whole. Starting with the debates surrounding the draft law in 2005, many speakers considered this transition a necessity on account of global trends. They spoke of the "new global economic order"[4] or, even more abstractly, of the "global direction."[5] A few connected the economic order to the degree of civilization within a

---

4. 2005/21: 49–50.

5. 2005/21: 48–49; 50–51. Some MPs spoke as though the entire world was heading in this direction (25–26). It was repeatedly stated that more than 110 states had already introduced an antitrust law, and such international organizations as the United Nations, the EU, and the Arab League had published guiding principles on competition protection and antitrust laws (56, 29, 30). For some MPs, this indicated the simple need to follow the same path; others used it as an argument against further delaying the passage of an Egyptian antitrust law (51).

country.[6] Many members of parliament stressed Egypt's international obligations, which would force the country to enact the law. It is not entirely clear whether Egypt's membership in these organizations per se, or certain agreements with them, obliged the ministers to pass the antitrust law.[7] Generally, the MPs did not see their country as being in a position to actively use global developments for its own interests but rather viewed Egypt as an actor that had difficulty following mainstream (civilizational) trends and fulfilling commitments within existing international agreements.[8] In short, the antitrust law was simply something Egypt had to have on an international level.

Recognizing that the economic system was not free for their choosing, many members of parliament focused on how to prevent the negative impacts brought about by the market economy. The rules of the market itself prohibited monopolies,[9] which therefore necessitated regulation.[10] Primary attention was paid to the increasing role of the private sector, on which the state heavily relied for investment and production in the

6. A few spoke of the "whole civilized world" (12–13) that Egypt needed to follow, while others argued that the fact that so many countries had already introduced an antitrust law showed that civilization alone could not be the criterion for the existence of such a law (52). Only once is "civilization" used in connection with the term "capitalism," but not in an idealized way; it is stated that the greed capitalism evokes in "civilized" capitalist countries makes an antitrust law a necessity in these countries.

7. Among these organizations were the UN (50–51), the World Trade Organization (25–26), the EU (25–26, 50–51, agreement 44), the Euro-Mediterranean Partnership (31–32), the Common Market for Eastern and Southern Africa (COMESA, 31–32), and the Arab League (31–32, 50–51, 54).

8. Strikingly, only the rapporteur of the joint committee that had developed the draft law talked about the potential for international cooperation leading to coordinated actions against huge multinational companies whose market activities had negative consequences in developing countries like Egypt (2005/21: 11). Cooperation among other states was also not deemed to be an option, even as another speaker shared his observation that governments in other countries also intervene against international or supranational companies that have an effect on domestic economies.

9. 2005/21: 30–31.

10. 2005/21: 21, 28, 52, 59.

eyes of the MPs.[11] Particularly large entities needed to be regulated to protect consumers and markets from monopolies, mergers, and takeovers.[12] Here the fear of huge companies surfaced, as greed was perceived to be the leading characteristic of private actors. In the past, large conglomerates had belonged to the state, which bore a social responsibility.[13] Because of the economic transformation, the state's role had changed from that of a socially responsible entrepreneur to that of a regulator who was restricted to safeguarding the principles of the free market—the antitrust law was seen as an essential element within this new role. The opinion that the state should even be allowed to operate monopolies because they serve the common good, as opposed to serving the private sector, was voted down. This conflict was also visible in the discussion of the title of the law. The draft law spoke of "harmful monopolistic practices" before the government and the Shura Council's reviewed the draft and deleted the word "harmful" (2005/22: 13). Two NDP MPs feared that eliminating the word would prohibit state intervention in favor of people with limited income (13, 14). Again, their position did not win the vote.[14]

11. 2005/21: 41, 52–53.

12. 2005/21: 25–26, 30.

13. The source of fear with regard to private sector companies was the "capitalist greed" (31) thought to automatically lead to exploitation of the consumer. Antitrust laws should thus serve as a safety valve against the social "explosion" in Egypt through such greedy behavior. Less dramatically, the law was seen as the state's duty to intervene in the economy to regulate relations among producers and between producers and the consumers (53–54).

14. The ruling party MPs differentiated between beneficial and harmful monopolistic practices. "Harmful" was defined as having negative consequences for the people, especially in terms of prices, but it also presupposed an intentionally harmful monopoly, which excluded cases in which a market sector is controlled as a result of innovation or a lack of competition (13–14). By contrast, the head of the joint committee claimed that no beneficial monopolistic practices existed (13), whereas the minister of investment qualified this statement: any monopoly was harmful per se, but in the case of the state as monopolist, the benefit to society could outweigh any harm, and thus legitimate it. Again, whether a monopoly was exercised for the public good or for profit seeking was decisive. In any case, the word "harmful" remained excluded (14–15).

There were also several positive effects expected to arise from the law, beyond merely preventing the worst. Many parliamentarians had high hopes that it would be a boon for the economy in general[15] by ushering in economic dynamics and free and fair competition.[16] The effects expected included development and innovation along with modernization and high growth rates, even on a global scale.[17] More specifically, the MPs assumed that competition protection would support domestic and foreign investment[18] by strengthened confidence in Egypt as a stable and reliable country and market for investment.[19] An improved competitive climate would lead to lower costs and higher-quality production, to the improved distribution of goods, to increasing export rates, and to the creation of job opportunities.[20] Most important, consumer prices were expected to sink as a byproduct of enhanced competition.[21] Here, protecting competition was seen as a way to instill competitive justice, which would improve every part of the economy in a dynamic way.

In contrast to the idea of progress through development, another expected benefit of this law was a new balance (*tawazun*) among the producer, the consumer, and the supplier, or between supply and demand.[22] Moreover, the law was supposed to create an atmosphere of fraternization between producers, providing them the opportunity to strive for the common good.[23] The new balance could also affect smaller players, small-scale

---

15. 2005/21: 12–13, 60.

16. Terms used in 2005/21 were 'adalat al-munafasa (23) and *al-munafasa al-sharifa* (59, 60–61).

17. 2005/21: 36, 44, 51–52, 52.

18. 2005/21: 14, 31–32, 39–40, 44, 44b, 52, 55, 59, 60.

19. 2005/21: 39–40, 58b.

20. 2005/21: 14, 39–40, 23, 25–26, 56, 58, 59, 64.

21. 2005/21: 15–17, 51–52, 52, 58, 58b, 59, 60–61, 61–62. Some MPs specified price decreases as a result of price regulation through enhanced competition (59) and through protection from agreements between importers and suppliers on prices, quantities, and market shares (15–17). From this point of view, it was the consumer's right to be protected from controlled prices (62–62) that justified the antitrust law.

22. 2005/21: 12–13, 51, 58, 61–62, 64–65.

23. 2005/21: 64–65.

enterprises, or the populace in general, all of whom would be protected from the "big fish," or "whales."[24] How this was to be accomplished, however, remained unclear. While these MPs—all from the ruling party—expressed open concern for large economic entities, a number of NDP and independent MPs tried to avoid the impression of a discourse hostile to big companies: they were quick to explain that protecting small players through this law did not entail fighting the large ones.[25] Another group of MPs expected Egypt to simultaneously have a dynamic *and* balanced economy, with no need for government control. These visions of fraternization and the search for the common good as a direct result of free competition stood in contrast to the description of the status quo made by other assembly members, who pointed to the suffering of Egyptian people due to price increases, highlighting how far Egypt actually was from any kind of harmony.

On the whole, conflicting concepts of freedom, justice, and equality could be found in 2005: free competition was seen as a means for development as well as an opportunity for large players to exploit the weak. The definition of justice remained vague and rather loosely related to fair opportunities in a free economy. Equality found its expression in the idea of a new balance, which was not built on equal actors yet exhibited limited tolerance toward inequality. The idea of a harmonic whole persisted in many speeches, as did a fear of the private sector.[26]

24. 2005/21: 21–22, 31–32, 51–52, 52–53.

25. 2005/21: 28, 32–33. On the contrary, independent and ruling party speakers pointed out that this law actually supported large companies (36, 52) since Egypt needed companies capable of competing on the world market and investing in technology, research, and development (15–17). The "whales" were the ones who had the means to create job opportunities, especially for the younger generation (61). The minister of investment even tried to quell concerns by pointing out that, compared to such countries as the United States, the Egyptian "whales" were small anyway (42–44).

26. In contrast to these political and economic arguments, three MPs framed the necessity of the antitrust law in religious terms. Two hadiths and one episode of the *sira*, the life of the prophet, were cited (2005/21: 26; 45; 54). These references, however, said only that Allah banned monopolistic practices.

Three years later, the two contrasting visions of a free market economy became even more visible: in two debates in 2008 (2008/118 and 2008/139), MPs from the ruling party as well as from the Muslim Brotherhood, in cooperation with the minister of trade and industry, attempted to increase the efficacy of the Competition Protection Law by raising fines and introducing a leniency policy. The credo of all the speakers was that a free market economy was the desired outcome. However, the alliance in favor of strengthening the law based its argumentation on the idea of balance: improving the balance between differing interests, which included protecting the weak, meaning small and medium-sized enterprises.[27] It also meant taking action against the large "greedy" players.[28] Another type of balance was called for, namely the balance between deterring businessmen from committing monopolistic crimes while, at the same time, not threatening entrepreneurs with overly harsh regulations. Balance could also be found in the recurrent pledge that a free market system would not lead to chaos but to an organized system.[29] Part of the regulation included transparency, which needed to be created through a strong antitrust law that provided incentives for people to testify about monopolistic practices they had witnessed.[30] In sum, MPs from all parties and backgrounds aimed for balance and order in the economy, accepting inequality but including rules that prevented the system from drifting apart.

The well-known business tycoon Ahmad ʿIzz painted a completely different picture: for him, constraints on competition were out of the question. He described players in a free market economy as constantly "lying in ambush" (2008/139: 57): at any given moment, anybody could attempt to gain an advantage over other players, leaving any moral considerations aside. This situation would lead to a misuse of the leniency policy, as every player would give false testimony to improve their own company's position in relation to the competition. The economic system as interpreted

---

27. 2008/118: 12–13, 18.
28. Annex 2008/118: 24.
29. Annex 2008/118: 24, 2008/118: 12.
30. 2008/139: 53c, 58–59, 61–62, 66, 63a.

by 'Izz was reminiscent of a Hobbesian state of nature. This anarchic situation—in which anything can happen at any time, creating a permanent feeling of insecurity—clearly contrasts with the conceptions of a balanced and well-ordered economy mentioned above. 'Izz's conclusion drawn also differed: the businessman accepted the uncontrollable nature of the market and even argued that the state should not interfere at all. In contrast, a large group of MPs lobbied for the state's active role in establishing and maintaining a balanced market.

In March 2009, following extreme price hikes for basic goods in 2008, the government faced harsh critique for its inability to implement the antitrust law and its failure to control price increases and fight poverty, unemployment, and fraud. Considering that the world was facing a global financial and economic crisis, however, one might have expected a more fundamental discussion to have arisen about the right economic strategy or system. On the one hand, Egypt was still perceived as being in a transitional phase from a state-controlled to a free market economy, which meant supporters of the old system could have used the failure of the new one as an argument to turn back the wheel of time. On the other hand, the most dominant opposition force at the time was the Muslim Brotherhood, which could have fundamentally criticized Western capitalism and its violation of Islamic economic norms, such as the prohibition of interest (*riba*).[31] Yet, with very few exceptions, the concepts of justice and equality were far from being used as clear counterarguments or even ideologies of the prevailing capitalist order, but as a pledge for reducing inequality by way of policies within the given framework of a free market economy.

---

31. One can find a few remarks against the so-called American way based on *riba*, interest, which was forbidden in Islamic law (2009/67: 13). However, this reference remained vague and was not spelled out, for example, in terms of explaining how an Islamic competition protection law would look. Another broad claim that the shari'a was the ideal system remained on a very abstract level, even though the speaker referred to a classic Islamic thinker, Ibn Qayyim al-Jawziyya (1292–1350), whose work deals with economic questions in detail (2009/67: 13). No attempt was made to transfer Ibn Qayyim's assumptions to the contemporary world, which makes it difficult to judge the possible underlying ideas of this reference—beyond giving the speech an Islamist touch.

Opposition MPs—both independent and from the Muslim Brother-hood—criticized the government for favoring the rich and suppressing the poor,[32] while the majority of Egyptian businessmen were criticized for exploiting Egypt, amassing wealth, and leaving nothing for the people.[33] High prices on the local market after price drops on the world market were attributed to the greed of the private sector, which seemed to confirm old fears about private business;[34] corruption among elites was declared to be an additional reason.[35] The core problem, as several parliamentarians saw it, was the violation of distributional justice: they did not criticize inequal-ity as such, but the extent of it in contemporary Egypt. The government was accused of talking only about the economic growth rate, when, in fact, it was the distribution of the gains generated by that growth that should mat-ter to the politicians.[36] One solution was found in the wage system, which the opposition MPs had criticized for offering wages far too low to provide a decent living for small-scale farmers or employees in the government administration, even those with a university degree. Demands were made for a minimum national wage of 1,200 Egyptian pounds and for a maxi-mum wage (of ten times the minimum wage).[37] This demand was grounded in an ideal of limited inequality, and it sought to correct the unfairness of

32. 2009/66: 59, 2009/67: 3, 2009/67: 8–9.

33. "Give the bread to its bakers even if they ate three quarters of it, but the business-men would like to eat the whole loaf" (2009/67: 9).

34. 2009/68: 6.

35. One Muslim Brother MP used Qur'anic verses to indirectly say it was not pos-sible for a people to live with a high degree of corruption among its upper class and that this corruption would negatively affect the entire society (2009/67: 16): "And if the people of the towns had believed and guarded (against evil) We would certainly have opened up for them blessings from the heaven and the earth, but they rejected, so We overtook them for what they had earned" (7:96). "And when We wish to destroy a town, We send com-mandments to its people who lead easy lives, but they transgress therein; thus the word proves true against it, so We destroy it with utter destruction" (17:16). All translations of the Qur'an cited in this study are by Shakir (1986).

36. 2009/66: 62.

37. 2009/66: 63; 2009/67: 7. These demands had been put forward by the growing workers' movement.

wages that led to a life under the poverty line. Similarly, the government was criticized for providing insufficient social aid during the price hikes on food and basic goods. The extra 100 Egyptian pounds (around 17 US dollars) per month for a household of five was not enough for a decent living.[38] Yet another idea was investment distribution across different regions in Egypt. Private investors apparently did not care about a just distribution of investment and questions of development. Only the state could ensure the right to industrial development for all regions.[39] Complete planning for all sectors and administrations would help bring about social justice.[40]

All of these suggestions placed much greater emphasis on regulation of the market economy than before. In regard to the global order, opening the economy was no longer seen as the only way forward: instead, it represented the desire for autonomy from the external forces, driven by the widespread fear of giving foreign companies too much of a hold on the Egyptian economy (as I discuss further in chapter 4). This desire for autonomy also became apparent in the idea of self-sufficiency in the area of food and basic goods, which was praised as an achievement from the 1960s that had been lost due to policies favoring consumption over production.[41] All in all, though we see tendencies to discredit the market economy as a whole, a counterideology, such as a socialist or Islamic concept of the economic order, was absent.

In sum, the most remarkable observation for the period under study is that the debate started with two major sets of ideas: the first related to the complex of development and progress, whereas the second concentrated on

---

38. One MP demanded the extension of social aid from those who live at the *hadd al-kafaf* (subsistence line) to those at the *hadd al-kifaya* (sufficiency line), as the latter group, persons with limited income, suffered a great deal from the price increases and stagnating wages (2009/68: 15)—two terms referring to the shari'a's limits on wealth distribution. The latter offers enough for a satisfactory standard of living, whereas the first covers only basic needs. Both limits have to be evaluated regarding "the general economic conditions in the country as well as generally accepted conventions" (Manjoo 2008, 262).

39. 2009/68: 6.

40. 2009/68: 8.

41. 2009/67: 12.

the idea of a balance between economy and society. The first set of ideas had already disappeared by 2008, leaving only the idea of economic and social balance; however, proponents believed that simply enhancing free competition would lead to this outcome. In 2009, in contrast, central planning was put forward as a solution, which tended to clash with the idea of free competition. This was accompanied by the call for the autonomy of the Egyptian economy and self-sufficiency in the food sector. Only one independent member of parliament actually demanded a return to socialism, while the others redefined the market economy in their own way, which mainly involved regulation by the state. However, there were calls in 2009 to abandon the US model—a radical departure from 2005, when the global trend toward a free market economy was accepted as a given, without reflection on specific models or even on whether the country was at liberty to choose a model. A new dynamic for the independent formulation of economic policies seems to have emerged within the framework of a market economy, yet with much more state intervention. Concerning justice, it was not only the general market situation and its domination by a number of large players that was considered unjust in the 2009 debate, but also numerous questions of distributional policies, from social welfare to income distribution.

The Role of the State

The core tenet of any competition protection law is that free market economies need regulation by the state. The degree of state intervention and how it should be applied in various sectors can be the subject of heated political debate. This conflict potential is all the more pertinent as Egypt went through a long period of economic transformation that restructured relations between the state and the market. One can observe how political fights over this question developed in years of increasing socioeconomic protest, perceived by many to be the result of state withdrawal or outright lack of state intervention in the economic sector. One also finds very differentiated assessments of the various institutions that exercised state power, constituting a complex picture of trust and suspicion.

As covered in the previous section, there were two major economic expectations associated with the antitrust law in 2005: new, dynamic development and modernization of the Egyptian economy paired with the creation of a new balance among the producer, trader, and consumer. However, the MPs did not mention any direct role through which the state would achieve these aims in either dimension. Their position reflected a change in the role of the state from that of an entrepreneur with social responsibility to that of a regulator restricted to safeguarding the principles of the free market;[42] the antitrust law was taken as an essential part of this new role of the state. The state was seen as playing a significant role only in regard to price controls. While a few assembly members argued that prices would sink as a byproduct of enhanced competition,[43] most who mentioned the topic aimed at protecting the consumer through price controls by the state. A group of MPs asked for direct state intervention into the realm of price setting and justified this request by characterizing the existing situation as "a burden on the citizen," who already suffered under monopolies.[44] They argued that "the citizen on the street" blamed the members of parliament for not helping—people were losing hope, and the politicians were doing nothing.[45] These members of parliament saw the real benefit of the antitrust law as lying in the possibility of government-led price regulations and price setting for essential or strategic goods.[46] This was what they understood as "consumer protection": direct governmental intervention into the market.[47]

Contrary to the hope of many speakers, the minister of investment argued that the law was not intended to lead to price fixing by authorities

42. 2005/21: 26.

43. 2005/21: 15–17, 51–52, 52, 58, 58b, 59, 60–61, 61–62.

44. 2005/21: 44. Others complained about the "earthquake of prices" (61), "horrible increase of crazy prices" (56–57), and the "existing chaos" in the markets, especially for essential goods (58b). This view of the status quo was then criticized by the minister for investment, who declared there was no chaos in the market, since the government at that time exercised sectoral control of the economy (42–44).

45. 2005/21: 59.

46. 2005/21: 45–46, 49, 54, 56–57.

47. A few narrowed it down further, saying that the "philosophy" of the antitrust law should lead to sinking prices (45–46, 64), including the critique that the law explicitly banned price reductions (45–46).

in general but only in cases of prohibited agreements among competitors that infringed on the principles of free and fair competition.[48] This position was contradicted by Article 10 of the draft law, which allowed the council of ministers to determine the prices of essential products for a limited amount of time without considering these activities as anticompetitive. Whereas the draft entailed a list of goods, some parliamentarians tried to expand the number of products[49] as well as the duration for price setting. One even called for a stronger role of the state, proposing that the state not only have the option to intervene but that it be obliged to do so.[50] Other MPs opposed state interference in general and demanded the complete deletion of this article.[51] Ultimately, the parliament voted to delete any specifications in which products were conceived as being strategic, granting free rein in setting prices to include any item deemed necessary on account of monopolistic practices.[52]

This intensely debated question revolved around whether lowering consumer prices could be achieved by indirectly protecting the market, or

48. 2005/21: 42–44, 47. The minister's point of view was supported by a parliamentarian who expressed the fear that price reductions would lead to monopolies and that competition would actually be exercised by only a few businessmen. This, in turn, would lead to agreements about price reductions, which could destroy the new industries developing in Egypt at the time (49–50).

49. Some speakers preferred the term "essential products" (2005/26: 30, 34–35) and others preferred "strategic products" (29–30, 30), while one MP opted for the combination of both (30) and another spoke solely of "products" (33). The minister of trade thought this question did not matter at all. In general, they all intended to use terms that covered as wide a pool of products as possible. The draft law contained a paragraph with an enumeration of goods that were deemed essential, among them medicine, petroleum products, and all goods subsidized by the state and included in the ration card system. Some MPs wanted to add other items such as food (2005/26: 30), water, electricity (35), alum, and flour (33).

50. 2005/26: 30–31.

51. 2005/26: 29, 37.

52. 2005/26: 35–36. Attempts to limit the government's power in terms of the time period in which state intervention would remain failed as well (30, 31). Whether price determination also applied to the private sector, and if the state had to compensate producers whose production costs exceeded the fixed selling prices, remained unanswered.

if direct state intervention in setting prices at a lower level was the better solution. Both positions were expressed in the assembly, and, strikingly, the division did not run along party lines but rather divided the ruling party. Except for one Muslim Brother[53] who fought for the active determination of strategic and basic goods by the government, the debate was only between NDP members. The MPs involved were difficult to classify: they were neither well-known businessmen nor members of the army, and there was no geographic pattern in regard to their constituencies. Their interests, intentions, and motivations for propagating this specific opinion were not explicitly expressed either. Apparently, positions in favor of and against price regulations were both found within the party, and the free market ideology was not left undisputed. The solution they identified attempted to bridge the gap between the two camps, which opposed each other in regard to the role of the state. By giving the government carte blanche to set the price for any product for as long as the ministry wanted, they also left the door open for the council of ministers to remain inactive, if desired. Even the Competition Protection Authority did not attain a greater role in this procedure, although parliamentarians did fight for a strong and independent body in regard to other competences.[54] This proposed solution required a high degree of trust that the government would exercise an appropriate amount of interference in the market; this trust would, however, come to be lost in the following years.

In 2008, two MPs—one NDP and one Muslim Brother—worked together with the minister of trade and industry to amend the antitrust law in a way that would strengthen the state's role as a regulator for competition protection, but all of their attempts to do so were blocked in parliament. Because the Competition Protection Law had failed to effectuate price decreases—one of its main goals—the parliamentarians' general mood toward it was negative; indeed, the year 2008 was marked by skyrocketing

---

53. al-Shaʿir 2005/21: 45–46.

54. In the version approved by the assembly, the council of ministers only needed to ask the CPA for its opinion on any specific case; the authority's permission was not required. This was criticized by only one MP (30).

prices, especially for food. Many assembly members, both from the ruling party and the Muslim Brotherhood, argued for direct state regulation of consumer prices,[55] but the initiators of the amendments still believed prices would sink as a result of improved competition.[56] They therefore suggested raising fines against cartel activities to create a scare-off effect, and they also proposed introducing a fine based on the business volume generated by monopolistic practices. Moreover, they suggested new obligations to provide information to the CPA, along with a leniency policy to generate incentives for people to report monopolistic practices and violations.

Other segments of the ruling party introduced amendments that undermined the draft law, although they did not explicitly contest the norms it upheld. Fines were again reduced to a very low amount compared to gains from monopolistic practices.[57] Furthermore, another demand (*talab*), signed by twenty parliamentarians, called for reopening the discussion about Article 26 concerning the key witness regulation.[58] They proposed completely eliminating Article 26, and the measure

55. 2008/118: 15–16, 16, 16–17, 17, 21–22, 22, 22–23.

56. One of the initiators argued that prices might sink as a result of state regulation rather than as a result of direct intervention. To him, only a stronger state had the capacity to fight monopolies effectively (2008/118 annex: 23–24). The minister of trade and industry, Rashid Muhammad Rashid, tried to argue that not every price increase was a result of monopolistic practices; other reasons might include fluctuations on the global level (2008/118: 20–21). Nevertheless, Rashid also demanded a more active state role and increased intervention by the government against monopolies (13).

57. Suddenly, the majority within the NDP now supported a new version of the article in which the maximum fine was 300 million pounds, as opposed to a percentage of the illegal gains. Surprisingly, there was no justification put forward by rapporteur Isma'il Hilal or any other MP. In the annex of the protocol, the argument is put forward that a fine based on a percentage of sales risks being void in cases where no active sale had taken place (annex 2008/131: 30). The annex, however, does not mention that the committee and the Shura Council included a fixed amount in their proposal.

58. This happened to be in line with Article 152 of assembly's internal regulations, which stipulated that a discussion may take place about a previously approved article if new factors surface that make it necessary to reconsider the issue, or if the government, committee head, rapporteur, or ten members of parliament demand that discussion be reopened. The assembly also approved a new debate.

was ultimately approved even though they did not provide any serious justification for it.[59] In contrast to amendments proposed by the minister of trade and industry and the two members of parliament, this group of MPs aimed solely to buffer against attempts to strengthen the law, without suggesting their own political goal or vision. Fellow MPs regarded the counterinitiative as an attempt to keep the law both lax and weak, ignoring the socioeconomic problems present outside of the chamber.

The same criticism was applied to Ahmad 'Izz's proposed reintroduction of the leniency article, though with a 50 percent maximum penalty instead of a complete remission of the penalty. What may have been intended as a compromise was not deemed by the other bloc of parliamentarians as a serious attempt to strengthen the law. Instead, they issued point-blank accusations that 'Izz's proposal and the earlier proposed revisions of the fine article would destroy the effectiveness of the entire law.[60] Clearly, the gap between the two camps fighting over the role of the state was widening. Compromises could no longer be achieved due to the lack of trust in the camp that organized support among the ruling party and voted against other positions.

During the debate, the two blocs confronted each other on the question of whether large companies that violate antitrust stipulations should be seriously punished under the amended law. This conflict points to a more general cleavage that becomes evident when we consider which MPs supported low, fixed-amount fines on monopolists: Mustafa Kamal al-Sallab, a ceramics magnate; Dr. 'Abd al-Rahman Baraka, a banking tycoon; and Ibrahim Sa'd Muhammad al-Jawjari, a member of one of the wealthiest families from al-Mansura. These wealthy businessmen safeguarded their own or their group's interests by protecting monopolistic practices from

59. The only reason offered was a contradiction of Rashid's claim in the previous session that the remission of penalty for a key witness was practiced in many countries and had dramatically increased the effectiveness of antitrust policies. MP al-Jawjari simply stated that this was not true: on the contrary, this stipulation had been annulled in other countries (6), which was why Egypt should follow the international trend and remove Article 26.

60. 2008/139: 52–53, 61–62, 64, 67–68, 68–69, 69.

prosecution and punishment. Although they were all NDP members, this was not the explanatory factor, as a look at the opposing camp reveals. The attempt to strengthen the antitrust law was headed by minister of trade and industry Rashid, who was himself an NDP member and a known opponent of Ahmad 'Izz. He found support in the head of the committee for economic affairs and rapporteur of the joint committee, Mustafa al-Sa'id, who also opposed the lax fines. Sa'id, a professor for economics and a NDP member for decades, found himself allied with three Muslim Brothers[61] who were likewise fighting monopolists and corrupt businessmen. Another NDP member who engaged in the struggle to enhance the law was MP Khalil Quwayta, who submitted one of the two proposals for amendment. This mixed opposition against 'Izz became even broader in the attack against his proposal to reintroduce the leniency article: it included not only independent MPs[62] and Muslim Brothers,[63] but also NDP members, the army general Mahir al-Darabi, and Khalil Quwayta.[64]

Remarkably, the alliance for a stronger antitrust law placed much greater emphasis on justifying their position, arguing for an active state role to establish a social and economic balance. In contrast, the other bloc barely attempted to persuade their colleagues, and the few arguments they did offer were rather farfetched. This lack of effort gave the impression that this bloc was well aware of its decision-making power behind the scenes and that its members believed they did not need to legitimize their actions to others. This bloc's power was visible when the business elites presented a watered-down version of the leniency article with reduced fines. In this instance, they switched out the rapporteur of the joint committee, Mustafa Sa'id, who was in favor of the stronger antitrust law and had presented Rashid's earlier proposal; instead, they had Isma'il Hilal, owner of

---

61. 'Abd al-Halim 'Awad Hilal, Ahmad Muhammad Mahmud Diyab, and Sa'd al-Husayni.

62. Mustafa Bakri 2008/139: 50, and 'Ala' al-Din 'Abd al-Mun'im 2008/139: 64.

63. Hamdi Hasan 2008/139: 66–67, Hasan Jabr 2008/139: 58–59, Ahmad Ibrahim Mustafa Abu Baraka 2008/139: 66, Taymur 'Abd al-Ghani 2008/139: 67–68, 'Abd al-Halim Hilal 2008/139: 68–69, and Sa'd al-Husayni 2008/139: 69.

64. 2008/139: 52, 2008/139: 63.

an electricity company, present the committee's hastily changed position to the plenary. Silencing Sa'id, the well-respected professor of economics, demonstrated just how harshly the 'Izz camp was pushing its agenda. From that point forward, public criticism toward the NDP in regard to the weak version of the law disappeared.

The business elite's behind-the-scenes power effectively silenced critical voices; at the same time, they were increasingly silent about their own positions, which they knew were not widely regarded as legitimate. The impossibility of publicly justifying the weak regulatory role of the state became obvious in 2009: after the price hikes of 2008, the debate about the government's response to socioeconomic problems addressed the appropriate role of the state and the extent to which the government had employed state power accordingly. In general, while the ministers mostly shared the normative ideals of the MPs (Muslim Brotherhood and independent opposition), they deviated in their assessment of their own actions as well as of the status quo. The MPs demanded that the ministers activate the market, whereas the ministers claimed they had already done so.[65] The deputies regarded the role of the state as essential in the realm of distributional justice, explicitly in organizing the wage system and social transfers.[66] The minister of trade and industry, by comparison, shared the same ideas but claimed that the government's economic policies had fulfilled them.[67]

---

65. MPs demanded support for production, not consumption (2009/67: 11), and for activating market mechanisms (66: 49, 66: 57, 59, 66: 60). Here, they referred to the historical development of the market economy: after the beginning of *infitah*, no government had introduced institutions or administrative mechanisms to protect the market economy, which, in turn, had led to the biased market structures of today. The late introduction of such regulations and institutions as the Competition Protection Law and the CPA explained their weakness (2009/68: 10, 68: 8).

66. 2009/66: 62, 67: 7.

67. As evidence, he put forward the government increase in wages for state employees; however, he did so without referring to private-sector wages (2009/67: 24). He also claimed that mechanisms and authorities to support the market had been introduced (67: 25): production was increased and exports were regulated to stop the price increases and prevent shortages of goods (67: 25, 27). All of these points matched with points of

Yet, two differences remained: first, two MPs demanded the government's direct intervention in setting prices, as Article 10 of the Competition Protection Law allowed.[68] The ministers did not refer to this option at all. Second, one could observe that the parliamentarians drew a line between the state and the government; in some speeches, the state was presented as a victim of the government's policies. Price increases, for instance, affected the state, since it needed to buy goods at market prices in order to subsidize them. The greater the gap between market prices and subsidized consumer prices, the worse it was for the state budget.[69] Furthermore, the parliamentarians accused the government of being directly responsible for price increases and inflation through influencing the policies of the central bank.[70] Additionally, they accused the government of being corrupt.[71]

Altogether, the MPs no longer placed much trust in the government to use state power in a constructive way. Although they accused the government of being absent from the economy and incapable of controlling it, they likewise accused cabinet members of consciously violating Egypt's interests and pursuing their own instead. Thus, it was unclear whether the cabinet was willingly violating agreed-upon norms. The MPs' criticism

---

criticism from one or more parliamentarians. Al-Musalhi, minister for social solidarity, promoted the active role of the state in delivering welfare services, mainly by the means of ration cards and subsidies (68: 4).

68. 2009/66: 59, 67: 15. Strikingly, one of them, Kamal Ahmad, had rallied for the complete deletion of this article in 2005. Faith in the self-regulation powers of the market had obviously diminished over the years.

69. 2009/67: 20a, 20b.

70. They accused the government of pushing the central bank to incessantly print new money to devaluate the debt burden (2009/68: 8). Furthermore, they claimed that the government violated its fundamental obligation to protect the wealth of the Egyptian people (2009/66: 68). Instead, the government had sold Egypt and thereby betrayed the country (2009/67: 11, 20).

71. 2009/67: 16. Some MPs expressed despair, saying they had given up on this government and the hope that justice would be done for the crimes committed. Two MPs shifted their hopes of punishment for the politicians and monopolists to the afterlife (2009/67: 20; 68: 18).

was rife with contradictions as well: they attacked the government for not implementing a free system of supply and demand, and at the same time they asked for direct price manipulations by the state.

The government's positions in trying to appease every critique exhibited bias, too. The ministers claimed that prices had already begun to fall and that overall economic development was positive, but still they promised to further expand the social welfare system.[72] Their assertion that "everything is great" clashed with MPs' perception that "the crisis is near"; nevertheless, the normative standard of an active role for both the state and government was widely shared. Yet the picture of an active state as a distributor of subsidies, as the minister described, was rejected by the members of parliament who demanded structural changes to redistribution, including a minimum and maximum wage.

This criticism expressed in the interpellations stands alongside a large number of requests for information; most of these requests were quite similar to the content of the interpellations. The MPs tried to distinguish themselves from the government and to reflect common sense concerning the issue of increasing prices, especially in the cement and housing sector. Recurring elements in the discourse on the free market included social justice, protecting the poor from the greedy, the negative consequences of foreign investors, and, as a new element, foreign producers who hurt the Egyptian economy. Rhetorically, the parliamentarians sounded much like the opposition, stressing their role as representatives of the people and quasi-interrogating the government in the people's name. The exceptions here were three groups of MPs. As discussed in chapter 6 in detail, businessmen and powerful NDP members around Ahmad 'Izz requested business-related topics or brought up the topic of price increases without taking any critical positions toward the government. One can distinguish them from other NDP members who had a much more critical attitude

---

72. Al-Musalhi, for example, praised the government for increasing the number of ration-card owners to 63 million people in 2009. This means that almost 80 percent of the Egyptian people received state support to make ends meet. This high level of social welfare is neither sustainable nor a sign of a healthy economy.

and, at times, cooperated with Muslim Brothers and independent assembly members. The well-known NDP-affiliated critics of the earlier debates, however, were silenced.

The way that the debate developed over the years proved the survival of the century-old belief that a strong state intervening in the economy would lead to prosperity—as opposed to the new free market economy. Tensions among differing concepts of economic and political order were hidden under very broad regulations. The Competition Protection Law remained weak in the face of price increases and alleged cartels in many sectors. Although the model of the weak state won over state interference in the economy in every parliamentary vote, it was less and less justifiable among the parliamentarians, and it disappeared completely by 2009. The government was trapped by their justification that the free market would solve the prevailing problems and that social welfare would suffice in keeping social discontent in check. A large gap appeared between the government's legitimacy claims and the socioeconomic grievances that parliamentarians decried across party divisions.

The Role of Specific State Institutions

In addition to the more abstract question on the role of the state, debates over the implementing authority for the antitrust law gave a very concrete idea to legitimacy claims and beliefs concerning the state and the economy. There was broad consensus in 2005 that, even if the law were perfect, its actual effectiveness would depend on the implementing authority. Five factors were seen as crucial for the success of the future Competition Protection Authority: decision-making power,[73] independence,[74] expertise,[75]

---

73. Most of the MPs wanted a strong authority with the right to prohibit and approve economic activities. They rejected its role as a mere source of information and reports alone, as suggested by the minister of investment (2005/21: 23). The authority would not have the right to set prices (2005/21: 42–44).

74. They demanded the authority generally be independent (2005/21: 32–33, 62–63, 64–65), "independent like judges" (19–20), and neutral (27, 62–63, 65).

75. Many MPs argued that the authority needed the best employees with outstanding knowledge of economics and law, who were able to give detailed reports and make good

technical capacity, and access to information.[76] Regarding the second factor, an intense debate arose as to whom the CPA should be subordinate.[77] Most speakers argued for an authority with an objective and precise structure, distant from a government that was perceived to be under the influence of big business. The debate generally showed that the institutional design of the authority mattered: in the eyes of the MPs, it would affect the performance of the body, while authorities in general could remain autonomous and efficient.[78] This was underlined by a number of MPs who referred to a preexisting model for an independent institution, namely the Central Auditing Organization.[79] One could also observe that many assembly members sought the opportunity to take control and establish

---

decisions quickly (2005/21: 31–32, 51). The experts should be experienced themselves or should be trained in countries that were well versed in the realm of competition protection (2005/21: 57–58, 64).

76. 2005/21: 31–32, 51, 64–65. Especially at this moment of the debate, the diagnosis of monopolistic practices is related to a certain percentage of the market share, which is controlled by one economic unit. Here, one MP raised serious doubts about whether the authority would really have access to the information needed to assess the market situation (2005/21: 22–23).

77. It was debated whether the CPA should be subordinate to the prime minster, as the draft law suggested, or to the parliament or the president. For the underlying understanding of these respective institutions, see chapter 5.

78. The minister of investment and the head of the joint committee expressed their doubts about the authority being independent from the very beginning, and they warned against a potential lack of experience: the antitrust law was new to Egypt, everything was an experiment. To limit the severity of political and judicial mistakes, there were no jail sentences designated within the law (2005/21: 39). The minister brought up the example of France, where the authority had a consulting function for four years before it became independent (2005/21: 15–17). Beyond that, both warned that the authority could not be controlled and held to account without being subordinate to the prime minister (2005/21: 21). However, the ability of the government to deal with this "difficult and dangerous authority" was questioned as well (2005/21: 21–22).

79. It is striking that although the MPs praised the CAO, they made contradictory statements about its affiliation. Some said it was subordinate to the parliament (2005/21: 27, 59–60), some said to the president (2005/21: 13–14, 37), and others claimed the prime minister was responsible for it, but that it was nevertheless independent, because its

a realm of independence from the ruling elite. Hopes (at least) were high that such an authority could lead to real protection in the Egyptian economy, which was mostly interpreted as protection of the consumer, not of the free market for its own sake.

The government's proposal for amending the antitrust law included the "activation of the role of the Competition Protection Authority," even though the authority was presented as having undertaken large efforts to fight monopolistic practices.[80] In parliament, however, both NDP and Muslim Brotherhood MPs complained that the CPA should be stronger and more active, whereas the minister of trade and industry defended the authority.[81] The parliamentarians further criticized the CPA for being biased in its activities in various economic sectors.[82] The ideal of a stronger and more active authority was still expressed and considered as a realistic aim, yet the path to get there was not elaborated to any great extent. This pointed to a decreasing belief in the effectiveness of the authority. Still, it enjoyed higher credibility than the only other authority referred to, the Consumer Protection Authority (created in 2006), which was seen as responsible for regulating consumer prices, but as not having fulfilled its role in any way.[83]

---

director was independent. This type of arrangement, however, was not outlined in the draft antitrust law (2005/21: 39).

80. 2008/118 annex: 18. The main activity had taken place in fourteen "big cases" against cement, steel, meat, dairy products, and oil (Rashid, 2008/118: 13). However, there was still a need for improvement seen, for example, through higher fines for noncompliance and more obligations to inform the authority of business activities. The Shura Council considered the CPA as one pillar of free competition, but it also suggested improvements, such as a better cooperation with universities, business associations, and chambers of commerce (118 annex: 31).

81. 2008/118: 16, 16–17, 118 annex: 23. He defended the CPA as being dependent on complaints about monopolistic practices. Indeed, the number of complaints had been so low that the authority started to investigate on its own behalf (2008/118: 23–24).

82. Whereas the cement sector received a lot of attention, the steel sector remained practically untouched (2008/118: 22–23), which Rashid justified by pointing to the limited resources of the CPA (2008/118: 23–24).

83. 2008/118: 15–16, 22.

Parliamentarians completely lost their belief in the CPA during the debate in 2009, in contrast to the government, which praised the authority's success in fighting monopolistic practices.[84] Yet the numbers that the minister proudly presented were extremely low: nineteen convictions out of 11,000 complaints represented merely 0.2 percent, hardly an impressive conviction rate. Moreover, a total of 200 million Egyptian pounds in fines for four years of antimonopolistic activity across all sectors was just a drop in the bucket. This might also explain why none of the parliamentarians went into detail concerning the CPA. State control institutions were regarded as weak in general: the CPA was specifically criticized for being limited to the realm of fraud in trade and production and for not being authorized to set prices itself.[85] In contrast to the negative perspective on the CPA authorities, many oppositional MPs referred to the CAO as an official yet trustworthy institution. They used documents from the authority to defeat the government on its own ground: they attempted to refute the ministers' positive outlook on the socioeconomic situation by referring to the official numbers.[86]

Apparently, a general belief in state authorities existed throughout the period. The MPs tried to establish a strong Competition Protection Authority, although it was never thought to have fulfilled its role effectively. Several problems had already appeared during the establishment phase which prevented the CPA from becoming strong and active. Here, its subordination to the prime minister was particularly criticized. These obstacles were not debated in the subsequent years, likely since no one thought themselves to have the capacity to make a difference. However, the belief in an independent state authority remained: the Central

---

84. The introduction of authorities and mechanisms was praised as a success, including the CPA and its investigation in the cement, steel, and food sectors. Some cases were even brought to court, where fines of 200 million Egyptian pounds were ordered. Also, the Consumer Protection Authority was working effectively, pursuing 11,000 complaints. Nineteen companies were actually convicted, and civil society was integrated into the authority's work, such as in the preparation of market studies (Rashid 2009/67: 25–26).

85. 2009/68: 8, 16.

86. 2009/68: 12, 14, 17–18.

Auditing Organization was deemed to have maintained its autonomy and continuously enjoyed the trust of the MPs. The other authority that was mentioned, the Consumer Protection Authority, was seen to be just as powerless and ineffective as the Competition Protection Authority; no one engaged in any serious detailed debate about these institutions after 2008.

Who Wants What? The Economic System and the Role of the State

Throughout the debates over an appropriate economic model for Egypt, parliament and government views on the role of norms and practices evolved. At the beginning of the period of study, the parliamentarians were oriented toward an economic ideal seen as globally valid, which guaranteed both development and a balanced society. Hopes about what could be achieved with the introduction of the antitrust law were high, and almost all MPs welcomed it. The broad consensus across the parties was that the state should have an active role, intervening in the free market for the sake of society. Furthermore, one widely shared belief was that the aim of the law was the protection, not prohibition, of competition, and that this could be achieved through a strong and independent competition protection authority. Similarly, the assembly members agreed on learning from Western countries and their experiences with competition protection. During the subsequent debates in 2008 and 2009, it became clear that the MPs had lost their faith in the government as well as in the relevant state institutions, such as the Competition Protection Authority; this loss of faith went hand-in-hand with decreased expectations for the market economy—no one talked about modernization, innovation, or development anymore. Now the only aim still seriously discussed was a balance between different economic and social forces, with a special focus on the protection of the weak. The state was held responsible for ensuring this protection, which became the normative standard in the discourse. Remarkably, the proponents of a free market without state interference justified their position in public less and less, and ultimately remained silent.

Over time, the debates revealed a serious struggle over policies that cannot be explained by the cleavage between the ruling party and the opposition: proponents of an active state that regulates the free market were found on both sides. The increasingly visible isolation of one group of MPs around the business tycoon Ahmad 'Izz supports the argument that shared decision making among the ruling elite coalition as a stabilizing function of parliament is not a structural outcome. It depends on the more powerful actors' willingness to compromise, but obviously also on the specific policies they pursue and the extent to which these policies deviate from what is regarded as right or wrong. Furthermore, only voicing discontent without attempting to influence policy making fuels anger more than it helps calm the situation. The safety-valve argument cannot be substantiated when considering how low degrees of responsiveness led to recurrent and increasing criticism of the government's performance. This observation supports the general pattern of a contentious parliament in times of socioeconomic crises that reappeared over many decades (as outlined in chapters 1 and 2). In the next chapter, we will observe how negative evaluations on the policy level affected the identities of the MPs as representatives of the Egyptian people, and thus their relation to the respective constituencies and the public in general.

4

Parliament, Representation, and the Politicization of Identities

The previous chapter elaborated on how perceptions of the economic order and the role of the state developed during a period of increasing protest and the political rise of business elites. The following sections analyze how these changes affected the way in which members of parliament presented their relations with their constituencies and to the broader public. It is possible to see that, in the face of mounting public pressure, the target group of the parliamentarians shifted: from the consumer who hoped for sinking prices as a result of competition protection to the citizen, the people, and the street. The MPs' speeches reflect these developments in the relations between parliament and the constituencies, as well as the general public. They also reveal changes in the construction of Egypt's position in international relations. Interactions in parliament also shed light on the normative benchmarks regulating the proper behavior of parliamentarians—of "good" representation. These conflicts do not reflect a simple opposition–ruling party divide but rather overlapping institutional norms that existed in spite of allegedly differing world views among the parties and organizations represented in the assembly.

Representing the Nation: Egypt and the Outside World

The economic restructuring plan—of which the antitrust law comprised a crucial part—was portrayed in parliament as a global trend that Egypt simply had to follow (see chapter 3). As such, many delegates made references to Egypt and other nations, which reveals a great deal about the construction of the national identity. A look at not only how other nations were perceived but also which nations were mentioned at all is very telling. In 2005, only Western nations (the United States, Great Britain, and France) served as Egypt's models for the path to competition protection.[1] The United States was mainly presented as the capitalist country par excellence, and its fight against monopolies legitimated Egypt's own struggle against cartels and violations of free competition.[2] Egypt was referred to as a developing country on its way to closing the gap between itself and rich developed nations.[3] The debated antitrust law was seen as one step in this process, within which assistance from emerging economies such as South Africa was regarded as positive in terms of capacity building, for instance, that would allow Egypt to gain a degree of expertise that would enable it to train other Arab countries afterward.[4] Clearly, the parliamentarians still regarded Egypt as playing a leading role in the Arab world. For example, one member of parliament blamed the government for introducing the law too late, citing that even Tunisia and Jordan had introduced similar legislation long before.[5] Nobody voiced the possibility that Egypt might, in fact, stand to learn from these two countries and their experiences.[6] Moreover, no alternative plans for international or regional cooperation in the fight against monopolies could be found in any of the speeches.

1. 2005/21: 27, 28.

2. In particular, US government intervention against Microsoft encouraged the parliamentarians in their fight against the big players; one member of parliament from the liberal Ghad Party even explicitly equated Bill Gates with Naguib Sawiris, a famous Egyptian businessman (2005/21: 34). The minister of investment tried to mediate and claimed that even in the United States not everything was perfect (43), although this fact was overlooked and the United States remained the ideal model (2005/21: 54).

3. 2005/21: 62.

4. Minister of finance: 2005/21: 22.

5. 2005/21: 56.

6. Similar connotations could be found in remarks by the speaker of the assembly when praising the rule of law in Egypt, which still served as a model for the rest of the Arab world (2005/21: 38).

The positive outlook on Western states as a model still persisted in 2008[7] but would change drastically in 2009. It was at this point that the US model of capitalism was blamed for bringing Egypt into its current miserable situation.[8] Whereas in 2005 only one Muslim Brotherhood MP criticized "foreign" investors for pursuing their own interests and damaging Egypt's industry,[9] this view became widespread in 2009. Parliamentarians portrayed foreign companies to be exploiters of Egypt who only acted on behalf of foreigner interests.[10] One independent member of parliament made clear that his criticism was not aimed at the private sector as such, but specifically at foreigners and the recolonization of Egypt, highlighting that gains made in Egypt were repeatedly transferred to foreign countries.[11] Another independent deputy also alluded to Egypt's colonial past; he evoked Egypt of the nineteenth century, when foreign investors (who monopolized the cotton sector) and their governments dominated the country's debt administration, which resulted in a state of dependence for decades to come.[12]

The ongoing socioeconomic crisis evoked feelings of inferiority, which were fueled by an increasingly hostile view toward other countries.

---

7. In 2008, all references to other countries were positive examples of fighting monopolistic practices (2008/118: 37, 48, 56, 2008/139: 56, 58, 61 69). Among them were the Netherlands, Belgium, Croatia, Switzerland, Italy, and South Africa. Again, no Arab countries were referred to as models. Steel tycoon Ahmad 'Izz was the first to bring up the gap between developed countries and Egypt, while in the same speech praising Egypt for having a great and developed society and civilization (2008/139: 56). Similarly, another MP found the aim of the antitrust law to entail reaching a "respectable degree like developed countries" (2008/139: 66).

8. The assembly member accused the Egyptian government of having followed the United States down the path of unconditional support for entrepreneurs by granting easy access to loans. In Egypt, this led to a waste of public funds without any returns. He also disparaged the United States with a religious argument against interest (*riba*), citing the Qur'anic verse 2, 276: "Allah does not bless usury, and He causes charitable deeds to prosper, and Allah does not love any ungrateful sinner" (2009/67: 13).

9. 2005/21: 63.

10. 2009/66: 49, 65.

11. 2009/68: 7.

12. 2009/68: 9–10.

Muslim Brotherhood and independent opposition deputies referred to cases in which Egypt trailed behind other nations, citing economic indicators such as prices for certain goods, inflation rates, and investment rates.[13] Comparisons between Egypt's worsening economic situation and the economic success of other states were even used to bring in the regime question: one member of parliament spoke of countries with fair prices and higher wages (citing Lebanon and Germany), adding that, in contrast to Egypt, those governments could be held accountable or vanquished by the people (though the path to doing so was quite long).[14]

Assembly Members' Identities and Representation of Constituencies

This section looks at whether and how parliamentarians made particular reference to their constituencies in a literal sense (their electoral district) or in a broader sense of groups of supporters, such as functional groups, parties, or organizations. Concerning the first, delegates hardly made any references to their constituencies, either in 2005[15] or in 2008.[16] In 2009, however, this changed in two ways: first, two members of parliament used

13. 2009/66: 57–59, 62, 2009/67: 17. The minister for trade and industry, in contrast, tried to show that Egypt was much better off than the assembly members claimed (2009/67: 25, 28). Two MPs criticized his positive outlook, stating that he compared price indexes for certain goods without reference to local wages and prices for energy or raw materials (2009/68: 10, 12). The interpellants did not bring up the fact that they themselves proceeded in the same way.

14. 2009/66: 58.

15. There were only two connections made by NDP deputies, one to the governorate al-Buhayra and the miserable situation of the peasants in the cotton sector, where a monopoly had supposedly destroyed prices. As a consequence, it was impossible for the small-scale farmer to make a living from planting cotton anymore (2005/21: 48). Besides that, only one MP further referred to his constituency, which he declared to be the same as that of the minister for investment, Mahmud Muhyi al-Din. He intended to underline that the minister stemmed from a family in which all members "grew up in the service of Egypt" (2005/21: 56). This very subtle comment was the only reference to the correlation of family and constituency in this debate.

16. Only one delegate talked about the governorate of his constituency, al-Buhayra, and of the steel company there suspected of monopolistic practices (2008/118: 24).

examples of their own constituencies to underline and illustrate the socio-economic crisis;[17] second, the representation of constituencies became an issue in itself. In comments to responses made by the ministers, several interpellants were furious that the government denied the existence of price increases and the growing poverty and misery among many parts of the Egyptian population.[18] Two oppositional MPs went a step further and called on the NDP assembly members to represent the people and be conscious of the nation rather than of the government.[19]

In contrast to many other criticisms by the opposition, this direct attack against NDP deputies provoked three ruling party MPs to challenge the interpellants. One responded to the criticism by deriding the oppositional delegates' claim to be the real representatives of the Egyptian people. They stated that those MPs could not claim this prerogative on account of the simple fact that they had only won a minority of seats, and thus did not enjoy as much confidence as the majority. Further, by affronting other

17. One Muslim Brother deputy referred to his constituency, Port Said, several times and on various occasions: as an example of dramatic price increases for apartments; for contracts awarded to corrupt waste-disposal companies, which, in turn, led to garbage piling up on the streets; and to the distribution of land to government cronies to reward loyalty, thereby impoverishing average citizens (2009/67: 12; 2009/68: 15). Another direct link to his constituency was brought up by another Muslim Brother, who denounced the temporary working contracts at the al-Mansura hospital and demanded permanent contracts (2009/67: 22). Here, the connection with those represented was even more direct, as the MP himself had worked at the hospital and had been general secretary of its workers union from 1996 to 2001. Other regions referenced are Qalyubiyya (2009/67: 5), Matruh and Sinai (2009/68: 7), and Upper Egypt (2009/67: 17), which did not correlate to the MPs' constituencies.

18. Two MPs demanded that the minister for social solidarity ask his own constituents whether there had been price increases and whether they had needed to wait in line for bread (2009/68: 11, 19). The delegates claimed that the government was too far removed from the Egyptian people, who knew the reality and hence supported the interpellations (2009/68: 12, 16).

19. 2009/68: 9, 16. Both were members of the Muslim Brotherhood. The first MP even posed a question about the existence of poverty in Egypt directly to the majority bloc in the People's Assembly. The protocol simply says that "one" MP of the majority said "No!" out loud.

assembly members and questioning their loyalty, the interpellants were putting the dignity of the assembly itself at risk.[20] Similarly, another NDP comrade stressed that a parliamentarian's capital rested on the constituency and its people, and not, as he suspected of the opposition, in public attacks on the government in the yellow press and on satellite channels. The people had decided to give the majority to the ruling party, whether the opposition liked it or not. To him, fighting one another in parliament was not a criterion of democracy, and he referred to discussions that took place inside the NDP instead of the assembly hall as being democratic.[21]

Whereas direct links to the MPs' own constituencies could rarely be found during the period of study, the debate in 2009 shows that denying an assembly member's connection to the constituency was perceived as a grave attack on their credibility, as it questioned a crucial part of their identity as representatives. It is indeed telling that the NDP members based their claims of being the "real" representatives of the people on the fact that their party held the majority; this was presented as sufficient, and no further proof by way of their performance in the assembly was given. Democratic procedures, which could generate legitimacy for the parliamentarians as representatives, were localized within the NDP. This, however, entailed an inherent lack of transparency. How were citizens to evaluate the performance of their representatives when delegates refrained from publicly expressing the interests of their constituencies?

Apart from denying the representation of constituencies in the parliament, NDP members also doubted that citizens might feel a sense of representation by observing the performance of delegates in the media. During the debates, progovernment lawmakers presented a very negative picture of the media, especially satellite channels, with which the opposition was allegedly colluding. Instead of seeing media coverage as a way to reach voters, one NDP assembly member stated that a direct link between the parliamentarian and the people in his constituency was sufficient without the help of media—though he did not explain how this link might

20. 2009/68: 20–21.
21. 2009/68: 21.

be developed. This is astonishing insofar as large parts of Egypt's media landscape were still under state control. Private media was never outright regime-critical, as the major television channels and newspapers were owned by private businessmen with good connections to the ruling elite (Richter 2013).

This incident shows that the transparency created by the autocratic legislature led to a dilemma for some NDP delegates. Denying their identity as representatives of their constituencies and agreeing with the government's description of the status quo seemed to defy common sense. Open criticism also appeared to be difficult. Since the failed attempt by members of the ruling party in cooperation with oppositional parliamentarians to amend the antitrust law in 2008, critical voices from within the ruling party had been silenced. The only way out of this dilemma was to relocate the appropriate place for representation and contestation against the government from within the parliament to within the ruling party. Open dispute was presented as putting the dignity of parliament at risk. Instead, harmonic cooperation and exchanges of opinion were considered to be appropriate parliamentary behavior for an assembly member.

But the attempts to simply shift the locus of representation from parliament to the ruling party was contested as well. Affiliation with the NDP became a point of attack by the opposition, which claimed that party allegiance contradicted the idealized identity of a parliamentarian as the representative of a people. In 2008, for instance, Ahmad 'Izz, as secretary for organizational affairs for the NDP, was denounced for pursuing special interests.[22] In 2009, NDP membership was used to delegitimize actions by the ministers on account of their dependence on the party.[23] Defending

22. 2008/139: 52.

23. In a rare case of censorship, one must guess as to what the independent MP Jamal Zahran said to cause such an outcry in the assembly. The responses made clear that he touched on the issue of NDP assembly members and NDP ministers. The minister for judicial affairs and representative assemblies intervened and accused Zahran of violating the parliamentary tradition and principles of dialogue. The criticized unity of the ruling party and government did not present a problem to the minister; on the contrary, he considered this to be a natural fact (2009/68: 13). Zahran tried to raise another accusation

the ruling party, one of its members stated that he could not see any reason to feel ashamed for being a member of the NDP. On the contrary, the ministers were held to account more firmly within the party than in the People's Assembly. In contrast, he believed the cooperative style among members of parliament to be a real expression of patriotism; cooperation and a consideration for different opinions was his ideal of parliamentary activity.[24] Again, the parliament was presented as the place for unity and harmony, while the controversial exchange of opinions was to take place within parties.

In spite of the attacks on the government and the call upon NDP assembly members to distance themselves from the ministers, a few oppositional speakers pointed to NDP politicians as a source of evidence that would legitimate their own positions.[25] Trustworthiness and credibility were not simply denied to all members of the ruling party but instead varied according to specific policy preferences and degrees of responsiveness of individual NDP delegates. This underlines just how heterogeneous the ruling elite coalition was perceived to be and, further, that the opposition clearly related to those who shared their own point of view. The process involving the antitrust law revealed the existence of two camps within the ruling elite that fought for differing agendas.[26] As identification with the NDP became a political issue in 2009, it also made the conflict within the ruling party even more visible.

---

of bribery concerning the relation between the party and government but was stopped by the speaker of the assembly.

24. 2009/68: 22.

25. Among the ruling party members mentioned was Mustafa al-Sa'id, head of the parliamentary committee of economic affairs, who was cited as giving a warning about the economy being in danger (2009/67: 5). Ahmad Juwayli, the former minister of trade, was referred to as being on alert about a "revolution of hunger" (2009/67: 4). One MP mentioned professor 'Ali al-Din Hilal, a heavyweight in the NDP, who had informally told the MP that the real problem in Egypt was the monopoly in politics and the marriage of power and money (2009/68: 17).

26. The MP rhetorically asked whether the party belonged to the government or the other way around (2008/139: 68–69).

Apart from these disputes, parliamentarians seldom explicitly mentioned their party or organizational affiliations.[27] As noted above, it was not one's membership in the ruling party as such that decided the positive or negative evaluation of an assembly member, but rather their alleged or assumed activities as a parliamentarian.

Another element that makes the normative benchmark even more visible is the idea of representing "special interests." This appeared as a new dimension of an MP's identity in 2008 and was prompted through the active involvement of Ahmad ʿIzz. Even a fellow NDP member assumed him to be a monopolist and viewed any legislative involvement on his part to be a manipulation of the law according to his particular interests.[28] To claim that someone pursues special interests served to demarcate them as a bad member of parliament, as opposed to a good one who represents the people and the common good. Strikingly, both the delegates who attacked ʿIzz and the party comrades defending him used the issue of pursuing the common good as their benchmark.[29]

For the opposing members, ʿIzz's identity as one of the *rijal al-aʿmal* (businessmen) violated the parliamentary rules of objectivity and neutrality and hence annulled his right to use parliamentary procedures and tools. For ʿIzz, his distinctiveness gave him *more* credibility to participate in and lead the debate. ʿIzz drew a similar line of distinction between himself and the assembly members who accused him of pursuing special interests, but with a different set of conclusions. He presented himself as being a "competitor" and adopted a posture of expertise with regard to competition

27. In 2005/21, the Ghad Party members referred to their party and also to its liberal nature (2005/21: 17, 34, 65). One Nasserist expressed his gratefulness to the government for the draft law in the name of his party (2005/21: 25). Talʿat al-Sadat, a member of parliament for the Liberal Party and nephew to former President Anwar al-Sadat, attacked the ruling party as a power monopolist (2005/21: 19). In 2008/118, no one mentioned parties, neither in their own identification nor in categorizations of other actors.

28. 2008/139: 50, 52.

29. 2008/139: 52–53, 55, 59. They claimed that ʿIzz was not a monopolist, but rather working outstandingly for the nation. The real intention behind ʿIzz's proposal was transparency, competition protection, and to side with the Egyptian people (2008/139: 55, 59).

protection policies. As though speaking to little children, 'Izz illustrated that competition in the economic realm was similar to that in the political system (which MPs, as politicians, knew well) but without an orientation toward the common good.[30] He underlined his otherness from the assembly members through subtle references to "the elite," saying that even the elite in Egypt was confused about the complicated antitrust law.[31] This is noteworthy as the term "elite" was never used by anyone else in the entire period of study. This did, however, fit in quite well with the technocratic and business-oriented image of the NDP as a new guard centered around Gamal Mubarak and the government of Ahmad Nazif.

One can observe how the line of demarcation between the big businessmen and a heterogeneous alliance among parliamentarians became more visible over the years.[32] The interpellants made big business and the cabinet into the camps that must be fought against, which led to the naming and shaming of long lists of entrepreneurs.[33] Whereas in 2008 the opposition still deemed Rashid Muhammad Rashid, minister for trade and industry, to be on the correct side, this changed in 2009, when his role as a businessman was explicitly raised as an issue, with one delegate asking whether Rashid the minister could deal with Rashid the businessman.[34]

Islamic References and Identities

One of the most heavily debated topics of the last decade under Mubarak was the political participation of the Muslim Brotherhood. As the analysis above has demonstrated, parties did not play a significant role as a point of reference. The Brotherhood was still legally banned at that time and, for that reason, may not have been mentioned by name, but it was publicly known which delegates belonged to the organization. One could therefore assume that, to distinguish themselves from the other parties and establish a thorough connection to their electorate, Brotherhood parliamentarians

30. 2008/139: 56.
31. 2008/139: 56.
32. For the detailed analysis of this alliance, refer to chapter 5.
33. 2009/67: 9, 19.
34. 2009/67: 19.

would make a significantly higher use of Islamic references than any other group or party as a way to highlight their Islamist identity.

However, MPs identifying with the Muslim Brotherhood did not, in fact, make very heavy use of explicit references to the Qur'an, the hadith, Islamic scholars, or Islamic institutions.[35] In 2005, Islamic references were only used to justify the fight against monopolistic practices.[36] For instance, one Muslim Brotherhood MP told the story, found in a hadith, of someone complaining to the prophet about rising prices and then asking Muhammad to set the prices. The prophet refused and declared that Allah was the price maker, but he also said that Allah condemned the monopolist and blessed the taxpayer. He then confiscated what the monopolistic trader and producer possessed. To the delegate, the story's message was that the state should intervene against those committing the monopolistic practices but should not set prices. The hadith also served as a proof that the entire issue of monopolies had its origins in Islam.[37] Another Muslim Brother began his statement with the hadith (found in *Sahih Muslim*, one of the six canonical hadith collections in Sunni Islam): who monopolizes, is wrong.[38] The message was clear, and nothing new was added by this reference—it was simply expressed that monopolies should be prohibited. Indeed, he reinforced common sense by putting it into an Islamic wording and reference system.

The debates of 2008, in contrast, showed how the ruling party internally discussed the proper Islamic way to deal with monopolistic crimes.

35. In 2005, only four out of seventy-seven speakers made a reference to Islam. Three of them were members of the then-illegal Muslim Brotherhood, and one belonged to the NDP. In the 2008 debates, not one Muslim Brotherhood MP used Islamic references; only NDP members did. Among the eleven interpellants in 2009/66–68, four of the eight Muslim Brotherhood MPs cited the Qur'an, and only one used a hadith.

36. One NDP assembly member stood out from his party colleagues when he made an argument that began with a long religious formula praising the prophet Muhammad but did not actually refer to the content of the debate at all, only giving it a religious touch (2005/21: 48).

37. 2005/21: 26.

38. 2005/21: 45.

One NDP assembly member compared the dramatic price increases to the seven years of famine during the time of prophet Yusuf.[39] Another NDP MP argued against the leniency policy by claiming that this was against shariʿa in general and a violation of the prophetic hadiths, since, according to them, the corrupting, the corrupted, and the intermediary person should all be punished. Any release from punishment was seen as un-Islamic.[40] In 2009, however, Islamic references were used more often, typically in the form of a warning that members of the government would be punished for their crimes in the afterlife.[41] Only two Muslim Brotherhood delegates talked about *"riba"* (usury), which is quite remarkable in a debate about the government's neoliberal policies shortly after the global financial and economic crisis that had hit Egypt hard.[42] Speculation on the international markets, accompanied by skyrocketing food prices, in particular, could have provided plenty of material with which to condemn "Western" capitalism. In fact, four of the eight interpellants from the Brotherhood did not make any Islamic references beyond the *basmala*[43] and introductory formulas praising the prophet.

Whenever used, Qur'anic verses were typically either put at the beginning or at the end of a text. These sections were often juxtaposed with the core text concerning social, economic, and political issues. In the two cases when the Qur'an was cited at the beginning, the verses were rhetorically divided from the main text.[44] On the whole, the Qur'anic verses did not serve as a source of norms or rules, but rather as a way to present a threatening scenario for the ministers if they did not change their political course. The only exception was the reference to *riba*, but even here, although the Qur'anic verse condemned it, no specific demands, such as abolishing the capitalist banking system, were deducted from it.

39. 2008/118:21.

40. 2008/118: 54.

41. 2009/67: 16–18, 20.

42. 2009/67: 13, 17.

43. *Basmala* is the name for the Islamic phrase *bi-smi-llahi l-rahmani l-rahim* (in the name of Allah, the most gracious and the most merciful).

44. 2009/67: 8, 17.

Besides "Qur'an" and "sunna," the keywords usually associated with the Muslim Brotherhood are "shari'a" and "Islam is the solution"; both only surfaced on one occasion, and the religious portions were not connected to the rest of the text. On an abstract level, the delegate asked where hope was to be found and offered a rhetorical answer: in the Islamic shari'a—it was the ideal system for humankind in the political, economic, and social spheres. Here, he cited Ibn Qayyim al-Jawziyya, who praised the shari'a as representing perfect justice, mercy, and wisdom. Even though the content might not have been particularly insightful, the reference to Ibn Qayyim al-Jawziyya certainly was. Ibn Qayyim al-Jawziyya (1292–1350) was a Sunni Islamic jurist and theologian from Damascus and a student of Ibn Taymiyya. It is remarkable that despite his extensive writing on economics,[45] all he was cited for here was a vague statement in favor of Islamic shari'a, without any further elaboration. Additional shari'a terms were used to attack the government's social aid during the price hikes as grossly insufficient; one assembly member asked for social aid to not be "*hadd al-kafaf*" (at the subsistence line, meeting only basic needs) but rather "*hadd al-kifaya*" (at the sufficiency line, which offers a satisfactory standard of living).[46]

Interestingly, no one criticized the government for not being Islamic, for not implementing the shari'a, or on grounds one might expect from political actors classified as Islamists. Furthermore, one of the delegates who used Islamic sources and vocabulary most frequently explicitly accused the government of not fulfilling its constitutional duty (*wajibuha al-dusturi*),[47] although he did not specify which duties. Given the fact that the Egyptian constitution mentions the shari'a in several articles, including those concerning the duties of the state, the extent to which the constitutional duty should be regarded as an Islamic one is not entirely clear.

The analysis of the use of Islamic references shows that some Muslim Brothers stood out among their Islamist peers and among the majority of

45. See, for example, Islahi (1984).
46. 2009/68: 15.
47. 2009/67: 16.

the delegates. Yet citing Islamic sources was not a distinguishing feature of representatives of political Islam, especially considering that a number of ruling party members also made use of religious texts. It is striking that the references were mostly used to give additional justification to a position but not for raising a new norm or belief. In 2005, Brotherhood assembly members used early Islam and the hadiths to support the prohibition of monopolies. This corresponds well to the Muslim Brotherhood ideological world view, which comprehends Islam as universal and applicable at any time. Following this, the Qur'an and hadiths should offer a solution to every problem, including those of "modern" economies. As such, the connection to early Islam and the holy texts did indeed constitute a distinguishing feature among other delegates in creating a specific identity for delegates of the Muslim Brotherhood. However, it did not result in differing political positions but simply granted them additional legitimacy. In the middle of the socioeconomic crisis in 2009, the Islamic identity (just like the other dimensions discussed here) became politicized in that religious sources were mainly used to create an additional threatening scenario for the government about punishment in this world as well as in the afterlife.

Representing Whom? The Citizen, the Consumer, and the Street

As most assembly members did not direct their speeches to their own constituency or supporter groups and avoided articulating any "specific interests," their words were generally directed at a wider public. There were, however, significant differences in who the delegates targeted in their policy proposals, that is, on whose behalf they believed they acted. In 2005, most of the speakers talked about "the consumer" who needed to be protected and who would feel the effects of the antitrust law.[48] The term "consumer" was mentioned 129 times; by comparison, "citizen" appeared only twenty times.[49] Another common pattern was to refer to "the people"

---

48. 2005/21: 14, 34.

49. There did not seem to be a pattern among the users of each term, and in some cases both appeared next to each other. Only once was the direct link between citizen and

(twenty times) and "the society" as the target groups for whom the law should make a difference. The same applied to "the weak," who needed to be protected against "the big fish" or "the whales." Here, as well, both ruling party members and oppositional parliamentarians employed a similar dichotomy. The very broad concept of society was used as a counterweight against economic reasoning. State intervention that harmed free competition was justified with positive effects for the "the society" and sometimes "the people."[50]

In 2008, the pattern changed. While "the consumer" was still called upon the most (twenty-one times) and references to "the people" remained common (seventeen times), "the street" or "the Egyptian street" became more prominent (seven times) and references to "the citizen" sank to only three instances.[51] Strikingly, beyond the connection with the people, some MPs explicitly identified with their addressees: one member of parliament spoke about "we as the people."[52] Or they stressed the representative character of parliament, stating that parliamentarians had to proclaim what "the people" (al-sha'b) say, namely, that trust in the government and the People's Assembly had almost evaporated.[53]

Two contributions were noteworthy in their connection to "everyday citizens." In the debate about the antitrust law, for the first time, one assembly member referred to "the workers," stating that he was in contact with workers in cement companies who kept him informed about price setting

---

member of parliament constructed (interestingly, by an NDP member). He blamed the ministers for their intention not to intervene in price regulation. To support his point, he brought up that "the citizens on the street" asked the delegates why they neither talked nor acted as the prices increased (2005/21: 59).

50. 2005/22: 13–14, 14, 14–15.

51. One MP called to "the simple citizen" and "the street"; both terms were used to indicate the reality of normal people (2008/118: 17).

52. 2008/118: 17.

53. 2008/118: 21. He also used this reference to blame the government for cooperating with the big companies, suspected of committing monopolistic practices, and that he, as a member of parliament, could not stay quiet about what "the people" said (2008/118: 22).

within those enterprises. Another MP used words such as "street," "citizen," and "consumer" much more frequently than his peers.[54] As both of them were descendants of traditional and influential families from Upper Egypt/Suhaj, one could assume that their ties to the constituency and its needs were much stronger in these cases, and in times of socioeconomic hardship, pressure on these families to improve the situation was great.

Compared to 2005, the use of "consumer" relative to "the citizen" and "the people" had become inverted by 2009. The interpellants almost entirely deleted the term "consumer" from their speeches, with only the minister for trade and industry making use of it several times. This hints at the politicization of the debate and the issue of economic policies in general. The addressee of politics was not an economic entity but rather a political one: the citizen or the people. Independent and Muslim Brotherhood–affiliated speakers stressed that sole representation of the people lay in the People's Assembly and its members.[55] The aim of the interpellants was indeed to construct a direct link to an external audience, as the interpellation as such would not make any difference in the political process.[56] The speeches were not about expressing a different view, but about instigating the people to rise against the government.[57] The ministers also claimed to pursue the aim of improving the lives of citizens, but when talking about the measures to be taken, they referred to the protection of the consumer.[58] The MPs instead called upon the dignity and pride of the citizens and, in various forms, they revealed how the government was

54. Mahmud Abu 'Aqil and Ashraf Faruq al-Barudi (2008/118: 21).

55. 2009/66: 56, 61.

56. 2009/66: 56, 2009/67: 8.

57. Accordingly, they evoked the people's anger: the government betrayed the people (2009/67: 17), humiliated it (2009/66: 60, 68), and caused harm to it (2009/ 67: 14); the people lived in misery (2009/67: 11, 12) and died (2009/67: 9); the people would unite in action against the government (2009/67: 19); and the people could not take it any longer (2009/67: 21). They also called upon the misery of various classes ("the poor," the middle class [2009/67: 17]) and groups such as peasants, workers, university graduates, and the population of informal settlements ('ashwa'iyyat) (2009/67: 11, 19, 2009/66: 50, 62–64).

58. 2009/67: 23, 28, 31, 32; 2009/68: 5.

violating the sentiments of Egyptians. Expressions such as monopolists "sucking the people's blood" or direct calls to "become angry, o people!" could be found.[59] Some remarks even surpassed the realm of representing the people's sentiments and also spoke of the People's Assembly *feeling with* the people; for example, the parliament was said to have "shivered" with the grievances of the people when prices were raised in 2004.[60]

Conclusion: Representation and Identities, 2005–9

From 2005 to 2009, the construction and perception of identities related to the delegates, the public as the general addressee, and even the nation, whose people the delegates claimed to represent, evolved considerably and became increasingly politicized. Egypt's identity in relation to other nation states became a political issue when those other nations were no longer regarded neutrally. Instead of belonging to the same course of economic development, the outside world was only perceived of as "foreign" investors exploiting Egypt.

The identity of delegates themselves turned into an issue of debate when private businessmen were no longer regarded as legitimate members of parliament. Moreover, ruling party parliamentarians in general were attacked for being out of touch with the needs of their constituencies in instances when they avoided speaking of the socioeconomic crisis. This specific assault challenged the core identity of the NDP deputies and led to an unusually harsh self-defense. It emphasized that the relevance of many assembly members in the autocratic parliament was based on being the intermediary for a specific locality—denying this connection was an affront to the delegate's very position. This was underlined by NDP members from traditionally influential families in Upper Egypt with long-standing ties to a region. They visibly spoke differently about the public, mentioning specific groups and the addressees of policies much more frequently than other assembly members. However, the addressees generally changed over time, as speeches shifted in their construction from

59. 2009/68: 5, 2009/67: 19.
60. 2009/66: 57.

reference to acting on behalf of "the consumer" in 2005 to "the citizen," "the people," and "the street" in 2009.

During the same period, the normative benchmark for "good" or "real" representation remained by-and-large the same: pursuing the common good in contrast to representing particular or partisan interests. Accordingly, party and organizational affiliations played only a minor role. This norm became a challenge for the NDP parliamentarians when party members or the government were criticized for neglecting general welfare and when the parliamentarians' "representativeness" was questioned on account of their membership in the ruling party. The NDP assembly members could not remain silent, nor could they deny the socioeconomic problems at hand. Their way out was to appeal to a harmonious conception of parliament and declare the ruling party as the appropriate arena for contesting the policies of ministers. The norm of "not criticizing in public" also applied to controversies with fellow NDP members, as this, too, was declared to be an internal party affair. These elements of representation and identities highlight the interlinkage with the evaluation of what constitutes appropriate behavior on the part of different political institutions and within them. The next chapter carries out a systematic investigation of this matter.

5

Autocratic Institutional Norms and Contesting the Democratic Façade

In Egypt, institutional procedures and the rights of parliamentarians and parliament itself never remained static in more than 150 years of parliamentary history. This perpetual evolution has either been driven by the parliamentarians themselves or granted in a top-down manner to appease MPs and keep them firmly within the ruling elite coalition. This chapter takes a closer look at how members of parliament made use of the rights and tools at their disposal and how they fought over their meaning and scope. These debates provide us with insights about norms related to parliament but also about their institutional relations with government and the president. Across all dimensions, the speeches and actions were interwoven with the context of the autocratic regime and reveal a complex picture of the autocratic parliament.

Looking at institutional norms, one can observe the dialectic nature of institutions and actors: how institutional rules influenced the actors, and how the actors, in turn, shaped the institution. Procedural correctness was a norm claimed by all sides. But the autocratic nature of the parliament became apparent once the members of the ruling elite employed formal rules to justify their actions in a way that was completely distorted and simply intended to suit their own goals. This arbitrariness did, however, come at a cost as the legitimacy of these farfetched applications of rules was directly challenged by other MPs. Exceptions to adhering to the formal rules were only regarded as legitimate when justified as upholding the common good. In the name of "the people," opposition and ruling party MPs alike would refer to the common good as existing a priori, not as a result of a bargaining process.

Interinstitutional relations did not reflect a simple dichotomy of ruling party and opposition. We can see mistrust toward the NDP government, including among ruling party MPs, which points to intra-elite conflicts playing out between institutions. Oppositional MPs occasionally cooperated with ruling party peers and segments of the government. Such instances were guided by an evaluation of the legitimacy of political actors and institutions at a given time, with the result that alliances were constantly in flux.

The only exception to fluid interinstitutional relations was the general trust in the president's neutrality that prevailed even among oppositional members of parliament. This phenomenon reflects Mubarak's image as the balancer between different elite factions—one who tried to remain above interest conflicts—a role he was apparently still viewed as playing during the last five years of his rule.

Explicit Contestation of the Democratic Façade: The Regime Question

The ideal political order allegedly pursued by the ruling elite was that of liberal democracy. President Husni Mubarak repeatedly referred to Egypt's gradual development toward democracy.[1] However, the ideal of a separation of powers paired with parliamentary rights and procedures applied in equal measure clashed with the logic of the autocratic regime, as well as with the power asymmetries and inequality that resulted. One can observe many instances of criticism at the violation of liberal rights within the assembly, along with attempts to justify these violations. Most of the debates dealt with parliamentary tools and interinstitutional relations,

---

1. See, for instance, Mubarak's annual speeches to the joint meeting of the People's Assembly and Shura Council upon commencement of the new parliamentary session. During the period under study, he always spoke of Egypt's progress on the path to democracy and reform (*tariq al-dimuqratiyya wa-l-islah*). Speeches were available online before 2011 at http://www2.sis.gov.eg/Ar/Politics/PInstitution/President/Speeshes/00 (accessed Dec. 1, 2010, site discontinued).

and did not explicitly raise the regime question. Two exceptions are, however, worth noting.

In 2005, during the general debate over the Competition Protection Law, the discussion about the subordination of the Competition Protection Authority turned into a question of whether the prime minister should be in charge of the institution. One independent member of parliament, arguing against the concentration of power in the hands of the government, eventually admitted "the reality that everybody knows": "we are here in Egypt, not in a state where democracy and the basis of transparency are deeply rooted."[2] While it is surprising that a member of parliament could speak so frankly about the undemocratic nature of the Egyptian regime, the speaker's reply was similarly astonishing. Fathi Surur did not object to the statement but instead tried to water down the accusation by claiming that the rule of law did nevertheless exist in Egypt, something for which Egypt was admired by neighboring Arab countries. He thus presented the rule of law as a substitute for democracy and transparency.[3]

Another remark in 2009 underlined that parliamentarians were aware of the hollowness inherent in Mubarak's repeated promises of gradual reforms toward democracy. During an interpellation in 2009, one independent assembly member referred to statements by Prime Minister Ahmad Nazif, who had allegedly said on one of his visits to the United States that democracy was something that the Egyptian people did not understand.[4] These incidents clearly show that, to the extent that it had ever been effective, Egypt's democratic façade was disintegrated, as had the fear of stating the fact in public.

2. 2005/21: 38.

3. 2005/21: 38. The speaker, Fathi Surur, himself a law professor, was always referred to by MPs as an authority when it came to questions concerning the constitution, laws, and regulations, as well as legal formulations and procedures. His reaction to substituting the rule of law for democracy fits in with Egyptians' general high regard for their legal system, especially judges. This dates back to the anticolonial struggle and early nationalism of the turn of the nineteenth century, which was led by jurists educated in secular law, mainly in France.

4. 2009/66: 56.

Implicitly, however, when considering the use of parliamentary tools and procedures in interinstitutional relations, one observes more specific political norms, either applied or contested. Surprisingly, norm contestation was not simply structured as a conflict between a per se prodemocratic opposition and the ruling party as the defender of the authoritarian regime. In many cases the opposition also acted according to the logic of authoritarian regimes. Whether they did so out of necessity or conviction is a separate question outside the scope of this analysis.

Parliament and the Parliamentarians

The beginning of the period under study was marked by a relatively high degree of trust in the parliamentary institution and a positive attitude toward it. A number of assembly members claimed that the antitrust law had resulted from an initiative by the assembly. This position was held by ruling party members, of which one even described the legislative power of the People's Assembly as completely free in composing the law.[5] Members of the opposition, whose trust in the prime minister was already quite low, likewise stressed the active role of the parliament.[6] One oppositional MP from the Tagammu party described how a fight against monopolies was occurring in society as a whole, of which the People's Assembly was part.[7] Parliament was also regarded as impartial and, as such, able to ensure the neutrality and independence of the Competition Protection Authority, although this position was mostly, but not exclusively, voiced by members of the opposition.[8]

The picture became more blurred in 2008. First, a Muslim Brotherhood deputy from Bani Suwayf interrupted the debate about amendments to the antitrust law by presenting a completely different issue—seeking protection against extrainstitutional threats to his parliamentary activities. He explained that he had been insulted and threatened by the dean

---

5. 2005/21: 24.

6. 2005/21: 21, 54.

7. 2005/21: 13.

8. 2005/21: 37; 2005/22: 18–19, 20.

of Bani Suwayf University after requesting information from the People's Assembly committee on higher education about unspecified acts of violence at the university. For the assembly member, the dean's attacks in the press and within the university council represented "mental terror"[9] and disrespect to him as a member of parliament, and, moreover, to the whole of parliament.[10] The speaker of the People's Assembly tried to calm the MP and put the dean's comments in the newspapers into perspective as "the press wanting to sow the seeds of discord between the people and not saying the truth."[11] For Surur, the speaker of parliament, exaggeration and falsified reports seemed to be a normal feature in the media. He promised to protect parliamentarians in the People's Assembly, as well as in the committees, but mentioned that investigations against the member of parliament for actions at the university could not be stopped. Disciplinary measures against MPs were only allowed with permission from the assembly, as found in Article 25 of the law for the People's Assembly. Surur declared the assembly member's protection to be part of the speaker's formal obligations according to the assembly's bylaws. Asserting that the dignity of an individual member was equal to the dignity of the whole assembly, he declared that no one wanted to protect the MP more than the speaker of the assembly.[12] Surur then asked the Muslim Brotherhood deputy to formally protest against the investigations against him so that the speaker could intervene on his behalf.

Taking a slightly different tone, the minister for legal and parliamentary affairs intervened and declared the MP's attempts to stop the instigations against him to be futile. To succeed, he would have to prove that the attacks were the result of his request for information from the committee for higher education, which was almost impossible.[13] This opinion provoked criticism from another member, who blamed the minister for having prematurely pronounced a judgment. The same MP also interjected

9. 2008/118: 9.
10. 2008/118: 9–10.
11. 2008/118: 9.
12. 2008/118: 11.
13. 2008/118: 10.

several times with the words "we want to protect him,"[14] and he did not seem appeased by the speaker's promises. This does not come as a surprise, as both the aggrieved lawmaker and his ally were members of the Muslim Brotherhood. At the time, state repression of the Brotherhood was high on account of ongoing municipal elections, in which the regime was trying to avoid another victory by the Brothers, as in the 2005 parliamentary elections.[15]

The Brotherhood assembly members relied on the concept of indemnity, although without explicitly referring to the term. On the one hand, they obviously hoped that parliament could provide protection in times when state repression against the Muslim Brothers increased. On the other hand, the Muslim Brotherhood parliamentarians did not trust the speaker of the assembly in presenting himself as a guarantor of their rights and dignity. Surur, one of the heavyweights of the NDP, appeared as a wolf in sheep's clothing. Pointing to the formal framework for indemnity in general, he channeled their complaints into the system, but in so doing he gained control of their attempt to use parliamentary protection for actions outside the assembly. Typically, indemnity does not protect a parliamentarian from public criticism but rather from legal and official prosecution. Moreover, the dean's criticism of the MP was likely politically motivated and directed against the Brotherhood, not against the specific parliamentary activities of one member. Overstretching the concept of indemnity amounted to an attempt to counter repression against the Islamist organization outside of the People's Assembly by relying on parliamentary rights as a substitute for a lack of freedom outside of the institution.

14. 2008/118: 11.

15. The Muslim Brothers were quite strong at the Bani Suwayf University and launched demonstrations at the campus. The MP who was under attack in this instance had led one of these demonstrations a few months earlier to protest the detention of Muhammad Badi', a professor of veterinary sciences and member of the Guidance Bureau of the Muslim Brotherhood. Badi' would go on to become the Supreme Guide of the Brotherhood in 2010. "University Professors Stage Protests to Release Dr. Badee'," *Ikhwan Web*, Apr. 9, 2008, http://www.ikhwanweb.com/article.php?id=16624.

When parliament blocked amendments for stricter antitrust rules and fines in 2008, the way that the assembly members came to perceive parliament changed. One MP from the Muslim Brotherhood explicitly denounced the whole institution for supporting monopolies.[16] It also led to a debate about the equality of the assembly members, starting with the opposition questioning whether Ahmad 'Izz was allowed to submit a draft law proposal when he had "special interest" (*maslaha khassa*[17]) in the issue at hand.[18] Even an NDP parliamentarian asked how it could be that a request for debate was prohibited if a member of parliament was shown to have special interests, but a draft proposal was allowed.[19] A Muslim Brotherhood deputy claimed that 'Izz had enjoyed preferential treatment, such as in the processing of his proposals. The assembly member recounted how his own proposal for a new law stayed in parliamentary committees without being discussed for four years. In contrast, 'Izz's proposal was presented to the assembly the morning after being submitted to the proposal and complaint committee, and it received immediate approval to be forwarded to the committee for economic affairs. There, the draft law was discussed by about noon, and parliament was holding a final debate by that same evening. Four hours in one case and four years in the other, "this is the difference between Ahmad 'Izz and me," concluded the assembly member.[20]

Surur defended 'Izz, explaining that he, along with every other member of parliament, had rights guaranteed by the constitution, and having a profession—whether self-employed or not—was common among parliamentarians. Furthermore, the draft law in question was about restricting traders, so even if special interests were present, they were not part of the proposal.[21] Concerning the proposal's prompt treatment, Surur did not

16. 2008/131: 8.

17. 2008/139: 50, 52.

18. One independent MP speaks of the 5 billion Egyptian pounds in profit that 'Izz made from trading each year (2008/139: 50).

19. 2008/139: 52.

20. 2008/139: 66–67.

21. 2008/139: 50, 52–53.

see this as a problem since it enhanced public welfare (*al-salih al-'amm*).[22] Support for 'Izz also came directly from other parliamentarians, who praised him as a man who took the side of the Egyptian people, and, since he was a businessman, he had a comprehensive understanding of what was at stake.[23] 'Izz was praised for having a greater orientation toward God and the nation than anyone else, as was apparent in his proposal, which took a stand for transparency and competition.[24]

This defense of 'Izz and his preferential treatment as an individual "more equal" than the others brought another Muslim Brother to conclude that the parliament protected the monopolist: someone accused of monopolistic practices in the steel sector was now amending the antitrust law.[25] The common good, allegedly enhanced by 'Izz's proposal, was used by the NDP to justify the unequal application of procedures and to counter the accusations that 'Izz pursued special interests. This remained the only basis on which 'Izz was allowed to continue his involvement in the Competition Protection Law. A conflict of private and common interests was not acknowledged or identified.[26]

The complaint pertaining to the overrepresentation of special interests was also reflected in allegations from oppositional parliamentarians, who argued that the opinions of the minority were not being represented in the committee report on the 'Izz proposal. The government's statement was integrated into the final report without a ministerial representative having been present at the meeting,[27] violating Article 67 of the parliament's bylaws. The rapporteur and vice-head of the committee rejected the possibility of violations to the parliamentary rules, stating that the proposal was indeed debated, but, in the final vote, it passed committee, precluding the need to state who had supported it and who had not.

22. 2008/139: 67.

23. 2008/139: 59.

24. 2008/139: 54–55.

25. 2008/139: 67.

26. We will return to the usage and understanding of the common good in chapter 5 as it recurs in the overall Egyptian discourse.

27. 2008/139: 51–52.

Moreover, the government's position had been put forward by a member of parliament, which they claimed fulfilled the bylaw's requirements.[28] Surur, as the supervisor of rules and procedures, also referred to Article 67 of the bylaws, where he found that dissenting positions needed to be submitted in written form to be integrated into the final committee report.[29] As opponents of the proposal had not done so, the exclusion of their positions from the report did not constitute a breach of the rules.

The emphasis on playing by the rules is evident here once again, and expertise in the rules of procedure laid out in the internal regulation (*al-la'iha al-dakhiliyya*) was fundamental in the debate. Surur served as the watchdog and was praised for his outstanding legal knowledge several times during the debate. This was necessary, not simply because the game was to be played by the rules, but also because formal rights were the basis of the discourse and they needed to be reinterpreted and adapted according to the particular needs of the speaker. These observations showed how the formal framework was taken very seriously and how it structured agency. The room to maneuver created through the implementation of rules reveals the dualistic nature of the institution: rules shaped the actors' behavior and actors shaped the rules. Success in parliamentary decisions was determined by power relations, specifically by the most influential segment within the ruling elite. Yet, the opposition, in turn, used the unequal application of rules to uncover the logic of authoritarianism and to contest the democratic façade. The justifications put forth by the ruling party often lacked coherence, thereby revealing the true nature of the regime.

This became even more visible when, in 2009, several parliamentary tools meant to hold the government accountable were put into practice. The debate in sessions 66 through 68 of 2009 was originally supposed to consist of eleven interpellations, 144 requests for information, two questions, and four requests for a general debate; these were directed at the prime minister and eight ministers. The most powerful one was represented by interpellations with the power to withdraw confidence in the

28. 2008/139: 51.
29. 2008/139: 52.

government according to chapter 6 of the internal regulation on parliamentary control. Compared to this tool, generally employed by opposition MPs, the other tools used in this debate—which were most frequently used since the introduction of the People's Assembly, as seen in chapter 2—were comparatively weak in terms of direct consequences for the executive. As demonstrated by the heavy usage by ruling party members, these other tools were nevertheless important in terms of the intermediary function of parliament. For most MPs who relied on the support of constituencies, these tools provided a way to demonstrate that the MP took care of certain issues, for instance, by fighting for more information from the government.[30]

For the government, the urge to justify their actions could prove to be an annoyance or even a serious problem if the actual policies violated widely held norms and therefore proved difficult to justify to the public. This might explain why, at the beginning of the session, the speaker of the assembly presented the agenda of the debate in a different manner. Citing the internal regulations of the People's Assembly, Surur declared that all interpellations and requests would be merged into a single discussion, as all involved a similar topic.[31] The interpellations would be presented first, but divided into two groups: the first five interpellants would have twenty minutes to deliver their talk, while the other six interpellants were limited to ten minutes (Surur did not explain the reason for this allotment). After responses from the ministers, each interpellant would have an additional five minutes to comment, after which a general debate would take place. Referring again to the internal regulation of the assembly, MPs who had raised a request for information or a question would have the first opportunity to comment in the debate. Afterward, requests to speak and requests for a general debate would be delivered.[32]

30. Among other control tools in the internal regulation, there were also committees of inquiry, petitions, and complaints, the indictment of ministers, and the monitoring of local administrative affairs (as part of a decentralization process).

31. 2009/66: 23.

32. 2009/66: 47.

Ultimately, however, there was no general debate, comments from the 144 MPs were never heard, and the request for a general debate was never presented (see table 7). After the last comment from the eleventh interpellant, a group of parliamentarians requested that the debate about the interpellations be separated from the discussion about the requests for a briefing and a general debate. Immediately following approval by the majority, two other requests were directed to the speaker. The first involved the establishment of an inquiry commission for a scandal concerning the privatization of a cement company, which had been brought up in several interpellations. The second—allegedly submitted at exactly the same moment as the first—was a request to transfer the debate to the agenda (*intiqal ila jadwal al-a'mal*). As Surur explained, if handed in at the same time as another request, the internal regulation of the assembly would prioritize any request for transfer to the agenda. Without referring to it explicitly, Surur invoked article 204 of the internal regulation of the People's Assembly.[33] As such, this request was put to vote first and the majority agreed on it.

What we can observe here is that the scope of action within which the opposition tried to operate was limited in two instances: first, when a large number of requests and interpellations were initially brought under one umbrella and, second, following the interpellations procedure, when the discussion was practically terminated before it even began. In fact, the opposition had expected this to happen, as the second interpellant revealed in his introductory remarks to his interpellation:

> What this is about today is, as Mr. Speaker of the Assembly has said, that we address the public opinion. This is right because these interpellations, the previous interpellations and the upcoming interpellations will be transferred to Allah's mercy and to the agenda. But we demand for an account. We open ourselves towards the public opinion in order that the public opinion and the Egyptian people know that their assembly is not far away from them.[34]

33. I thank one of the anonymous reviewers for the helpful information on this procedure.

34. 2009/66: 56.

Table 7

Use of Parliamentary Tools in 2009

Original agenda	Eleven interpellations	Response of prime minister and eight ministers	Eleven comments of the interpellants	General Debate: • 144 requests for information • Two questions • Request to speak • Request for a general debate
Actual course of the debate	Eleven interpellations	Response of three ministers	Eleven comments of the interpellants	Nonexistent

Source: Egyptian Parliament, Official Gazette, *al-Jarida al-rasmiyya*, 2009, no. 66–68.

For the MPs, interpellations were an opportunity for parliament to be seen as representing the people. The interpellant reflected on the actions of parliament during the previous price hikes and acknowledged that, at times, parliament "woke up" to reality and became active in representing the people's will.[35] Evidently, the expectations of discussing the interpellations within the assembly were rather low and the procedure for transferring them to the agenda was well-known. But it is noteworthy that, despite the arbitrary power of the NDP's overwhelming majority, its members justified their actions using the internal regulations of the People's Assembly. This underlines the ambivalence of institutional rules: although they may empower criticism, they also entail the possibility of constraining parliamentary activities.

Not only was the debate cut short, the interpellations also provoked protest from the opposition. Eleven interpellations had been submitted against the prime minister and eight ministers; but before the interpellations started, the speaker sought the assembly's permission to select senior officials to represent five of the ministers. The majority quickly approved it, but oppositional MPs criticized the move, which triggered a debate about the very idea of interpellations.

An independent assembly member first addressed the issue of the presence of senior officials during the session. He argued that they were

35. 2009/66: 57.

supposed to provide support for the ministers, not act as their proxies.[36] Another member of parliament from the Wafd Party later carried this further, pointing out that the senior officials were not even in attendance and that this was a sign of disrespect for the assembly. Surur responded that the proxies did not need to be present but *may* take part in the session, which heated the debate further still. The independent member of parliament cited Article 135 of the constitution, which required that the prime minister and the ministers *listen* to the assembly and specified that state officials were permitted to support the ministers but not replace them. If the ministers did not listen to the members of the assembly, they could not respond to them, which made the whole concept of interpellations meaningless.[37]

Mufid Shihab, minister for legal and parliamentary affairs, clarified that all of the interpellations were carefully studied and then apologized for the absence of some of his colleagues who could not attend due to unspecified circumstances. In addition, he promised that, since every minister sought to inform the assembly to the best of their abilities, the absent ministers would soon submit their answers in written form. Beyond that, Shihab argued, the assembly had the final say as to whether the government had replied satisfactorily. Meanwhile, the attending ministers would have a responsibility to reply and would do so with the help of the appointed officials.[38] Again, however, the independent oppositional assembly member stressed the importance of the ministers' personal attendance. An interpellation is an accusation directed toward a minister in person. Comparing interpellations in parliament to those used in private law, the lawmaker argued that a culprit cannot be substituted by another culprit.[39]

This analogy was rejected by the speaker, who declared that crimes were one thing and politics another. Surur then expressed his opinion

36. 2009/66: 47–48.
37. 2009/66: 53–54.
38. 2009/66: 54.
39. 2009/66: 55.

about the nature of interpellations: the assembly simply granted the government a forum for political discussion to speak to the public. It was up to the minister to attend or be absent. What really mattered, according to Surur, was not that the minister replied to the interpellations, since he knew that the majority would side with him anyway, but rather that his absence would be a missed opportunity to sway public opinion. Shihab supported Surur and demanded an overview of when ministers attended plenary and committee sessions. His aim was to show that ministers usually did attend and to prove that the government desired cooperation with the assembly, which was an important discussion forum, and that the opinions of lawmakers were of use to the ministers.[40]

As is evident here, the opposition did not tire of attacking the government for neglecting the parliamentarians' formal rights. The dispute that arose had to do with the significance of interpellations, revealing distinct conceptions in the relationship between parliament and government. On the one hand, the opposition used the interpellation as *a parliamentary tool to hold the government accountable*. This became obvious in the question of whether an interpellation inherently obligated a minister to appear at the People's Assembly. It also entailed a much more conflict-based conception of politics: a minister being interrogated as a criminal was a very different picture from the one used by the ruling party. On the other hand, the government framed interpellations as *an optional opportunity to speak to the public*; criticism and unpleasant interrogation were not part of this harmonious model. It even excluded the parliamentarians altogether, as they were neither active in criticizing the ministers nor were they considered to be the addressee of the ministers' responses. As the speaker of the assembly explicitly stated, a minister's response to the parliamentarians did not matter at all, as the majority would always support him anyway. Although this reflected the political reality in an autocratic regime, it could not be convincing justification within a debate on the nature of interpellations. Additionally, if it was public opinion in general which was meant to be the target, then the opposition was excluded from this concept. In fact,

40. 2009/66: 55–56.

the very idea of representation seems to have been eliminated, as well. There was simply a direct connection between the government and the public. Not even a debate about interpellations with party comrades appeared to be of value to the NDP ministers.

These findings show the unintended consequences of liberal mechanisms in the formal setting of a parliament. Instead of simply creating a democratic façade, formally granting rights (such as the right of interpellation) created expectations and demands to actually see these rights exercised. This placed the ruling elite in a difficult position: they could either give in to the oppositional demands or justify their neglect of these rights. Attempts at justification, however, revealed the autocratic conceptions of the political order held by the elite; even the speaker of the assembly himself declared the parliament to be irrelevant. This turns the whole argument of parliament as an enhancer of regime legitimacy upside down. Instead of serving as a democratic fig leaf, the *parliament was a mirror, revealing the autocratic face of the regime to the public.*

All of these examples reveal the dual nature of institutions: they empower and constrain. For the opposition, it was clear that parliamentary rights and tools created a space for action against the ruling party and the government. In the case of indemnity, the mere attempt by the opposition to assert this right was observed as an overreach that went beyond its formal and original intent. Usually, however, the oppositional deputies faced constraints in effecting outcomes. Even though the NDP majority always prevented the opposition from implementing the tools of control, the institution also constrained the NDP, as their members still had to justify their actions. The more arbitrary a decision, the more effort was required to persuade others of its legitimacy. This showed the trade-off that the ruling party had to make when exercising its power arbitrarily. Whereas decision-making power allowed the ruling majority to do virtually anything it desired, a belief in the rectitude of their actions as the basis of legitimacy was put at risk when the autocratic nature of the regime violated the norms of the self-declared liberal and democratic institutions.

At the end of the period under investigation, the image of parliament as a forum for a harmonious and friendly exchange of opinions was evoked in order to restrict the use of parliamentary rights and to avoid criticism. The opposition still used the tools available to them to express their opinions and challenge the government's actions. Significantly, those actions had become so difficult to justify in public that the only way out for the members of the ruling party was to declare parliament itself irrelevant.

Parliament–Government Relations

Whereas the attitude toward parliament was relatively positive at the beginning of the debates studied here, one finds a mixed picture in the assessment of the government by 2005, which further deteriorated over the next several years. When assembly members and ministers remarked on their perception of the relation between the powers—how things actually were and how they ought to be—the ideas ranged from perfect harmony to open conflict. In general, ministers tried to appease parliamentarians by citing the great cooperation among the council of ministers, the People's Assembly, its committees, and the Shura Council.[41] In the discussion of whom to thank for introducing the antitrust law, some MPs attributed its success to the government, including an oppositional MP from the Nasserist Party.[42]

Initial points of conflict arose in regard to implementing the law, particularly about the role of the prime minister in the daily operations of the future Competition Protection Authority and in issuing executive regulations for the law. Across all parties, MPs feared that power would accumulate in the prime minister's hands, and some even viewed him as the very source of the monopoly problem. The first open declaration of mistrust arose regarding criticism of the original plan to subordinate the CPA to the prime minister.[43] First, it was argued that the workload that came along with the CPA was too great to be handled by someone as busy as the prime minister, who would be unable to fulfill the important duties of the authority. Effectiveness, however, was not the major concern: besides the workload, one independent member of parliament stated that it

41. Minister of investment, 2005/21: 15.
42. 2005/21: 25, 32, 51.
43. 2005/21: 13–14, 14, 27, 27–28, 37, 59–60, 62–63.

was a matter of fact that the prime minister was generally affiliated with a party. As large-scale producers were typically members of the ruling party and were inclined to safeguard their interests, the CPA's independence would be questionable if the prime minister, as a party comrade of big business, was at the helm.[44] A parliamentarian from the Muslim Brotherhood explicitly spoke about his unease with such a high degree of power residing with the prime minister, who had been held responsible for several economic scandals and existing monopolies on fertilizer and cement, and therefore could not be trusted to lead the CPA. He warned against putting the cat in charge of the storeroom key[45]—an Arabic proverb that is equivalent to "appointing a fox to guard the henhouse"—and asserted that responsibility for safeguarding the neutrality of the authority rested with the People's Assembly, as well as with the president of the republic.[46]

Apparently, the prime minister was not considered an independent institution. The verbal exchange became heated when the speaker of the assembly pointed out that, according to the constitution, control of authorities was a responsibility of the prime minister. An independent MP clarified that the CPA could be under the supervision of the prime minister but must not directly answer to him. Since the minister in charge of the authority would decide about its structure and budget, the entire power of the CPA would be in the hands of the prime minister. He openly justified his doubts by referring to Egypt's undemocratic regime and the lack of transparency.[47] In doing so, the MP made clear that the subordination of the competition authority to the prime minister was problematic within an autocratic regime. This dispute reframed the entire debate about the independence of the CPA: instead of treating it as a structural question from within a political system, the MP tried to circumvent the power structure of the current system and exclude the authority from the influence of the autocratic elite. Although the MP truly might have believed it

44. 2005/21: 37.

45. *"Fa-la yumkin an 'nimsik al-qutt miftah al-karar'"* (2005/22: 18). Colloquial Arabic used to be put in single quotation marks in the parliamentary minutes.

46. 2005/22: 18–19, also 2005/22: 20.

47. 2005/21: 38. See also the beginning of this chapter.

was possible to protect the CPA from such influence, his comments were likely intended to publicly shame and blame the government or, more broadly, the ruling elite.

Other parliamentarians expressed their mistrust in the prime minister more cautiously. As an alternative to the prime minister, one MP from the Tagammu Party, but also another one from the NDP, advocated for designating someone else with the status of a minister to head the authority. This would ensure the highest degree of independence and clarity in the authority's operations, and it would also appease the public.[48] Another independent assembly member expressed his suspicion of the government a bit less provocatively by warning that *future* governments could be manipulated by businessmen and competitors.[49] Minister of parliamentary affairs Kamal al-Shadhili responded to the criticism by pointing to parliament's strong role in the current construction, as the prime minister was held to account by the People's Assembly.[50] He also defended the NDP as being open to everyone, not only to businessmen. The minister literally said that "every guest" was welcome within the party.[51]

This debate is striking from two perspectives. It is surprising that the president, who must formally pass an electoral process, was deemed to be distant from special interests. No one mentioned the possibility that a businessman could ever become president. Mubarak, the balancer between different interest groups, seemed to be removed from political competition, reminiscent of the role usually ascribed to kings in monarchies. In a similar vein, parliament was considered to be neutral, even though the ruling party always held the majority. That the opposition regarded the People's Assembly as an independent institution is quite surprising.

The lack of trust in the prime minister was also apparent in the discussion about executive regulation of the law. The draft stated that the rules for competition would be issued by a prime ministerial decree one

48. 2005/22: 17–18, similar 19.
49. 2005/22: 20.
50. 2005/21: 39.
51. 2005/21: 37.

month after the antitrust law came into force. This stirred criticism, as the prime minister was perceived to already have too many responsibilities in regard to competition protection. Independent and Muslim Brotherhood–affiliated deputies argued in favor of the president assuming the regulatory responsibility instead.[52] One NDP deputy even brought forward the concern that, since the law itself did not include much in terms of content, definitions, principles, or procedures, executive regulation would create a means to define the law anew, instead of merely clarifying procedural details.[53]

By contrast, the head of the joint committee argued in favor of the prime minister issuing regulations, as this would guarantee a high degree of flexibility for traversing this terrain still unknown in Egypt.[54] The minister of finance tried to appease the parliamentarians, saying that nothing new would come from the regulation, as such methods for competition protection were globally known.[55] Similar to the previous debate, it was argued that having the prime minister in charge would even increase the influence of the People's Assembly, which could control him.[56] Here, we may observe the deputies' side of the struggle for legislative power, as they tried to prevent the law from becoming a vague framework within which the prime minister could do anything he pleased. The head of the committee did not appear very trustworthy, arguing that nothing new would come of the law while concurrently praising the flexibility of executive regulation.

Ultimately, the protest fell on deaf ears, and the prime minister remained in charge of virtually all aspects of the Competition Protection Authority. In the same year, however, as discussed in chapter 3, the members of parliament deliberated on how to regulate the setting of prices for basic goods, and whether the law was to predefine a list of goods and a fixed time period. The final solution gave the government complete power

52. 2005/22: 22, 22–23.
53. 2005/22: 23–24.
54. 2005/22: 23.
55. 2005/22: 24.
56. 2005/22: 24–25.

to decide on the items and the duration. As only one MP protested against the final vote, we may assume that the council of ministers as a whole still enjoyed a certain level of trust in 2005.

The other controversial issue concerned the role of the government in the implementation of the law. Assembly members from various parties, including the NDP, opposed any prominent role for the prime minister in supervising the CPA and issuing executive regulations.[57] Even though other members of the NDP and members of the cabinet tried to sway these critical voices, the controversy revealed that some ruling party members did not trust the prime minister and were willing to express their skepticism in public. It is striking that these critical voices from within the NDP became more vocal after the general debate was over. This could indicate an attempt on their part to present their divergent opinions, albeit not at the most crucial moment with the greatest public attention. It is telling that all of these attempts to restrict the prime minister's competences failed in the voting procedure.

Hopes for an effective and broad solution that would bring prices down led to a very open-ended Article 10, which gave all latitude of judgment to the government; the final formulation allowed him to do anything and obliged him to nothing. This result was achieved by a cross-party alliance of four MPs: two Muslim Brothers, one member of the NDP (Faruq al-Miqrahi, an army officer) and one member of the Wafd. This was also one of the few times that oppositional MPs were successful in the parliament's voting process and that their proposal was accepted by the majority. A more binding solution proposed by NDP member Khalil Quwayta, which obliged the council of ministers to limit prices, was not accepted.

A similarly amicable relationship with the government was evident when a group of parliamentarians cooperated with one minister in 2008 to amend the antitrust law. Many assembly members thanked the government, the minister of trade and industry, and the parliamentary

---

57. Among the parliamentarians who criticized the draft for not guaranteeing the CPA's independence were members of the Liberals, the Muslim Brotherhood, New Wafd, and Tagammu, an independent deputy, and NDP members (2005/21 and 2005/22).

committee for economic affairs for their work on the revisions. A closer look showed that there was an especially close relationship between NDP members and the executive, but also that two Muslim Brothers expressed their respect and support for the minister of trade and industry.[58] The minister himself referred to his amendments as the implementation of the president's philosophy that was presented as being based upon increased state intervention.[59]

However, when the amendments to the antitrust law were turned upside down by the relevant committee in session 131 of 2008, Muslim Brotherhood MPs questioned the power and assertiveness of the government. While the government had been in favor of strengthening the Competition Protection Law, the parliament would now support monopolies.[60] Similarly, another Muslim Brother argued against the 'Izz proposal and complained that the party actually ruled over the government, and not the other way around. He requested that 'Izz, as the head of the NDP and leading figure in the NDP parliamentary group, should be brought under control by the government[61]—an astonishing demand from a parliamentarian, particularly a member of the opposition. Still, the good intentions of the cabinet as a whole were not yet questioned.

This changed in 2009, when parliamentary debate consisted almost entirely of blunt attacks against the government and its inability to rule the country and protect the interests of the Egyptian people. In asking for the withdrawal of confidence from the cabinet, the interpellants all claimed that monopolies had evolved on the Egyptian market, pushing up prices, and that the government had done nothing. Yet there were three different ways in which this accusation was built. The first was that the government had been absent during the crisis, as it had not done anything to prevent skyrocketing prices. Whether this absence was intentional or due to their incompetence was not always made clear. One independent MP stated that

58. 2008/118: 22, 43.
59. 2008/118: 13.
60. 2008/131: 8.
61. 2008/139: 68–69.

the government believed that the state should not play an active role and that this was why the government left the market "to the greedy searching for quick gains,"[62] without control and regulation. The absence of the government was visible for him in Egypt's low public expenditure quota compared to other capitalist countries.[63] This absence was also strongly felt in the field of exports: rising prices in the food sector, in spite of a national production surplus, were explained through the chaotic export situation.[64] Most interpellants, however, pushed the argument that the government was incapable of ruling the country or managing privatization processes. In the case of the cement industry, they described how successful state-owned companies were sold to the associates of high-placed politicians for incredibly low prices and how the companies were repeatedly resold at high profits until ending in the hands of foreign investors, thereby creating a monopoly of foreigners in a strategically important industrial sector. Moreover, after the companies were privatized, cement prices steadily rose.[65]

In all of these accusations against the entire cabinet, trust in former ally Rashid had disappeared and the assembly members even explicitly questioned his political loyalty, as he was a businessman himself.[66] At the same time, the interpellants took the Shura Council to be on their side, as partners in a fight against the monopolists.[67] Social solidarity minister 'Ali al-Musalhi, in turn, understood government policies to represent the implementation of the president's electoral program of standing up to price increases,[68] thereby using this reference to the unquestioned authority of the president as the source of legitimacy for his own policies.

Apart from the interpellations raised by the opposition—making an antigovernment stance very likely—144 requests for information were also

62. 2009/66: 59.
63. 2009/66: 59.
64. 2009/66: 65.
65. 2009/66: 49–50, 66.
66. 2009/67: 19.
67. 2009/67: 15.
68. 2009/68: 4–5.

submitted, which eventually had to involve ruling party members, as well. It was possible to identify nine groups of parliamentarians who submitted the exact same request, representing more than one-half of all requests. These deputies, with very few exceptions, were all members of the ruling party, including a number of very well-known businessmen and representatives of influential families.

Three groups consisted solely of businessmen and powerful NDP members. Two of them posed requests mostly related to business.[69] The third group asked about the increase of the inflation rate, the measures that the government had taken to halt the rise, and the influence on the prices of goods and services.[70] The requests ultimately remained superficial and neutral. The most surprising aspect was that high-ranking NDP members contradicted their own government, which claimed that prices were actually sinking. The MPs might have sought to intentionally weaken the government, but perhaps they were trying to bolster their

69. Group 1, around Ahmad ʿIzz, included only NDP members. Among them was Mustafa al-Sallab, a ceramics magnate who had already supported ʿIzz in 2008. Several members of this group were involved in scandals of land privatization (ʿAtif ʿAbduh), corruption (Hamdi Shalabi), and smuggling and gambling (Yasir Salah). Hasan Nashʾat al-Qassas became infamous in 2010 for being among the three MPs who demanded that security forces use live ammunition against protesters in front of the ministry of interior. The request for information from this group concentrates on the negative effects of price increases on economic activity. Only at the end does it mention the violation of social justice. Strikingly, no specific actors were blamed, nor were any particular actions requested. In group 2, there were ʿAbd al-Rahman Baraka, a banking tycoon and loyal ally of Ahmad ʿIzz, Mahmud Khamis, another businessman, and Hasan al-Mir, convicted in 2011 for making illegal profits from his parliamentary seat. Along with six other NDP members, they asked for information about the flood of products of unknown origin into the Egyptian market and its influence on the prices of Egyptian products. This quite specific request appeals to fear of the influence of foreign players on the market, but it might also be linked to personal affairs.

70. Among the parliamentarians of group 3 were Magdi ʿAllam, a member of the NDP board, Muhammad al-Salihi, a member of the policies committee headed by Gamal Mubarak, businessman Imbarik Abu al-Hajjaj, who had close ties to Ahmad ʿIzz, and two MPs from families with a background in politics (Amir Hasan Abu Hayf and Muhammad ʿAbd al-Maqsud).

own legitimacy by blaming the cabinet for failures, or, possibly, merely reflecting what actually might have been on people's minds. Still, these three groups stood out in terms of their neutrality and lack of criticism, not only in contrast to the opposition but also compared to many fellow NDP members.

In two of the other groups, NDP deputies cooperated with the opposition. Members of group 4 called the price increases unjustified and claimed that they were caused by greed. The MPs asked what measures the government had taken to find a way to sell goods at accessible prices, and to put an end to the exploitation of the citizens.[71] Similarly, group 5 requested more information about the permanent price increases, especially of goods on which the poor classes depended.[72] Other purely NDP-led groups dealt with topics of public relevance, such as cement prices and the shortage of affordable housing due to price increases in the construction sector.[73] Only one of the NDP groups echoed the opposition in asking

71. The most prominent member was Ahmad Shubayr, former goalkeeper for the Egyptian national soccer team. The rest of the group consisted of NDP parliamentarians, one independent MP (Hammam al-Daqishi), and one Muslim Brother (al-Muhammadi al-Sayyid Ahmad). Even the NDP members were quite heterogeneous, including one member of a traditionally influential family from Upper Egypt ('Ala' Makadi) and an army general (Muhammad Shabaka).

72. One remarkable figure in group 5 is Mustafa al-Katatni, cousin of the well-known Muslim Brother Sa'd al-Katatni, who was the head of the Brothers' parliamentary group at the time. Other MPs with important family ties in this group are Hazim Hammadi (whose forebears had been members of Egypt's very first parliament), Mahmud Abu 'Aqil from Suhaj, and a member of the Muslim Brotherhood (Rajab 'Amish). This group asked for the implementation of the antitrust law first and foremost for the cement companies that had increased their prices to an unjustified extent.

73. Within group 6, there was Ibrahim al-Jawjari, a member of one of the wealthiest families from al-Mansura, and Ashraf al-Barudi, who belonged to a traditionally influential family from Suhaj. Isma'il Hilal, who had presented the weakened version of the amendments (2008/131), was also part of the group. Rida Wahdan enjoyed questionable fame for being accused of fraud and rigging elections. Together with three other NDP members, they asked for an enumeration of the measures the government had taken to regulate the market in Egypt, especially in the housing sector, which was troubled by large price increases for housing units despite sinking prices at the global level.

for information as to why the state had left the market and the citizens unprotected.[74]

These very different approaches to using requests as a form of parliamentary tool by NDP members again reveals the presence of two factions within the NDP bloc. The big business owners could clearly be distinguished from a heterogeneous alliance that included army generals and traditionally influential families. In contrast to 2008, discontent with the status quo was no longer channeled against the 'Izz camp, but rather against the government. Yet the critical voices, once raised aloud, were now placed on the agenda—by the majority within the assembly. The well-known NDP-affiliated critics of earlier debates appear to have been silenced. The government was trapped by its justification that the free market would solve the existing problems and that social welfare would suffice in keeping social discontent in check. Their inability to exhibit any responsiveness reveals a large gap between legitimacy claims and beliefs.

One would usually expect ruling party assembly members to side with the government in parliamentary and semipresidential systems. The conflict might have reflected an intra-elite struggle taking place between two institutions—government and parliament—as previously observed in Egypt's parliamentary history; however, the minister of trade and industry who had spearheaded the attempt to limit the 'Izz camp's influence was obviously silenced and apparently abandoned openly acting against 'Izz. It is more probable that, on account of the intermediary nature of parliament, the socioeconomic crisis was even too large for businessmen to deny. Although most likely only paying lip service, they adapted to public and parliamentary discourse and the overall acknowledgment of the worsening situation among large parts of society. This reflects the pattern found in chapters 1 and 2, whereby a socioeconomic crisis would be channeled through parliament and into the government. Yet the 'Izz

---

74. A few scandalous MPs gathered in this group: Ahmad 'Abd al-Salam Qura was sentenced to seven years in prison for corrupt land deals, and Ahmad Abu 'Aqrab was among the three MPs who demanded the use of live ammunition on prodemocracy demonstrators in 2010.

camp, which had the greatest influence on decisions, still behaved differently from other segments of the ruling party and remained isolated. Its credibility in actually holding the government accountable remained low, particularly since it relied on a weak form of oversight, the parliamentary request.

Conclusion: The Parliament and Institutional Norms

The liberal content of formal parliamentary tools often clashed with the autocratic nature of power asymmetries and the actual impossibility of holding decision-makers accountable by using tools such as interpellations and the withdrawal of confidence. The tension created by liberal elements within the authoritarian context led to a constant struggle over the meaning of rules, which created a certain degree of transparency and brought the authoritarian regime logic to light, along with breaking down the democratic façade. The tension increased as the ruling elite (both in parliament and government) became unable to justify their actions. In his attempts to defend the behavior of ministers, the speaker of the assembly practically erased the connection between the parliament and the Egyptian people. But the opposition at times also tried to expand parliamentary rights beyond their intended scope as a substitute for a lack of legal protection outside of the assembly or to withdraw parliamentary rights from their adversaries in the ruling party, challenging the general legitimacy of businessmen as political actors.

Interinstitutional relations were never static but rather evolved in response to conflict and even included ad hoc alliances between ministers and opposition parliamentarians. At the same time, ruling party assembly members differed from each other in their parliamentary actions. Some of them showed a considerable amount of distrust in the government and tried to limit its power whenever possible. Over the years, one can observe how openly voiced evaluations of the government became increasingly negative: starting with mistrust in the prime minister in 2005, it spread to the belief in the absence of the government's power in 2008 and in 2009, and, ultimately, to viewing the cabinet as lacking even the willingness to solve social and economic problems. In contrast, and shared among opposition and NDP parliamentarians, only the president was consistently regarded as being neutral and beyond the sphere of influence of special interests. Parliament itself was held to be independent across parties and only lost credibility as a whole in 2008, when the "'Izz camp" too blatantly pushed through its interests. As discussed in chapter 4, the identity of NDP MPs as true representatives was thrown into question in 2009, and even the speaker of the assembly diluted the role of parliament—although opposition deputies still identified their actions with parliament and, in turn, with the needs of citizens.

These observations highlight the fact that all of the actors were operating within an autocratic regime logic and in the specific context. Of course, it is impossible to determine if adhering to existing rules, such as not criticizing the president, reflected conviction or recognition of a red line they dared not cross. But as even the opposition demanded more powers for the president—instead of handing them to the government—and when we consider parliament to be a neutral institution without any chance of ever gaining a majority, it seems that the integrated political actors, at least, had accepted the status quo and played according to the rules of "the only game in town." Other norms, *autocratic norms*, were apparently applied to judge what was right or wrong in regard to political institutions.

The most striking uncontested norm that was applied in many instances by both ruling party and opposition was "the common good above everything." It is not a norm as such that fits the authoritarian regime, as it is likely that practically every parliamentarian in the world would at least rhetorically claim to pursue it. The people's interests were used by every group as a justification for its own actions and as a benchmark for the evaluation of others, without explicitly defining just what these interests were and what they were composed of. Furthermore, the reference to the people's interest outplayed other norms such as the equality of parliamentarians. As a matter of fact, suppressing plurality and legitimizing the breaking of institutional rules in the name of "the people's interest" were used by both the ruling party and the opposition and remained unquestioned throughout the debate. The common good was used as a normative benchmark that existed before and independent of political debate. It was employed in a way that seems fairly similar to Rousseau's *volonté générale*, which dismisses deviant opinions as expressions of a *volonté particulière*. Special interests were also used as the normative counterpart to the common good in the parliamentary debates to delegitimize conflicting positions.

What became clear from the norms that were both explicitly debated and implicitly applied is that most of the institutional debates were not associated with the greater regime question. Whenever the latter issue was tackled, such rare occurrences revealed that "the democratic transition" proclaimed by the ruling elite was deemed to be nothing more than empty words. The democracy paradigm was not used as a benchmark in debates. Instead, liberal rights, such as MPs' individual privileges and parliamentary tools, were invoked, made use of, defended, and even circumvented. Obviously, no one actually believed in a transition from the autocratic institutional framework into something democratic; but, at the same time, no one seemed to be aware of the plethora of practices and norms that the actors themselves reproduced and the extent to which these suited an autocratic regime. As a consequence, these undebated norms have continued to affect Egypt even after the 2011 revolution.

6

The Autocratic Parliament
beyond Mubarak's Egypt

What lessons can we learn from long-term Egyptian parliamentary development and more recent parliamentary debates, and can these lessons be applied beyond Mubarak's Egypt? This chapter demonstrates that analysis of pre-2011 parliament offers a better understanding of parliament's role(s) in the context of regime destabilization prior to the 2011 uprising, shedding light on how the country's interinstitutional life might explain political developments from 2011 to the military coup in summer 2013. While earlier institutional experiences shaped practices and norms, new actors post-2011 also quickly learned how to make use of institutional rights and procedures. I end by identifying five general characteristics of the autocratic parliament that influence parliament's relation with power, legitimacy, contention, stability, and regime change in an autocracy.

Parliament as an Indicator of and Catalyst for Change

The 25 January uprising did not come out of the blue. Power rifts within the ruling elite and a full-fledged legitimacy crisis had been previously developing and had paved the way for mass mobilization that eventually brought down the long-standing dictator Husni Mubarak. The microanalysis of parliamentary actions in chapters 3, 4, and 5 revealed power struggles and a growing legitimacy crisis. Analysis of the 2005–10 parliamentary debates and the lines of conflict and cooperation reveals two emerging camps among the parties and institutions by 2010. One bloc within the NDP cooperated with the minister of trade and industry, the Muslim Brothers, independents, and opposition parties. The other bloc mainly consisted of businessmen who supported the alleged monopolist Ahmad 'Izz and always won out in parliamentary votes. Critical voices within the NDP were silenced over time.

These power relations in parliament emerged alongside a decreasing belief in the efficacy of the government's major economic policies, as well as growing skepticism about the legitimacy of political actors and institutions. In 2005, there was broad consensus with regard to norms on economic policy, along with widely shared expectations that these norms would be satisfied by the antitrust law. By safeguarding the positive effects of a free market, the law was expected to bring new balance to society and to promote dynamics that would produce economic development. This conviction was shared across party lines and institutions, and it can thus be regarded as a benchmark that the government was supposed to fulfill. By the first evaluation of this law in 2008, a broad alliance contested its effectiveness along with the implementation of normative consent. It was plain to see that the hope for dynamic development had been lost and soon disappeared from the debate. The hopes for a new social balance and progress in the struggle against inequality remained intact, and a bloc spanning party lines and institutions searched for ways to achieve those aims. Oppositional voices and segments of the ruling party and government worked together, galvanized by the discontent with the economic situation expressed outside of the assembly, such as the nationwide labor strikes and food riots that reached a climax in 2008.

The business elite within parliament blocked attempts to strengthen the law without providing any considerable amount of justification for their actions. This led parliamentarians to question the political identity of assembly members associated with the 'Izz camp. The latter were attacked for violating the political norms of procedural equality, and their status as representatives of the people was challenged on the grounds that they appeared to instead be proponents of their own particular interests. Norm contestation spilled over from the economic realm and impacted identity and political norms. Despite its alleged lack of legitimacy, the 'Izz camp still managed to achieve its ends by making use of its decision-making power behind the scenes and its influence with NDP members who cooperated, or at least agreed with, the opposition. This intensified the protests against norm violations, mainly among Muslim Brotherhood assembly members, and ultimately the basis for cooperation among elements within the opposition and the NDP fell apart.

By 2009, the government was again aligned with the interests of the business elites and denied even the existence of a continuing socioeconomic crisis that mobilized thousands of people who demonstrated even in front of government and parliamentary buildings. Instead, the ministers saw positive development, stressing that they were responding to economic hardship by providing subsidies and social welfare. This very limited response failed to structurally fulfill the normative ideal of limited social inequality ensured by an active state. The growing discrepancy between government claims and reality bred a sense of hopelessness on the part of MPs that something could be done to stem the crisis. In contrast to 2008, when criticism was transformed into legal proposals, opposition assembly members pursued interpellations instead. A decision-making bias in favor of business elites also had repercussions for the perception of the parliament itself. In 2008, oppositional parliamentarians viewed the assembly as supportive of monopolies and openly called for the government to bring the 'Izz camp in line. In 2009, the clash between the idea that parliament represents the people, on one hand, and the clear lack of responsiveness by government and NDP MPs, on the other hand, made the opposition stress its identification with the people's anger and indignation—emotions that would come to the fore in January 2011.

As the socioeconomic crisis unfolded, the parliament became a mirror for the deteriorating living conditions of ordinary Egyptians. At the same time, parliament served as a magnifying glass for processes that were otherwise hidden. This was mainly true of internal frictions within the ruling party, although it also revealed cooperation across party lines and among institutions. With the parliamentarians' expectations for economic restructuring failing to materialize, the legislature also turned into a prism that gathered the discontent outside the assembly and directed it at an ever-less-responsive ruling party and government. As oppositional lawmakers used every legal means possible to contest governmental legitimacy, the business elites turned up pressure on NDP assembly members to refrain from criticizing the regime's policies.

The most striking example relates to the topic of consumer prices, an extremely important benchmark for the evaluation of the free market economy, as demonstrated in chapter 3. In 2009, as parliamentarians drew the conclusion that deregulation of the market had not addressed the problem of rising price levels, the government simply denied the existence of a problem. This clashed with the reality experienced by many Egyptians. In 2010, world market prices for food had again increased, and inflation rates surpassed the level of 2008. Egypt imports 40 percent of its food and 60 percent of its wheat, making it the world's largest wheat importer. Prices for wheat skyrocketed due to shortages in supply from countries like Russia, which had suffered from fires that destroyed the harvest, and Australia, which was hit by floods, resulting in a record high inflation in December 2010.[1]

Besides developments on the world market, there were also structural problems, such as high demographic growth and a scarcity of agricultural land, that contributed to the general price increases. In 2010, the voices of dissent grew louder, placing the blame on "the marriage of money to power"[2] in Egypt that favored importers and weakened producers.[3] NDP parliamentarian Faruq al-Miqrahi even spoke of the "wheat mafia," a group of importers who sold their goods at inflated rates to the government, which in turn resold the wheat to bakeries at a subsidized price. The price difference added a burden to state expenses and, hence, to the taxpayer.[4] Various civil society organizations such as Kifaya, the April 6 Youth Movement, the Youth for Justice and Development Movement, and Watan hurr (Free Homeland) protested the rising prices throughout the

1. "Minister: Egypt Imports 40% of Its Food," *Egypt Independent*, June 8, 2010, http://www.egyptindependent.com/news/minister-egypt-imports-40-its-food.

2. 'Isam Sharif, quoted in "Activists Protest Rising Food Prices before Ministers Council," *Egypt Independent*, Aug. 9, 2010, http://www.egyptindependent.com/news/activists-protest-rising-food-prices-ministers-council.

3. "Who Sabotaged Our Wheat Supply?," *Egypt Independent*, Aug. 14, 2010, http://www.egyptindependent.com/opinion/who-sabotaged-our-wheat-supply.

4. "al-Miqrahi: Mafia al-qamh tanhish lahm al-misriyyin," *Al-Bashayer*, Apr. 9, 2010, http://www.elbashayer.com/news-93766.html.

year, sometimes in front of the People's Assembly. Parliament was thereby reinvoked as the symbolic place for representing the people.[5] The crisis of representation and lack of responsiveness to socioeconomic grievances found their expression in the revolutionary slogan "*'aysh, hurriyya, 'adala ijtima'iyya*"—"Bread, Freedom, Social Justice."

As described in chapters 1 and 2, parliament had long been a place for balancing interests, both internal and public, throughout various historical stages. However, the fading responsiveness and the silencing of critical voices from within the ruling party turned the parliament into an instrument of the NDP's business wing, whose members designed laws as they saw fit, relegating the People's Assembly to the oft-cited "rubber-stamp" function. A lack of responsiveness can come at a high cost and power-consolidation measures can easily backfire. Such was the case in the parliamentary elections at the end of 2010. To further consolidate its power and resolve the issue of a weak internal discipline resulting from the common practice of victorious independent candidates only later joining the NDP, the ruling party reorganized its selection procedure for candidates.[6] The results were shocking, and many labeled the 2010 elections the worst Egypt had ever witnessed. The share of seats held by oppositional candidates decreased from 30 percent to 10 percent,[7] and the critical camp

---

5. "Watan Hurr to Protest Price Increases Monday," *Egypt Independent*, Aug. 5, 2010, http://www.egyptindependent.com/news/watan-hurr-protest-price-increases-monday.

6. Official candidates had to sign a pledge that if they were not selected by the party as the official candidate they would not run as independents. Furthermore, the party list was announced at the last moment before the registration period ended, ensuring that disappointed NDP members would not run on their own behalf. At the same time, the NDP leadership decided to nominate more than one NDP candidate in around 60 percent of the constituencies, thereby channeling competition among various candidates into the ruling party. In the runoff elections, however, the NDP would join the forces once again and almost always win the majority against an opposition candidate. Another crucial change was decreased judicial supervision. "NDP Candidate List Exposes Internal Rifts," *Egypt Independent*, Nov. 15, 2010, http://www.egyptindependent.com/opinion/ndp-candidate-list-exposes-internal-rifts.

7. The Muslim Brotherhood boycotted the runoffs due to the extent of electoral fraud.

within the ruling party was shut out of the parliament. All of the NDP parliamentarians who had fought to strengthen the antitrust law in 2008 lost their seats, among them Mustafa al-Saʿid, the head of the economic affairs committee, Khalil Quwayta, who had been active in lobbying for a stronger antitrust law in 2008, and Faruq Miqrahi, who had fought to limit the prime minister's influence in the implementation of the antitrust law in 2005. All of Ahmad ʿIzz's allies who had rallied behind him in previous years made a reentry. The overall lesson learned from these elections was that the ʿIzz camp had taken over.[8]

It was not entirely clear why the plurality within parliament was not maintained. Some speculated that the presidential elections planned for 2011 forced the ruling party to ensure a safe majority within the legislature, especially since it was speculated that Husni Mubarak intended to pass power down to his son Gamal during, or soon after, the elections. This, however, is not a convincing argument, as even 70 percent for the NDP would have ensured that any required legislative approval would be obtained. Instead, it seemed that representing public grievances by using a pluralistic parliament was no longer seen as opportune.[9] The issue was not only about the social situation, but also about structural conflicts over the correct economic policies and the appropriate role of the state. This is supported by the fact that the former assembly members excluded from parliament were the ones who had contested the way that economic restructuring had been implemented, as it violated widely shared norms, and they were also the ones who had been silenced within the assembly prior to 2010.

Although the business wing of the NDP had likely intended to silence its critics, the unintended consequence was the alienation of broader segments of the ruling party and further public resentment. As a result, the newly elected People's Assembly was not accepted as legitimate. It became

<hr />

8. "Aqulu li-Ahmad ʿIzz wa-Aʿwanihi: Hasbuna Allah wa-Niʿma l-Wakil," *Al-Yawm al-Sabiʿ*, Feb. 10, 2011.

9. Mona El-Ghobashy, "The Liquidation of Egypt's Illiberal Experiment," *Middle East Report Online* (blog), Dec. 29, 2010, http://www.merip.org/mero/mero122910.

the object of contestation, and, as I argue, a catalyst for the mass uprising of 2011. Opposition forces mobilized public protest and called for a "Day of Rage" on December 12, 2010. This same label was applied to January 25, the first day of the public protests that would lead to Mubarak's fall and in reference to which the entire uprising became known as the January 25th Revolution. Moreover, they founded a shadow legislature—the so-called popular parliament (*barlaman sha'bi*)—and thereby contested the newly elected assembly's claim of being the legitimate parliament. Although all previous elections had also been manipulated, sometimes by means of violence, the elections of 2010 seemed to have crossed a threshold of what was considered tolerable, fair, or appropriate even within the existing regime.[10]

A certain degree of representation of opposition forces, along with a balanced distribution of seats within the broader ruling coalition, had been fundamental to bestowing legitimacy upon the institution. When both factors were eliminated through blatant vote rigging, the normative foundation of the parliament as being representative within an autocratic framework crumbled. On top of that, the elections had primarily been manipulated to the advantage of the alliance of businessmen. This group had not only exercised decision-making power to advance its own interests at the expense of ordinary Egyptians, it also had not complied with the economic norms shared by parts of the ruling party and the opposition. Even before the 2010 elections, the legitimacy of those assembly members as representatives of the people had been challenged and their practices within the institution criticized. The negative evaluation of all of these elements contributed to the perception that the new parliament as a whole was illegitimate.

The parliament's legitimacy crisis had indeed been one of the sparks that ignited the fire of revolution. On January 25, 2011, several youth movements joined forces with independent trade unions, unleashing an unexpected dynamic. It is often forgotten that the protesters' demands on

---

10. This assessment was expressed in interviews with a former NDP parliamentarian, an oppositional politician, and a political consultant in Cairo in June 2011.

the first day did not entail a call for an end to Mubarak's presidency or the regime but rather an end to the emergency state, the trial of officers who committed crimes against the Egyptian people, and labor-sponsored demands for a higher minimum wage and independent trade unions.[11] Gradually, awareness of the power resting in the people, those who had started to occupy Tahrir Square, grew and encouraged the participants to demand an end to the regime, which would become their overarching goal. They did not respond to the concessions that the regime offered, and the protests were further enlarged when mass strikes brought Egypt to a standstill starting on February 9.[12] On the third day after the initiation of these strikes, Mubarak's resignation was announced and the Supreme Council of the Armed Forces took over (Albrecht and Bishara 2011).[13]

Once Mubarak had been forced out of office, the army generals, who were a major force within the power structure of Egypt, seized the opportunity to consolidate their position. They exploited the vulnerability of the business elites who had expanded their power base within the political system at the expense of other parts of the ruling coalition. The generals ordered the imprisonment of the Mubarak clan and the well-known "whales," among them Ahmad 'Izz.[14] Ironically, the army, which had been deeply involved in the Egyptian economy since the 1950s, was not negatively affected by the process of economic restructuring promoted by the business elites. The military was compensated for the partial loss of power and money resulting from a wave of privatization, and members

11. "Al-Quwwa al-Siyasiyya Tu'akkid Isti'dadaha li-'Yawm al-Ghadab' Ghadan," *Al-Masry al-Youm*, Jan. 24, 2011.

12. For a detailed analysis of the role of labor in the Egyptian revolution, including the institutional development of an independent trade union federation during the protests, see Weipert-Fenner (2012).

13. It is beyond the scope of this book to provide a comprehensive account or even an explanation of the January 25 uprising that, after eighteen days, brought down President Mubarak. For further analyses of the January 25th Revolution, see, for example, Korany and El-Mahdi 2012, Sowers and Toensing 2012, Soudias 2014.

14. "Steel Tycoon with Links to a Mubarak Is Sentenced," *New York Times*, Sep. 15, 2011.

of the army received high positions in the privatized companies. By early 2011, the armed forces still controlled a substantial part of the economy, estimated to be between 5 percent and 15 percent of the GDP (Cook 2007). Yet this relationship might have been perceived as precarious, as the army's privileges also depended on Husni Mubarak, president and former army general, who had been the broker between conflicting interests for decades. However, as his health deteriorated, his son Gamal, a civilian, came to be seen as the likely successor. Gamal's leaning toward private businessmen and technocrats posed a threat to the old balance, one that loomed larger as the businessmen's unwillingness to negotiate with other elite groups became obvious and the elections of 2010 cemented their dominant position in the parliament. With the January 25th Revolution, the army took the opportunity to eliminate this threat to its privileges. In so doing, it profited from power conflicts and the lack of political legitimacy ascribed to the business elites, which was the result of developments within parliament that were carried out by parliamentarians and became visible in the analysis of parliamentary debates.

The Struggle over the New Institutional Order, 2011–2013

The years 2011 to 2013—from the ouster of President Husni Mubarak to the ouster of President Muhammad Mursi—were marked by constant attempts of three groups of actors to ensure a new institutional order that favored their respective interests: the army, in the form of the Supreme Council of the Armed Forces (SCAF); the Muslim Brotherhood through the Freedom and Justice Party (FJP); and a heterogeneous camp of "civil" forces that included secular parties (both left and liberal) and movements. During the process, the Supreme Constitutional Court (SCC) would play an important role as well.

The struggle over the new institutional order was characterized by a two-front power struggle that prevented any cooperative approach to institution building. The key word *madani* (civil) was ascribed to one side in both of the conflicts, the first between Islamists and secular (self-declared civil) groups and the second between military and civil forces. Each group cited a different basis for its legitimacy: members of the Muslim Brotherhood referred to their electoral victory; the army portrayed itself as the guardian of the Egyptian republic and protector of the Egyptian people; and many liberal parties and youth movements claimed "street legitimacy" in the form of public protests and the occupation of the public space as an alternative expression of the people's will.

What is striking is that each group's claim to legitimacy was built on the premise that it was the one and only representative of "the Egyptian people." By extension, the other groups were simply representing special interests (Islamists, the army) or thugs and foreign agents. As during the prerevolutionary period, this norm—the advancement of the common good above all else—was used as a benchmark to determine the legitimacy of someone's actions or identity. Yet it became clear that this concept of a unified, uncontested common good, which existed beyond the negotiation process, was very problematic. Deep mutual mistrust led to a heated fight over formal rules to compensate for the lack of confidence in the political intentions of other actors. The Muslim Brothers tried to formally institute and protect their power from a judiciary that repeatedly dissolved newly established and elected institutions, whereas the "civil" opposition forces always pushed for more precise formal rules to safeguard rights and liberties, particularly in the constitutional process.

One can differentiate between three phases of institutional development leading up to the July 2013 crisis that all reveal how much was at stake in the phase of reinstitutionalization, not only for prodemocratic forces but also for the army generals who, in the end, reinstalled a military dictatorship. Institutions matter, one could observe once more, and apparently it was worth fighting for them (or for one's preferred design for them). The process became a year-long struggle, one that proved to be messy and at times violent. It was marked by trial and error, miscalculations, and unintended consequences, and was heavily influenced by diverse prerevolutionary experiences with institutions.

Phase 1: Constitution or Elections First?

Egypt faced a tabula rasa, at least from an institutional perspective, when President Husni Mubarak stepped down and the SCAF took control. The generals suspended the constitution of 1971 and dissolved both the People's Assembly and the Shura Council. Only the government headed by Prime Minister Ahmad Shafiq, which had been hastily appointed by Mubarak during the mass protests, survived the immediate postrevolution purge, and only temporarily.

The most important conflict during this first phase revolved around whether the first step should be to elect new representatives to political institutions so that legitimate actors could draft a new constitution, or to instead (by some means) create a representative constituent assembly responsible for establishing democratic procedures and institutions. Secular left and liberal groups fought for the latter option. The huge organizational advantage enjoyed by the Muslim Brotherhood had created a high probability of a landslide victory for its Freedom and Justice Party (FJP), and the civil forces feared the consequences of a victory by Islamists without a constitutional framework that would obligate them to respect the rights of women and non-Muslims. In contrast, the army and the Muslim Brotherhood were in favor of quick elections; the Brothers, in particular, were confident of their electoral success and wanted to gain control of parliament and the government as soon as possible. Moreover, they hoped to transform electoral gains into influence in the constitutional process as well. The position of the army in this power game was to save the privileges of the generals, yet this aim was pursued by way of several constitutional declarations, at times carried out suddenly and at times discussed in secret talks and partially leaked to the public.

As the first move in the process of reinstitutionalization, the SCAF appointed Tariq al-Bishri[15] to head the committee tasked with amending the constitutional provisions related to parliamentary and presidential elections. The committee consisted of jurists and was therefore more of a technocratic body meant to smooth out the electoral process than a politically representative assembly meant to usher in substantial change in the

---

15. The nomination of al-Bishri, the former judge on the State Council and a well-known intellectual, was first interpreted to be a good sign, as he had also advised the antiregime movement Kifaya. Copts, however, were critical of the appointment, since al-Bishri sympathized with the Muslim Brothers, although he was never a member.

political system.[16] The timetable for Egypt's transition presented by the committee foresaw parliamentary elections first, followed by presidential elections, and finally the seating of a constituent assembly. The majority of amendments dealt with the election of the president, but some also addressed an increase of judicial oversight of electoral processes. They also annulled antiterrorist Article 179, which had been introduced in 2007, and authorized restrictions on liberties and rights in the name of counterterrorism. The measures could be used as a substitute for the state of emergency, which had been repeatedly extended by parliament since 1981 but was increasingly being contested. The deletion of the antiterrorism article was accompanied by stricter limitations on declaring and upholding an emergency state.[17] Despite opposition from civil political groups who demanded a new constitution first, the amendments were approved in a public referendum on March 19 with 77 percent support.

Less than two weeks later, the generals surprised the public by issuing a constituent declaration of 63 articles, most of which were copied from the 1971 version, with just minor changes. The declaration included all of the articles that were amended by the referendum. It was not entirely clear whether the SCAF wanted to appease the "constitution-first" supporters, or if a broader strategy was hidden beneath the minor adjustments and omissions to the articles. The declaration also included ambiguous statements about sequencing the reintroduction of political institutions.[18] But if appeasement was the goal, the move failed to achieve its objective: the

16. Only one member, Subhi Salih, had a political background, as a member of the Muslim Brotherhood. He was nominated as a lawyer and well-known legal expert, but he had also been a member of the People's Assembly from 2005 to 2010. Joshua Stacher, "Egypt without Mubarak," *Middle East Report Online*, Apr. 7, 2011, http://www.merip.org/mero/mero040711.

17. For the text of the amendments, see http://www.referendum.eg/homepage.html (accessed Nov. 16, 2012).

18. For a thorough analysis of the declaration, see Nathan Brown and Kristen Stilt, "A Haphazard Constitutional Compromise," *Carnegie Middle East Center*, Apr. 11, 2011, http://carnegie-mec.org/publications/?fa=43533#.

generals' nonchalance in implementing an interim constitution without putting it to vote, just one week after a constitutional referendum had been held, stoked fears that the army's promises of a transition toward democracy were hollow.

"Civil" left and liberal groups, including several youth movements, started a campaign to pressure the generals to hand over power to an interim civil government. The campaign also pushed for a new constitution prior to elections to prevent the winners from dominating the process of creating the institutions of the new political structure. Violent clashes with security forces grew in intensity and frequency and destroyed the illusion of the army working hand in hand with the people, as propagated during the uprising in January and February 2011.

Instead of giving in to the activists' demands, the SCAF prepared another text that was drafted in secret talks. Deputy Prime Minister 'Ali al-Silmi publicly presented the supraconstitutional principles to political parties in November 2011. To ensure buy-in from liberal forces, the generals offered protection of some civil liberties, while also including provisions that safeguarded the army's privileges. The document stipulated financial autonomy for the army, a veto right for the SCAF on any legislation concerning military affairs, and a plan for the composition of the constituent assembly that denied input from any future parliament. The document also referred to the army as the "legitimate protector of the constitution." This entailed the right to veto any article that "contradicts the basic tenets of the Egyptian state and society and the general rights and freedoms confirmed in successive Egyptian constitutions including the Constitutional Declaration issued . . . on 30 March 2011 and subsequent constitutional announcements."[19] It also granted the generals the right to intervene in the constitutional process if they deemed it necessary. It seemed that the Supreme Council of the Armed Forces simply sought to

19. Translation cited in Yezid Sayigh, "The Specter of 'Protected Democracy' in Egypt," *Carnegie Middle East Center*, Dec. 15, 2011, https://carnegie-mec.org/2011/12/15/specter-of-protected-democracy-in-egypt-pub-46245.

feather their own nest before elected political powers—most probably the Muslim Brothers—took over the transition and the constitutional process.

Although the so-called al-Silmi document offered compromises, the idea of granting the army exceptional rights on a long-term basis was completely rejected across all political camps. Opposition was particularly strong among the Muslim Brothers and the Salafists, who rejected any limitations on what they assumed would be their dominant influence over the process of writing the constitution. Together with the youth movements, they organized the million-man march on November 18, 2011. When the Islamists withdrew at night, civil groups refused to leave Tahrir Square and were subsequently attacked by military forces on Muhammad Mahmud Street, marking the beginning of bloody contestations between street activists and the army.[20] In two waves of violent clashes in downtown Cairo from November 19 to November 24 and in mid-December, the army acted with outright oppression, in blatant disrespect of human rights. The violence employed by security forces turned the area around Tahrir Square into a battle zone.

For the Muslim Brotherhood, the situation constituted a delicate balancing act between forestalling the army's slow grab for power by allying with the liberal forces, while avoiding an aggressive and violent confrontation with the military. The Brothers feared that any destabilization of the situation would lead to the postponement of the first round of parliamentary elections scheduled for November 29. Throughout the period of violence in downtown Cairo, paired with varying degrees of electoral fever in the rest of the country, the supraconstitutional principles, although not off the table, were pushed to the background, making the actual powers of the elected parliamentary institutions a matter of uncertainty (Moustafa 2012).

20. Michelle Dunne, "How Will the Supra-constitutional Principles Be Amended?," *Atlantic Council*, Nov. 17, 2011; "HRW [Human Rights Watch]: Morsy Must Reform Security after Mohamed Mahmoud Clashes," *Egypt Independent*, Nov. 19, 2012, http://www.egyptindependent.com/news/hrw-morsy-must-reform-security-after-mohamed-mahmoud-clashes.

Phase 2: A Return to Routine Politics?

The struggle over the new political institutions also included the parliamentary electoral system, which was altered three times before the votes were finally cast. To overcome the shortcomings of the majoritarian voting system that had been in use since the 1990s, the first solution presented in May 2011 reduced the percentage of seats distributed by way of the majoritarian system to two-thirds of the total, with one-third filled by means of a proportional system. In July 2011, this was changed to a fifty-fifty formula, and, in late September, the final solution set out that two-thirds of the parliamentarians were to be elected through the proportional system and one-third on an individual basis. To make one-third of the total of 496 seats electable by majority vote, Egypt was subdivided into eighty-three constituencies, each of which sent two members to the People's Assembly. The constituencies, which had previously accounted for 222 seats, were geographically enlarged, weakening the influence of local kinship. The other 322 seats were distributed among forty-six electoral districts, each of which sent between four and twelve parliamentarians to Cairo on a party basis.[21]

It proved nearly impossible to quickly train electoral staff and observers in the complexity of this voting system. This was also a central problem for the newly founded parties, whose electoral campaigns needed to be adjusted to the new electoral formula, the final version of which was determined less than two months before the elections. In spite of these and other insufficiencies, most electoral observers declared the three election rounds in November, December, and January of 2011–12, including the runoffs, to be free and fair. Voter turnout was just slightly above 50 percent, and the results were clear: the Muslim Brotherhood's Freedom and Justice Party won 44 percent and the Salafist al-Nur Party 22 percent of the seats. The strongest non-Islamist forces in parliament were the Wafd Party, with 8 percent, and the newly founded Egyptian Social Democratic

---

21. "The Effects of Egypt's Election Law," *Foreign Policy*, Nov. 1, 2011. The Shura elections held in January and February 2012 used yet another electoral map.

Party, with 3 percent (Electoral Institute for Sustainable Democracy in Africa 2012, 45–46).

The first post-revolutionary parliament sat for less than five months before the Supreme Constitutional Court dissolved the People's Assembly in June 2012, citing the unconstitutionality of the electoral law. Although this is, of course, too short a period to identify major institutional developments, several observations can be made that illustrate the degree to which parliamentary actors had internalized the logic of the authoritarian regime as well as how rapidly actors learned and adapted to the new possibilities afforded by a parliamentary seat.

The clash of new and old regime logics was nicely illustrated in the opening session of the newly elected People's Assembly on January 23, 2012. As the oldest assembly member, the Wafd representative Mahmud al-Saqqa presided over the parliament until a speaker was elected. The FJP nominated their stalwart, Sa'd al-Katatni, but, to their surprise, they faced competition from 'Isam Sultan, a former Muslim Brother who had left the organization in the mid-1990s for the newly founded Wasat Party. Sultan had formed an alliance with some liberal and even Salafist parliamentarians beforehand; with this support behind him, he stood up and demanded the right to speak and announce his candidacy. He was stopped by al-Saqqa for violating the Mubarak-era rules of the speaker's elections, which prohibited speeches concerning the choice of the speaker before the speaker had been elected. This obviously absurd and antidemocratic provision was upheld by the FJP's assembly members and resulted in raucous shouting from the Wasat MPs. In the end, Sultan received the right to speak, although this did not prevent al-Katatni from becoming the speaker.

A number of incidents stirred contention among the opposition in parliament toward the majority party and revealed that the Muslim Brotherhood exhibited similar behavior to the NDP before 2011. For instance, the distribution of committee leadership posts was dominated by the FJP, which chaired twelve of the nineteen committees; of the seven that remained, three were reserved for al-Nur members and four committees were headed by non-Islamist MPs. Among the latter, the only committee of importance was the committee for constitutional and legislative affairs. This division of the political spoils was criticized by the non-Islamist parties, who noted that they controlled 35 percent of the seats in parliament but only 20 percent of committee chairs.[22]

One subject of serious dispute was the Port Said soccer game, which had ended in the massacre of seventy-four people and the injury of a thousand others. Non-Islamist deputies inquired about the failure of the security forces and about the brutal violence used against activists who protested in front of the ministry of interior in the aftermath of the Port Said incident. In response to the public outcry, parliament installed commissions to investigate both issues. Even though some mistakes by the security forces were made public, the position taken by the ministers and the FJP blamed the ultra-fans of both teams, whose tense relation had been well known before. In addition, Facebook had allegedly served as a tool for the ultras to organize, and private satellite channel programs were accused of having instigated the aggressive behavior by sowing divisions. The violent clashes around the ministry of interior were, however, mainly attributed to thugs, manipulated by foreign powers trying to destabilize Egypt.[23] This was similar to the line of argumentation made by the SCAF post 2011 and the ruling party under Mubarak before the revolution. During the debates analyzed in chapters 3–5, some had argued that private television channels caused dissent by leveling false accusations; at that time, however, this line of argumentation was used by prominent NDP figures. The FJP very quickly adopted this kind of rhetoric in its new position as the majority party.

The gravest violation of democratic procedures occurred at the end of April 2012. To pressure the SCAF into dismissing Prime Minister Kamal al-Janzuri and his cabinet and allowing the FJP to form a new one, the speaker of parliament announced on April 29 that the People's Assembly sessions would be suspended for a week. Moreover, al-Katatni directly warned the government that 185 interpellations had been submitted to

22. "Islamist Takeover at the People's Assembly," *Al-Ahram Weekly*, Feb. 2–8, 2012, no. 1083.

23. "Twin Crisis in Parliament," *Al-Ahram Weekly*, Feb. 9–15, 2012, no. 1084; "Parliamentary Backbiting," *Al-Ahram Weekly*, Feb. 16–22, 2012, no. 1085.

him. The suspension was not decided on through a vote in parliament, a fact that ultimately made the liberal and leftist assembly members and even the Salafist al-Nur party protest al-Katatni's declaration. They simply refused to leave the assembly, and 175 members supported a petition submitted to the speaker to annul his decision. They openly raised accusations that the Muslim Brotherhood would hijack parliament. Even the Salafist MPs were clearly more worried about their parliamentary seats than about their large coalition partner.[24] Indeed, the behavior of the FJP parliamentarians was reminiscent of the intra-elite struggle carried out within interinstitutional relations (between parliament and government), as seen before in Egypt's autocratic parliament. The sole difference was that all other MPs—independents or from other parties—were not willing to play by the old rules.

Additional examples underline the degree of agency that had been created through institutional procedures and rules and how this had the potential to turn into open conflict. At the beginning of the legislative period, every assembly member had to swear an oath to the Egyptian state and its constitution. Several MPs rephrased the oath to express their personal beliefs, including one Social Democrat and former revolutionary activist who swore on the January 25th Revolution, and some Salafist parliamentarians who referred to shari'a in their pledges of fealty. Al-Saqqa, the interim speaker, intervened several times but could not ensure that each parliamentarian abided by the original version.[25] Other incidents in subsequent sessions raised question about the appropriate role of religion in parliamentary life; for example, one Salafist assembly member made a call to prayer during a parliamentary session. The FJP tried to forestall further interruptions by responding with a reference to the prophet's tradition, and hence stayed in the realm of Islamist argumentation.[26]

24. "Political Hysteria," *Al-Ahram Weekly*, May 3–9, 2012, no. 1096.

25. "Chaotic Start to Egypt's First Democratically Elected Parliament," *New York Times*, Jan. 23, 2012.

26. Mayy el Sheikh, "Islamist's Call to Prayer Ruled Out of Order in Egyptian Parliament," *The Lede* (blog), *New York Times*, Feb. 7, 2012, http://thelede.blogs.nytimes.com /2012/02/07/islamists-call-to-prayer-ruled-out-of-order-in-egyptian-parliament/.

These observations are indicative of both continuity and innovation in parliamentary practices by new actors as well as old actors in new positions. Matters of public relevance were channeled into the assembly while, at the same time, the majority party tried to instrumentalize the institution. Friction and conflicts became visible. Yet even as MPs inside the assembly fought over power and legitimacy, the dissolution of the body was already underway.

Phase 3: The Fight between the Institutions, June 2012–June 2013

The first important interinstitutional conflict occurred within the judiciary in mid-May 2012, when the Supreme Administrative Court ruled the existing electoral law, and thus parliament, to be unconstitutional. The case was transferred to the Supreme Constitutional Court, which was expected to issue a verdict quickly. To forestall a dissolution of the People's Assembly, in which the distribution of seats greatly favored the FJP, the majority party introduced a draft law that forbade the SCC from having a say in laws passed by three-fourths of parliamentary votes or in the assembly itself. This sparked intense protest from the SCC judges as well as human rights activists.[27] In the end, the judges won out, eventually dissolving parliament on June 14, 2012, right before Mursi was elected president on June 24.[28] The SCC decision prevented the Muslim Brotherhood from ever controlling both the legislative and executive powers at the same time. Mursi sought to reinstall the People's Assembly, but his decision was legally contested. The parliament remained dissolved for more than three years.

Another interinstitutional battleground was the question of the constituent assembly. Just before the final dissolution of the People's Assembly, the Brotherhood assembly members joined forces with the ultraconservative Salafists to elect another constituent assembly.[29] This time, the selection

27. "Draft Law Clash," *Al-Ahram Weekly*, May 24–30, 2012, no. 1099.

28. Issandr el Amrani, "In Translation, the SCC's Verdicts," *The Arabist* (blog), June 18, 2012, http://www.arabist.net/blog/2012/6/18/in-translation-the-sccs-verdicts.html.

29. The first constituent assembly had been elected in March 2012. Yet they voted for 65 percent Islamist MPs and public figures, turning a blind eye to calls for a representative

of candidates was based on a previous agreement between various actors representing different political and religious groups, syndicates, and law experts. However, the major division between Islamist and non-Islamist groups would continue to overshadow the negotiations. Furthermore, the battle over the future political order turned into a race of constitutional declarations. The Supreme Council of the Armed Forces released amendments to the March 2011 interim constitution on June 17, 2012—the day of the presidential runoff between Ahmad Shafiq and Muhammad Mursi—in a clear attempt to impose limitations on the future president's powers by making the SCAF the commander in chief. The SCAF also declared itself responsible for nominating the defense minister.[30] At the same time, these amendments legitimized the military's oppressive tactics against political activists by allowing the deployment of military police and secret service against civilians.[31] On August 12, 2012, the newly elected president, Muhammad Mursi, the Muslim Brotherhood's candidate, abrogated the previous constitutional declaration by the SCAF.[32] This first appeared to be a civilian counterattack, as Mursi restored all executive and legislative powers that he, as president, had originally held in the constitutional declaration of March 2011. Yet he also confirmed all army privileges mentioned in the previous SCAF declaration. While Mursi sent the two army leaders—Muhammad Husayn Tantawi, the minister of defense and general commander of the armed forces, and the army's chief of staff, Sami 'Anan—into early retirement, he likewise appointed field marshal 'Abd

---

assembly. With just six Copts and six women, out of a total of one hundred people, this composition was not regarded as legitimate. This led liberal, social democratic, and leftist parties to boycott the elections to the assembly and to leave the body after it was convened. It was then dissolved by a decree from the Supreme Administrative Court the following month.

30. This ensured the generals' decision-making role on matters of peace and war with Israel and safeguarded the annual 1.2 billion dollars of US military aid Egypt received.

31. For further details, see Weipert-Fenner (2013b).

32. For an English translation of the declaration, see "English Text of President Morsi's New Egypt Constitutional Declaration," *Ahram Online*, Aug. 12, 2012, http://english.ahram.org.eg/News/50248.aspx.

al-Fattah al-Sisi as minister of defense. Taken together, these changes seemed to result from a supposedly new power-sharing deal emerging with the army, which retained its privileges yet remained in the background (Pioppi 2013).

Mursi furthermore secured the right to appoint a new constituent assembly in case the existing one was dissolved once again. The latter move ensured that the Muslim Brotherhood's control over the constitutional process remained independent of the judiciary. In the event the existing assembly was ruled unconstitutional, the president could simply reinstall another assembly in line with the Brothers' interests. In spite of this, the Supreme Administrative Court transferred the question of the constituent assembly to the Supreme Constitutional Court in October. Meanwhile, most blocs that were supposed to ensure that the assembly would be recognized as representative of Egyptian society again withdrew from the body. These ranged from the Egyptian Bloc (Free Egyptians, Egyptian Social Democratic Party, and Tagammu Party) to the Karama Party, the Socialist Popular Alliance Party, and the Democratic Front Party.[33] About two weeks before the SCC ruling on the constituent assembly was expected, Mursi intervened once more with another constitutional declaration. On November 22, just a day after his successful mediation between Hamas and Israel, Mursi declared himself, as well as the legislative and constituent assemblies, immune to jurisdiction. He tried to set incentives for the edict's acceptance by firing the public prosecutor responsible for acquitting officials accused of organizing violence against protesters in the January 25th Revolution. However, this move proved to be completely miscalculated, as public protests mounted against his concentration of power. Still fearing that the SCC would dissolve the constituent assembly, Mursi and the FJP rushed the drafting process through, and on November

33. The number of withdrawals of prominent individuals increased, including activists (Manal al-Tibi), politicians ('Amr Musa), and representatives of syndicates (journalists and farmers) and Christian churches. "Journalists, Farmers' Syndicates Withdraw from Egypt's Constituent Assembly," *Ahram Online*, Nov. 20, 2012, http://english.ahram .org.eg/NewsContent/1/64/58676/Egypt/Politics-/Journalists,-farmers-syndicates-with draw-from-Egyp.aspx.

30 the assembly passed the entire draft version, which was put to public referendum only two weeks later.

The protests against Mursi's decree were then joined by demonstrations against the rushed drafting process, the lack of representation for certain groups in the process itself, and the omission of civil rights in the text. A closer look at the constitutional text provides a more nuanced, though still ambivalent, picture.[34] In fact, although the human rights and civil liberties one would expect in a liberal democratic constitution were present, they were largely limited by a stipulation that their specific implementation would be regulated by law. Leaving rights to be further defined by laws was a widely held practice under Mubarak to hollow out formal democratic rights: the respective laws were either never passed or they left all interpretive power to the government. An example of this stipulation in the 2012 constitution was workers' rights mentioned in the text, the enforcement of which depended on specific regulatory laws.[35] Secular parties and civil society criticized the considerable loopholes in the socially conservative formulations concerning public order, public moral, and the genuine character of the Egyptian family. Besides legal concerns, their allegations were driven by deep-seated mistrust in the Muslim Brothers' willingness to implement the constitution in a democratic, inclusive manner that respected women's and minority rights. This mistrust was further fueled by concessions made to the army and Salafists. First, and most importantly, the army was appeased by the constitutional draft that ensured future defense ministers would always be chosen from among the officers. The army kept control over its financial affairs, though with some civilian oversight in the form of a newly formed national defense council. Civilians could still be put on trial before military courts. Second, the role

---

34. Irene Weipert-Fenner, "Der unbekannte Text: was steht in Ägyptens umkämpfter Verfassung?" *Sicherheitspolitik* (blog), Dec. 13, 2012, http://www.sicherheitspolitik-blog .de/2012/12/13/was-steht-in-aegyptens-umkaempfter-verfassung/.

35. "Not for All Egyptians," *Egypt Independent*, Nov. 20, 2012, http://www.egypt independent.com/node/1253686; "The Draft Constitution: Where We Stand on Social Rights," *Egypt Independent*, Nov. 19, 2012, http://www.egyptindependent.com/node /1252381.

of religion required a balancing act between the ultraconservative Salafists and liberals, which still raised considerable criticism. Crucial here was the conflict over Article 2 of the old and the new constitution, which claimed that shari'a is the main source of legislation in Egypt. The Salafist wing tried to replace the word *source* with *rulings*, which was contested by secular groups as well as Muslim Brothers and al-Azhar representatives. The latter argued that rulings were in flux, whereas the constitution should settle issues in the long run. With the Brothers' veto, Article 2 remained untouched, but the debate shifted to a new Article 219, which read "The principles of Islamic shari'a include general evidence, foundational rules, rules of jurisprudence, and credible sources accepted in Sunni doctrines and by the larger community" (IDEA 2012). Article 219 also constituted a novelty, as, for the first time, the state religion was narrowed to Sunni Islam. The term *rulings* also raised criticism when it was added to Article 68 on gender equality, which would only have been granted when not in conflict with the rulings of the shari'a. The provision, which would have opened the door for discrimination against women, was dropped on November 7. Although the constitutional draft included articles that guaranteed state care for divorced women, it did not empower women but rather kept them in need of external protection. Further provisions defined an active role for the state in setting the school curriculum for Islam classes and in the protection of religion from insults against prophets.[36]

From an institutional perspective, the new political system enlarged parliamentary powers and, remarkably, continued the course set out in the 2007 amendments. The legislature, now called Majlis al-nuwwab (Chamber of Deputies), like the parliament from 1879 to 1882 and 1923 to 1952, had the right to withdraw confidence from the government (Article 126) and had greater influence in selecting the prime minister.[37] The regula-

---

36. See Nathan Brown, "Egypt's Constitution: Islamists Prepare for a Long Political Battle," *Carnegie Endowment for International Peace*, Oct. 23, 2012, http://carnegie endowment.org/2012/10/23/egypt-s-constitution-islamists-prepare-for-long-political -battle/e4wv).

37. If the president's choice failed to gain a majority in the assembly, he would have to pick a member of the majority party from within parliament. If this candidate was not

tions also elevated the Shura Council to a full legislative body (Article 131) and they kept the budgetary directives from the 2007 version of constitutional amendment, including the right to amend the budget (Article 117).

None of the parliaments under these regulations would ever see the light of day. The new constitution was overthrown along with President Muhammad Mursi. After months of the so-called *Tamarrud* (rebel) campaign, which culminated in mass protests on June 30, 2013, the army intervened and deposed Mursi on July 3. Since then, Egypt's shaky transformation process has become a clear return to authoritarianism. Human rights abuses are widespread, targeting Islamists and secular groups alike, while political freedoms and rights are much more limited than they were during the final decade of Mubarak's reign. In this context, a new constitution was drafted in late 2014 and a new parliament was elected in fall 2015, but it was, unfortunately, just another re-creation of an autocratic parliament.

General Lessons: The Five Characteristics of the Autocratic Parliament

Analyzing the Egyptian parliament over almost 150 years has brought to light five lessons about how the autocratic parliament is linked to power and legitimacy as well as to regime stability and destabilization. First of all, for nearly 150 years, the autocratic parliament as a whole never became a lobbyist for democratization in Egypt. This does not necessarily mean that it could never become one. What we can draw from this observation is that there is no inherent trajectory toward democracy in a parliamentary institution. This is not surprising when we consider that the majority of MPs were part of the greater ruling elite coalition—mostly second-tier elites. Why should they promote the change of a regime that granted them a share in privileges, resources, and decision making (which, in turn, allowed them to keep their position by fulfilling their personal or respective clients' interests)? Of course, when the regime is unable to fulfill its

---

elected either, the parliament itself appointed a candidate. These regulations, of course, only prove effective in a democratic order with the possibility for cohabitation.

part of the relationship over a longer period of time, this trust will erode; depending on power constellations and legitimacy beliefs, a change within autocratic political systems and regime subtypes (such as from monarchy to military regime) might seem less attractive than the shift to a democratic regime. Yet there are a lot of "maybes" in this equation. Without excluding the possibility of parliament becoming a prodemocracy force altogether, we must acknowledge that the autocratic parliament *works according to the logic of an authoritarian regime.*

Second, in the analysis of this very logic, we can see that parliament grew stronger in different autocratic political systems, expanding its power in two different ways. On the one hand, we can find an *incremental expansion of rights*, with parliament increasing its participation in the areas of consultation, agenda setting, and decision making. In most cases, the actual use of the rights granted and the acquisition of practical knowledge on how to use them predate the expansion of formal rights. Expertise and experience, informal rules, and institutional knowledge paved the way for incremental steps forward. As a result, rights continued to expand until the end of the period in four out of the five political systems.[38] This also holds true for the means available to hold the government accountable. The tools of interpellations and questions date back to the 1860s, yet their usage generally only increased some time after a new parliamentary body had been installed. Parliament's answers to the king's speeches from the throne (and later those of the president) at opening parliamentary sessions repeatedly evolved into a serious critical reply to executive policies. The internal structure of the parliament developed (through the establishment of committees, for example), and we see the expansion of policy fields in which parliament's consultation, approval, or legislative participation was needed, including for budgetary and tax matters. All in all, the expansion of parliamentary rights generally occurred slowly and incrementally, yet

38. The only exception was the constitutional monarchy, during which parliament increased its powers early on, then faced a harsh curtailment of rights in the constitution of 1930. After the old constitutional order was reinstalled, the majority party in parliament was dominated by large landowners, and it mainly engaged in struggles with the king and with the British, leading to a loss of legitimacy of the political system as a whole.

not necessarily in a contentious manner. At times, this expansion became visible through symbolic change, such as when, in 1879, the parliamentarians renamed the representative body from Majlis shura al-nuwwab to Majlis al-nuwwab. The elimination of the word *shura* signified that the body had overcome the limitation of merely providing consultation.

On the other hand, parliamentary power also expanded when the head of state and the core elite *granted rights to the members of parliament as concessions* to ensure their goodwill and cooperation. In contrast to the parliament-led empowerment, this often happened very quickly and at a moment when the executive faced a crisis due to foreign policy issues (military defeat, unpopular alignments), domestic problems (unpopular socioeconomic reforms, financial or socioeconomic crises), or the intervention of external actors (imperialism, international financial institutions). Parliament then gained importance either as a counterforce to the head of state's political adversaries, or as his supporter against a contentious public. Concessions included the expansion of consultation and decision-making power, with budgetary and tax matters falling under particular parliamentary scrutiny (1870s, 1914/15, 1967, 1990s). Whether this happened out of necessity in a struggle for survival or because the core elite considered empowering parliament an easy way to bolster regime support, the effect was always the same: the co-opted forces in parliament learned how to use their new rights. In so doing, parliamentarians very quickly came to conceive these rights as an entitlement rather than as granted from above.

This brings us to the third major lesson: parliament has the potential to become contentious. We observed heated disputation inside parliament directed mostly toward the government, in very rare cases toward the head of state, and also toward fellow parliamentarians. This contentious behavior was exhibited not only by opposition MPs, but also by members of the ruling party. Contestation was observed in regard to political actors, the policies they passed, and their institutional actions. Actors, policies, and institutions were evaluated according to norms, shared beliefs about what was held as right or wrong at a specific point in time. The general rule across all cases is that *breaking norms on a large scale or at a fast pace causes contention*. Institutional lines of conflict occurred in relation to which actor was held responsible for it. Parliament made these developments visible and could fuel existing discontent; it could be seen as the institution responsible for breaking norms, or as the one challenging another institution for doing so.

Institutional norms were among those contested. *Limiting or withdrawing parliamentary rights caused contention* among the parliamentarians and, at times, even an explicit refusal to obey. This finding goes against the widespread assumption that the core elite can manipulate the political system and its institutions as it wishes. What may have easily been granted to the assembly at one point could not be as easily removed once the parliamentarians came to think of the concessions as "normal" rights attached to their office. Each time parliament extended its participation into the realm of political discourse or even decision making, it did not easily cede these rights (1879–82, 1930–36, 1976–80). In these cases, only major changes (external military intervention or leadership change) resolved the conflict with the executive.

Norms also mattered greatly in terms of policies, yet we find that some policy areas matter more than others. Throughout all of the political systems studied here, *socioeconomic issues played a pivotal role* inside the assembly, both in relation to the executive and in terms of the public's perception of parliament and the entire political system. Inside the assembly, parliamentarians lobbied for policies in relation to their own economic background: landowners would focus on agricultural policies (from the first parliament in 1866 on), while private businessmen focused on economic liberalization (toward a biased version of crony capitalism that would benefit them). As a simple relationship of exchange, elites sought to gain something from their integration into the political system and from their support for the regime. In so doing, parliamentarians simply abided by clientelist logic: they received benefits from the head of state via their parliamentary seat and, in turn, remained loyal to the regime. But things proved to be more complex than this in reality.

Over the decades, the assemblies also channeled general socioeconomic discontent into parliament and used it as leverage against the executive. This can be explained by the role of MPs as intermediaries or brokers whose power relied on the support of their constituencies and the loyalty of these constituencies to the regime. The parliamentarians, as *nuwwab al-khidmat* (deputies of services), needed to deliver services and resources to their constituencies. As a result, the MPs—as brokers—had incentives to take an active role in crafting socioeconomic policies that would ensure a constant flow of socioeconomic benefits toward their clients. Given the limitations on resources (in most countries in the world), they would need to exert pressure on the executive in the mid to long term so that services and resources would continue to be channeled to their constituencies, and to stop, or at least slow down, reforms that cut back on social welfare policies. Discontent can grow slowly as resource flows dry up, or it can explode in the wake of sudden, harsh measures, such as al-Sadat's attempt to reduce bread subsidies in 1977. The latter not only caused public protests but also turned parliament into an even greater critical voice of the *infitah* reforms. One of the first moves of al-Sadat's successor, Mubarak, was to reduce the pace of reforms and to compensate and balance different elite groups.

A closer look at the dynamics of norms reveals that the different fields of legitimacy claims and beliefs (policy, polity, and identity of single actors) are interrelated. A constantly negative evaluation of major policies can influence perceptions of the decision-making group and political institutions. This can potentially grow into a full-fledged regime crisis, as witnessed in the last years under Mubarak.

Fourth, *asymmetric power distributions shape interinstitutional actions*, yet one can never speak of a monopoly on power held by a single side. As such, interinstitutional relations involve negotiation and bargaining, which are always based on an assessment of power resources as the bargaining capital held by a certain actor and the relevant others. These processes proved to be rife with *miscalculations and unintended consequences*. On the one hand, the parliamentarians were forced to consider their actual power and the regime's dependence on them or the represented groups. On the other hand, the ruling elite also had to estimate the effect of its actions on the various actors whose cooperation it needed, as well as the extent to which it actually relied on them. We can observe a constant process of trial and error as to who can act and to what extent. Miscalculations regularly arose in these complex struggles, which were both enabled and constrained by parliament. For example, soon after al-Sadat opened the political arena—most probably as a way to increase his legitimacy—he believed he could easily backtrack when parliament became an outspoken critic of his economic and foreign policies. Yet the harsh deliberalization measures drew heated criticism from oppositional parliamentarians. Oppositional forces made miscalculations as well. When the electoral law designed by the ruling elite was ruled unconstitutional twice in the 1980s, the oppositional parties and the Muslim Brotherhood overestimated their political weight and tried to blackmail the regime into granting them more rights by boycotting the elections in 1990. Apparently the ruling elite did not take much heed, and the result was a parliament without relevant opposition.

A recurrent pattern is revealed in the numerous forms that interinstitutional and internal power relations can assume in an autocratic parliament: parliament always negotiated with or against the government in order to achieve its aims and, in so doing, it exhibited a responsiveness to major policy issues. In most cases, the head of state was above such struggles. During these times, public and group-specific needs were channeled into the assembly, and as long as the government remained responsive to these demands, contention was largely avoided. Compromise on both sides safeguarded a balance between different interests. However, as the fifth parliamentary characteristic shows, the *balance was lost whenever responsiveness decreased* as a result of a major party (the Wafd in the 1940s), a group within the party (the business wing of the NDP in the 2000s), or the head of state (Tawfiq before the British occupation, al-Sadat at the end of the 1970s) opting to exercise power without taking other interests or beliefs into account. Responsiveness was also perceived as low when interinstitutional struggles rather than pressing policy issues dominated political life (pre-1952); this behavior contributed to the public perception of political paralysis. Strikingly, with the exception of al-Sadat (who was assassinated in the middle of his legitimacy crisis), all examples of such *diminished responsiveness resulted in a breakdown of the political system or regime subtype* (1882, 1952, 2011).

Building on these five characteristics, the autocratic parliament can be an *indicator, catalyst, and an agent of change within an autocracy.* As such, it can also provide additional insights into democratization, yet not as a prodemocratic force. As the intermediary between different political groups and the executive, the autocratic parliament can shed light on fault lines within the ruling elite as well as legitimacy crises, hinting at "windows of opportunity" for regime change. At the same time, there is no inherent determinism that leads parliaments to evolve into democracy. Authoritarian regimes are flexible and can deal with crises. Still, it is important to distinguish extraordinary times of conflict and imbalance between different elite groups from a "normal" level of dispute regarding policies, political actors, and institutions. Departures from this "normality" allow us to detect and assess developments that may indicate change within a regime or even the potential for a change of regime. As observed in several cases here, political "business as usual" took place when parliament and the executive respected a certain consensus on major norms with regard to policies and political actors and institutions. This consensus, however, was never static but always developed, usually in a steady and incremental manner. Breaches of such consensus have caused contestation and even led to regime destabilization. Parliament, as an institution, allows us to observe and detect when a new consensus has been found, when a group that has violated norms returns to the old established order, or when the regime has been shaken as a whole, leading to a major political reconfiguration.

Once such a rupture does occur, the autocratic parliament can help us better understand the ensuing political transformation processes. By studying institutional practices before and after major events such as the ouster of an autocratic ruler, we can learn much about the continuity and change of political norms and practices and better explore the gray areas of democratization. Regime change is never a clear-cut shift from one state of equilibrium to the next; how new and old political actors behave is shaped by their prior experiences in the authoritarian regime, as is the new institutional order they create. Bargaining processes and institutional practices learned and developed in the autocratic parliament may also be applied to other political systems and regimes. Oversight rights, committee work, plenary debates, and similar practices within an authoritarian parliament can serve as a toolkit for democratic parliaments; some tools might require democratic readjustment while others might simply continue to work in the new regime. A number of institutional developments under authoritarian rule—such as greater legislative participation or increased oversight rights—might retrospectively be interpreted as the evolution of democracy. While we know that these liberties can be reversed by the authoritarian elite, the rights and the practices that evolve around them may present themselves as a pool of established political procedures for a democratic regime once, and if, transformation takes place.

When comparing the "before and after" of parliamentary practices and trying to judge whether a "real" process of democratization is underway, it is crucial to remember that a number of shortcomings ascribed to autocratic parliaments happen to also be general paradoxes of any parliament. There will always exist a certain degree of tension within the parliamentarians as representatives who serve both their own constituencies and the people's interest in general. Moreover, informal power hierarchies among the members of parliament, whom we deem to be equal, will always persist. Party politics can heavily influence the behavior of parliamentarians once elected, even if the member of parliament is formally independent. Finally, decision making always proves a messy endeavor: it is a quid pro quo bargaining process that does not accord to the idea of the parliamentarian as a gentleman or lady who only pursues higher aims (Loewenberg 2016). Keeping these inevitable tensions in mind should prevent us from using an idealized version of democratic parliaments as a benchmark for evaluating their counterparts in autocracies or regimes in transformation. Formal rules, both in autocracies and democracies, only grant us limited insights into how parliaments actually function and why they matter. We must always compare them to their institutional practices, which evolve over time and which shape the regimes we seek to better understand. This is the only way that we can engage in a truly comparative study of democratic and autocratic parliaments, and of the gray areas in between.

Bibliography

Index

Bibliography

Egyptian Parliament, Official Gazette, *al-Jarida al-rasmiyya*

Much of my research is based on an analysis of debates and speeches during Egyptian parliamentary sessions from 2005 to 2009. These parliamentary minutes were published in the official gazette of Egypt, *al-Jarida al-rasmiyya*. In 2010, these documents were available on the official homepage of the parliament, and I was able to access and save these files for use in my analysis. My sources include minutes from the following dates and sessions; the page numbers refer to the official gazette in which the minutes were published.

Jan. 2, 2005, no. 21, p. 9–66.
Jan. 3, 2005, no. 22, p. 12–31.
Jan. 16, 2005, no. 26, p. 3–60.
June 8, 2008, no. 118, p. 8–60.
June 8, 2008, no. 118, annex, p. 1–35.
June 16, 2008, no. 131, p. 4–13.
June 16, 2008, no. 131, annex, p. 34–35.
June 18, 2008, no. 139, p. 49–60.
June 18, 2008, no. 139, annex, p. 81–88.
Mar. 22, 2009, no. 66, p. 22–68.
Mar. 22, 2009, no. 67, p. 3–23.
Mar. 22, 2009, no. 68, p. 3–23.

Other Sources Cited

Abdalla, Nadine. 2015. "Neoliberal Policies and the Egyptian Trade Union Movement: Politics of Containment and the Limits of Resistance." In *Neoliberal Governmentality and the Future of the State in the Middle East and North Africa*, edited by Emel Akçali, 123–43. New York: Palgrave Macmillan.

Abd-El Elah, Wafaa, Wadouda Badran, and Azza Wahby, eds. 1996. *Privatization in Egypt: The Debate in the People's Assembly*. Cairo: Center for Political Research and Studies—Faculty of Economics and Political Science.

Abdel Fattah, Nabil. 2008. "The Political Role of the Egyptian Judiciary." In *Judges and Political Reform in Egypt*, edited by Nathalie Bernard-Maugiron, 71–89. Cairo: American Univ. in Cairo Press.

Abdel-Malek, Anouar. 1975. *Idéologie et Renaissance Nationale: L'Egypte Moderne*. Paris: Éditions Anthropos.

Abdelrahman, Maha M. 2014. *Egypt's Long Revolution: Protest Movements and Uprisings*. Abingdon, Oxon: Routledge.

Abi-Hamad, Saad. 2012. "The Colonial State and Its Multiple Relations: A Case Study of Egypt." *Comparative Studies of South Asia, Africa and the Middle East* 32 (1): 1–12. https://doi.org/10.1215/1089201X-1545372.

Abul-Magd, Zeinab. 2010. "Rebellion in the Time of Cholera: Failed Empire, Unfinished Nation in Egypt, 1840–1920." *Journal of World History* 21 (4): 691–719.

Adler, Emanuel. 1997. "Seizing the Middle Ground: Constructivism in World Politics." *European Journal of International Relations* 3 (3): 319–63.

Aglan, Sabry. 2003. "Industrial Development: Progress and Challenges in the Future." In *Egypt in the Twenty-First Century: Challenges for Development*, edited by Mohamad R. el-Ghonemy, 160–80. London: Routledge.

Albrecht, Holger. 2013. *Raging against the Machine: Political Opposition under Authoritarianism in Egypt*. Syracuse: Syracuse Univ. Press.

Albrecht, Holger, and Dina Bishara. 2011. "Back on Horseback: The Military and Political Transformation in Egypt." *Middle East Law and Governance* 3: 13–23.

Albrecht, Holger, and Oliver Schlumberger. 2004. "'Waiting for Godot': Regime Change without Democratization in the Middle East." *International Political Science Review* 25 (4): 371–92.

Alissa, Sufyan. 2007. "The Political Economy of Reform in Egypt: Understanding the Role of Institutions." Carnegie Papers 5. Washington: Carnegie Endowment for International Peace.

Altman, Israel Elad. 1981. *Middle East Contemporary Survey*. Vol. 4. Boulder: Westview Press.

Amin, Galal. 2011. *Egypt in the Era of Hosni Mubarak, 1981–2011*. Cairo: American Univ. in Cairo Press.

Arafat, Alaa al-Din. 2009. *The Mubarak Leadership and Future of Democracy in Egypt.* 1st ed. New York: Palgrave Macmillan.

'Awad, Huda, and Hasanayn Tawfiq. 1996. *Al-Ikhwan al-Muslimun wa-l-Siyasa fi Misr. Dirasa fi al-Tahalufat al-Intikhabiyya wa-l-Mumarasat al-Barlamaniyya li-l-Ikhwan al-Muslimun [sic] fi Zill al-Ta'addudiyya al-Siyasiyya al-Muqayyada (1984–1990).* Cairo: Markaz al-Mahrusa li-l-Nashr wa-l-Khidmat al-Suhufiyya wa-l-Ma'lumat.

Awadi, Hesham al-. 2004. *In Pursuit of Legitimacy: The Muslim Brothers and Mubarak, 1982–2000.* Library of Modern Middle East Studies 46. London, New York: Tauris.

Ayalon, Ami. 1995. *Middle East Contemporary Survey.* Vol. 16. Boulder: Westview Press.

———. 1997. *Middle East Contemporary Survey.* Vol. 19. Boulder: Westview Press.

Baaklini, Abdo I., Guilain Denoeux, and Robert Springborg. 1999. *Legislative Politics in the Arab World: The Resurgence of Democratic Institutions.* Boulder: Lynne Rienner Publishers.

Badrawi, Malak. 2000. *Political Violence in Egypt, 1910–1924: Secret Societies, Plots and Assassinations.* Richmond: Curzon.

———. 2005. "Financial Cerberus? The Egyptian Parliament, 1924–52." In *Re-Envisioning Egypt 1919–1952,* edited by Arthur Goldschmidt, Ami Johnson, and Barak Salmoni, 94–122. Cairo: American Univ. in Cairo Press.

Baer, Gabriel. 1962. *A History of Landownership in Modern Egypt, 1800–1950.* London: Oxford Univ. Press.

Barakat, 'Ali. 1977. *Tatawwur al-Milkiyya al-Zira'iyya fi Misr, 1813–1914, wa-Atharuhu 'ala l-Haraka al-Siyasiyya.* Cairo: Dar al-Thaqafa al-Jadida.

Beattie, Kirk J. 2000. *Egypt during the Sadat Years.* New York: Palgrave Macmillan.

Beinin, Joel. 2001. *Workers and Peasants in the Modern Middle East.* Cambridge: Cambridge Univ. Press.

———. 2010. *Justice for All: The Struggle for Workers' Rights in Egypt.* Washington: Solidarity Center.

Beinin, Joel, and Marie Duboc. 2013. "A Workers' Social Movement on the Margin of the Global Neoliberal Order, Egypt 2004–2012." In *Social Movements, Mobilization, and Contestation in the Middle East and North Africa,* 2nd ed., edited by Joel Beinin and Frédéric Vairel, 205–27. Stanford: Stanford Univ. Press.

Bell, Stephen. 2011. "Do We Really Need a New 'Constructivist Institutionalism' to Explain Institutional Change?" *British Journal of Political Science* 41 (4): 883–906.

Bernard-Maugiron, Nathalie. 2008. "The 2007 Constitutional Amendments in Egypt, and Their Implications on the Balance of Power." *Arab Law Quarterly* 22 (4): 397–417. https://doi.org/10.1163/157302508X374429.

Binder, Leonard. 1978. *In a Moment of Enthusiasm.* Chicago: Univ. of Chicago Press.

———. 1988. *Islamic Liberalism: A Critique of Development Ideologies.* Chicago: Univ. of Chicago Press.

Bishara, Dina. 2018. *Contesting Authoritarianism: Labor Challenges to the State in Egypt.* Cambridge: Cambridge Univ. Press.

Blaydes, Lisa. 2011. *Elections and Distributive Politics in Mubarak's Egypt.* Cambridge: Cambridge Univ. Press.

Blunt, Wilfrid Scawen. 1922. *A Secret History of the British Occupation of Egypt: Being a Personal Narrative of Events by Wilfrid Scawen Blunt.* New York: Knopf.

Blyth, Mark. 2002. *Great Transformations: Economic Ideas and Institutional Change in the Twentieth Century.* Cambridge: Cambridge Univ. Press.

Botman, Selma. 1991. *Egypt from Independence to Revolution, 1919–1952.* Syracuse: Syracuse Univ. Press.

Brown, Nathan J. 2002. *Constitutions in a Nonconstitutional World: Arab Basic Laws and the Prospects for Accountable Government.* Albany: State Univ. of New York Press.

Brownlee, Jason. 2007. *Authoritarianism in an Age of Democratization.* Cambridge: Cambridge Univ. Press.

Buehler, Matt. 2013. "Safety-Valve Elections and the Arab Spring: The Weakening (and Resurgence) of Morocco's Islamist Opposition Party." *Terrorism and Political Violence* 25: 137–56.

Bush, Ray. 2007. "Politics, Power and Poverty: Twenty Years of Agricultural Reform and Market Liberalisation in Egypt." *Third World Quarterly* 28 (8): 1599–1615.

Bush, Ray, and Habib Ayeb, eds. 2012. *Marginality and Exclusion in Egypt.* London: Zed Books.

Cannon, Byron. 1988. *Politics of Law and the Courts in Nineteenth-Century Egypt.* Salt Lake City: Univ. of Utah Press.

Chamberlain, M. E. 1977. "The Alexandria Massacre of 11 June 1882 and the British Occupation of Egypt." *Middle Eastern Studies* 13 (1): 14–39.

Chen, An. 2015. *The Transformation of Governance in Rural China: Market, Finance and Political Authority*. Cambridge: Cambridge Univ. Press.

Cole, Juan Ricardo. 1993. *Colonialism and Revolution in the Middle East: Social and Cultural Origins of Egypt's 'Urabi Movement*. Princeton: Princeton Univ. Press.

Collombier, Virginie. 2007. "The Internal Stakes of the 2005 Elections: The Struggle for Influence in Egypt's National Democratic Party." *Middle East Journal* 61 (1): 95–111.

Colombe, Marcel. 1951. *L'Évolution de l'Egypte*. Paris: Maisonneuve.

Cook, Steven A. 2007. *Ruling but Not Governing: The Military and Political Development in Egypt, Algeria, and Turkey*. Baltimore: Johns Hopkins Univ. Press.

Cooper, Mark N. 1982. *The Transformation of Egypt*. Baltimore: Johns Hopkins Univ. Press.

Cuno, Kenneth M. 1992. *The Pasha's Peasants: Land, Society, and Economy in Lower Egypt, 1740–1858*. Cairo: American Univ. in Cairo Press.

Davis, Eric. 1983. *Challenging Colonialism: Bank Miṣr and Egyptian Industrialization, 1920–1941*. Princeton: Princeton Univ. Press.

Dean, Bahaa Ali el, and Mahmoud Mohieldin. 2001. "On the Formulation and Enforcement of Competition Law in Emerging Economies: The Case of Egypt." Working Paper 60. Cairo: Egyptian Center for Economic Studies.

Deeb, Marius. 1979a. *Party Politics in Egypt: The Wafd and its Rivals 1919–1939*. London: Ithaca Press.

———. 1979b. "Labour and Politics in Egypt, 1919–1939." *International Journal of Middle East Studies* 10 (2): 187–203. https://doi.org/10.1017/S0020743800 034760.

Dekmejian, Hrair. 1968. "The U.A.R. National Assembly: A Pioneering Experiment." *Middle Eastern Studies* 4 (4): 361–75.

———. 1971. *Egypt under Nasir: A Study in Political Dynamics*. Albany: State Univ. of New York Press.

Eggert, Friederike. 2011. "Wettbewerbsrecht in Ägypten—Ausgangspunkt für Reformen gegen Korruption." *Zeitschrift für Vergleichende Rechtswissenschaft* 110: 171–96.

Egyptian Initiative for Personal Rights. 2009. "Challenges Facing Health Expenditure in Egypt. Report on the Proceedings of a Roundtable Discussion." Cairo: EIPR, https://eipr.org/sites/default/files/reports/pdf/Health_Expenditure_in_Egypt.pdf.

Eldakak, Ahmed. 2012. "Approaching Rule of Law in Post-Revolution Egypt. Where We Were, Where We Are, and Where We Should Be." *U.C. David Journal of international Law and Policy* 18 (2): 261–307.

Electoral Institute for Sustainable Democracy in Africa. 2012. "EISA Election Witnessing Mission Report Egypt. The People's Assembly and Shura Council Elections November 2011–February 2012." https://www.eisa.org.za/pdf/egy2012eomr.pdf.

Elshobaki, Amr. 2009. *Les Frères Musulmans des Origines à nos Jours*. Paris: Karthala.

EzzelArab, AbdelAziz. 2002. *European Control and Egypt's Traditional Elites: A Case Study in Elite Economic Nationalism*. Lewiston: Edwin Mellen Press.

———. 2004. "The Experiment of Sharif Pasha's Cabinet (1879): An Inquiry into the Historiography of Egypt's Elite Movement." *International Journal of Middle East Studies* 36 (4): 561–89.

———. 2009. "The Fiscal and Constitutional Program of Egypt's Traditional Elites in 1879: A Documentary and Contextual Analysis of 'al-La'iha al-Wataniyya' [The National Program]." *Journal of the Economic and Social History of the Orient* 52 (2): 301–24. https://doi.org/10.1163/156852009X434364.

Fahmy, Ninette S. 2002. *The Politics of Egypt: State-Society Relationship*. London: RoutledgeCurzon.

Fahmy Menza, Mohamed. 2013. *Patronage Politics in Egypt: The National Democratic Party and Muslim Brotherhood in Cairo*. New York: Routledge.

Farah, Nadia Ramsis. 2009. *Egypt's Political Economy: Power Relations in Development*. Cairo: American Univ. in Cairo.

Finianos, Ghassan. 2002. *Islamistes, Apologists et Libres Penseurs*. Pessac: Presses Univ. de Bordeaux.

Finnemore, Martha. 1996. *National Interests in International Society*. Ithaca: Cornell Univ. Press.

Friedrichs, Jörg, and Friedrich Kratochwil. 2009. "On Acting and Knowing: How Pragmatism Can Advance International Relations Research and Methodology." *International Organization* 63: 701–31.

Galbraith, John, and Afaf Lutfi al-Sayyid Marsot. 1978. "The British Occupation of Egypt: Another View." *International Journal of Middle East Studies* 9 (4): 471–88.

Gandhi, Jennifer. 2008. *Political Institutions under Dictatorship*. Cambridge: Cambridge Univ. Press.

Gandhi, Jennifer, and Adam Przeworski. 2007. "Authoritarian Institutions and the Survival of Autocrats." *Comparative Political Studies* 40 (11): 1279–1301. https://doi.org/10.1177/0010414007305817.

Geddes, Barbara. 1999. "What Do we Know about Democratization after Twenty Years?" *Annual Review of Political Science* 2 (1): 115–44.

Gelvin, James. 2006. "The 'Politics of Notables' Forty Years After." *Middle East Studies Association Bulletin* 40 (1): 19–29.

Gershoni, Israel, and James Jankowski. 1987. *Egypt, Islam, and the Arabs: The Search for Egyptian Nationhood, 1900–1930.* Oxford: Oxford Univ. Press.

Goldschmidt, Arthur. 2013. *Historical Dictionary of Egypt.* 4th ed. Historical Dictionaries of Africa. Lanham: Scarecrow Press, Inc.

Gordon, Joel. 1989. "The False Hopes of 1950: The Wafd's Last Hurrah and the Demise of Egypt's Old Order." *International Journal of Middle East Studies* 21 (2): 193–214. https://doi.org/10.1017/S0020743800032281.

Green, Daniel. 2002. "Constructivist Comparative Politics: Framework and Foundations." In *Constructivism and Comparative Politics,* edited by Daniel Green, 3–59. Armonk: Sharpe.

Hadenius, Axel, and Jan Teorell. 2007. "Pathways from Authoritarianism." *Journal of Democracy* 18 (1): 143–56.

Hall, Peter A., and Rosemary C. R. Taylor. 1996. "Political Science and the Three New Institutionalisms." *Political Studies* 44 (5): 936–57. https://doi.org/10.1111/j.1467-9248.1996.tb00343.x.

Harik, Ilya. 1973. "The Single Party as a Subordinate Movement: The Case of Egypt." *World Politics* 26 (1): 80–105.

———. 1974. *The Political Mobilization of Peasants: A Study of an Egyptian Community.* Bloomington: Indiana Univ. Press.

Harrison, Robert T. 1995. *Gladstone's Imperialism in Egypt: Techniques of Domination.* Westport: Greenwood Press.

Hashem, Ahmed, and Noha el-Mikawy. 2002. "Business Parliamentarians as Locomotives of Information and Production of Knowledge." In *Institutional Reform and Economic Development in Egypt,* edited by Noha el-Mikawy and Heba Handoussa, 49–60. Cairo: American Univ. in Cairo Press.

Hay, Colin. 2004. "Ideas, Interests and Institutions in the Comparative Political Economy of Great Transformations." *Review of International Political Economy* 11 (1): 204–26.

Hicken, Allen. 2011. "Clientelism." *Annual Review of Political Science* 14 (1): 289–310. https://doi.org/10.1146/annurev.polisci.031908.220508.

Hinnebusch, Raymond A. 1981. "Egypt under Sadat: Elites, Power Structure, and Political Change in a Post-Populist State." *Social Problems* 28 (4): 442–64. https://doi.org/10.2307/800057.

―――. 1985. *Egyptian Politics under Sadat: The Post-Populist Development of an Authoritarian-Modernizing State.* Cambridge: Cambridge Univ. Press.

Hourani, Albert. 1983. *Arabic Thought in the Liberal Age, 1798–1938.* Cambridge: Cambridge Univ. Press.

―――. (1968) 1993. "Ottoman Reform and the Politics of Notables." In *The Modern Middle East: A Reader,* edited by Albert Hourani, Philip S. Khoury, and Mary C. Wilson, 83–110. Berkeley: Univ. of California Press.

Hunter, Archie. 2007. *Power and Passion in Egypt: A Life of Sir Eldon Gorst, 1861–1911.* London: I. B. Tauris.

Hunter, F. Robert. 1984. *Egypt under the Khedives, 1805–1879: From Household Government to Modern Bureaucracy.* Pittsburgh: Pittsburgh Univ. Press.

Huntington, Samuel P. 1991. *The Third Wave: Democratization in the Late Twentieth Century.* Norman: Univ. of Oklahoma Press.

'Id, 'Adil. 1984. *Al-Madabit Tatakallam: Mumarasat Na'ib Mu'arid fi Majlis al-Sha'b, 1976–79.* Cairo: Dar al-Marwa.

IDEA (International Institute for Democracy and Electoral Assistance). 2012. English translation of *The New Constitution of the Arab Republic of Egypt.* Accessed June 26, 2019. http://constitutionnet.org/sites/default/files/final _constitution_30_nov_2012_-english-_-idea.pdf.

Ihalainen, Pasi, Cornelia Ilie, and Kari Palonen. 2018. *Parliaments and Parliamentarism: A Comparative History of Disputes about a European Concept.* 1st paperback ed. European Conceptual History. New York, Oxford: Berghahn Books.

Ikeda, Misako. 2005. "Toward the Democratization of Public Education: The Debate in Late Parliamentary Egypt, 1943–52." In *Re-Envisioning Egypt 1919–1952,* edited by Arthur Golschmidt, Ami Johnson, and Barak Salmoni, 218–48. Cairo: American Univ. in Cairo Press.

International Crisis Group. 2008. "Egypt's Muslim Brothers: Confrontation or Integration?" *Middle East/North Africa Report* no. 76. June 18, 2008.

Islahi, Abdul Azim. 1984. *Economic Thought of Ibn al-Qayyim (1292–1350 A.D.).* Jeddah: King Abdulaziz Univ. Press.

Jabarti, 'Abd al-Rahman al-. 1994. *'Aja'ib al-Athar fi al-Tarajim wa-l-Akhbar: 'Abd al-Rahman al-Jabarti's History of Egypt.* 4 vols. Translated by Thomas Philipp and Moshe Perlmann. Stuttgart: Steiner.

Jankowski, James. 1970. "The Egyptian Blue Shirts and the Egyptian Wafd, 1935–1938." *Middle Eastern Studies* 6 (1): 77–95.

———. 2001. *Nasser's Egypt, Arab Nationalism, and the United Arab Republic.* Boulder: Lynne Rienner Publishers.

Jepperson, Ronald, Alexander Wendt, and Peter Katzenstein. 1996. "Norms, Identity, and Culture in National Security." In *The Culture of National Security: Norms and Identity in World Politics*, edited by Peter Katzenstein, 33–75. New York: Columbia Univ. Press.

Kailitz, Steffen. 2009. "Stand und Perspektiven der Autokratieforschung." *Zeitschrift für Politikwissenschaft* 19 (3): 437–88.

Kassem, May. 1999. *In the Guise of Democracy: Governance in Contemporary Egypt.* Reading: Ithaca Press.

———. 2004. *Egyptian Politics: The Dynamics of Authoritarian Rule.* Boulder: Lynne Rienner Publishers.

Katzenstein, Peter. 1996. *Cultural Norms and National Security: Police and Military in Postwar Japan.* Ithaca: Cornell Univ. Press.

Katznelson, Ira, and Barry R. Weingast. 2005. "Intersections between Historical and Rational Choice Institutionalism." In *Preferences and Situations: Points of Intersection between Historical and Rational Choice Institutionalism*, edited by Ira Katznelson and Barry R. Weingast, 1–26. New York: Russell Sage Foundation.

Kechavarzian, Arang. 2009. "Regime Loyalty and Bazari Representation under the Islamic Republic of Iran: Dilemmas of the Society of Islamic Coalition." *International Journal of Middle East Studies* 41 (2): 225–46.

Kienle, Eberhard. 2001. *A Grand Delusion: Democracy and Economic Reform in Egypt.* London, New York: I. B. Tauris.

Koehler, Kevin. 2008. "Authoritarian Elections in Egypt: Formal Institutions and Informal Mechanisms of Rule." *Democratization* 15 (5): 974–90. https://doi.org/10.1080/13510340802362612.

Korany, Bahgat, and Rabab el-Mahdi, eds. 2012. *Arab Spring in Egypt: Revolution and Beyond.* Cairo: American Univ. in Cairo Press.

Lagacé, Clara Boulianne, and Jennifer Gandhi. 2015. "Authoritarian Institutions." In *Routledge Handbook of Comparative Political Institutions*, edited by Jennifer Gandhi and Ruben Ruiz-Rufino, 278–92. London: Routledge.

Landau, Jacob. 1953. *Parliaments and Parties in Egypt.* Tel Aviv: Israel Publishing House.

Levitsky, Steven, and Lucan Way. 2002. "The Rise of Competitive Authoritarianism." *Journal of Democracy* 13 (2): 51–65. https://doi.org/10.1353/jod.2002.0026.

Lia, Brynjar. 1998. *The Society of the Muslim Brothers in Egypt: The Rise of an Islamic Mass Movement 1928–1942*. Reading: Ithaca Press.

Linz, Juan. 1975. "Totalitarian and Authoritarian Regimes." In *Handbook of Political Science*, vol. 3, edited by Fred Greenstein and Nelson Polsby, 175–411. Reading: Addison-Wesley.

Loewenberg, Gerhard. 2007. "Paradoxes of Legislatures." *Daedalus* 136 (3): 56–66. https://doi.org/10.1162/daed.2007.136.3.56.

———. 2016. *On Legislatures: The Puzzle of Representation*. Abingdon, Oxon: Routledge.

Long, Richard. 2004. *British Pro-consuls in Egypt, 1914–1929: The Challenge of Nationalism*. London, New York: RoutledgeCurzon.

Lust-Okar, Ellen. 2005. *Structuring Conflict in the Arab World: Incumbents, Opponents and Institutions*. Cambridge: Cambridge Univ. Press.

Magaloni, Beatriz. 2006. *Voting for Autocracy: Hegemonic Party Survival and Its Demise in Mexico*. Cambridge: Cambridge Univ. Press.

Maghraoui, Abdeslam. 2006. *Liberalism without Democracy: Nationhood and Citizenship in Egypt, 1922–1936*. Durham: Duke Univ. Press.

Mahdi, Rabab el-. 2010. "Labour Protests in Egypt: Causes and Meanings." *Review of African Political Economy* 38 (129): 387–402.

Mahoney, James. 2000. "Path Dependence in Historical Sociology." *Theory and Society* 29 (4): 507–48. https://doi.org/10.1023/A:1007113830879.

Mahoney, James, and Kathleen Ann Thelen, eds. 2010. *Explaining Institutional Change: Ambiguity, Agency, and Power*. Cambridge: Cambridge Univ. Press.

Makram-Ebeid, Mona. 1989. "Political Opposition in Egypt: Democratic Myth or Reality?" *Middle East Journal* 43 (3): 423–36.

Manjoo, Faizal Ahmad. 2008. "Tax Engineering Pertaining to Zakah and Waqf for Poverty Alleviation and Micro-Financing in South Africa." In *Islamic Finance for Micro and Medium Enterprises*, edited by Mohammed Obaidullah, Haji Abdul Latiff, and Hajah Salma, 259–87. Jeddah: Islamic Research and Training Institute, Islamic Development Bank.

March, James, and Johan Olsen. 1984. "The New Institutionalism: Organizational Factors in Political Life." *American Political Science Review* 78 (3): 734–49. https://doi.org/10.2307/1961840.

———. 1989. *Rediscovering Institutions: The Organizational Basis of Politics*. New York: Free Press.

Markaz al-Umma li-l-Dirasat wa-l-Tanmiya and al-Markaz al-Dawli li-l-I'lam. 2005. *Al-Ikhwan fi al-Barlaman 2000. Dirasa Tahliliyya li-Ada' Nuwwab al-Ikhwan al-Muslimin fi Barlaman 2000–2005*. Cairo: Markaz al-Umma li-l-Dirasat wa-l-Tanmiya.

———. 2008. *Al-Ikhwan al-Muslimun fi Barlaman 2005*.

Martin, Shane, Thomas Saalfeld, and Kaare W. Strøm. 2014. "Introduction." In *The Oxford Handbook of Legislative Studies*, edited by Shane Martin, Thomas Saalfeld, and Kaare W. Strøm, 1–28. Oxford: Oxford Univ. Press.

Mayer, Thomas. 1988. *The Changing Past: Egyptian Historiography of the Urabi Revolt, 1882–1983*. Gainesville: Univ. of Florida Press.

Mikawy, Noha el-. 1999. *The Building of Consensus in Egypt's Transition Process*. Cairo: American Univ. in Cairo Press.

———. 2002. "State/Society and Executive/Legislative Relations." In *Institutional Reform and Economic Development in Egypt*, edited by Noha el-Mikawy and Heba Handoussa, 21–36. Cairo: American Univ. in Cairo Press.

Mikawy, Noha el-, and Heba Handoussa, eds. 2002. *Institutional Reform and Economic Development in Egypt*. Cairo: American Univ. in Cairo Press.

Mitchell, Richard P. 1993. *The Society of the Muslim Brothers*. Reprint. Oxford: Oxford Univ. Press.

Moench, Richard. 1988. "Oil, Ideology and State Autonomy in Egypt." *Arab Studies Quarterly* 10 (2): 176–92.

Mommsen, Wolfgang. 1961. *Imperialismus in Ägypten: Der Aufstieg der ägyptischen nationalen Bewegung 1805–1956*. München: Oldenbourg.

Moustafa, Tamir. 2012. "Drafting Egypt's Constitution: Can a New Legal Framework Revive a Flawed Transition?" Brookings Doha Center-Stanford Paper 1. https://www.brookings.edu/wp-content/uploads/2016/06/new1-Drafting-Egypts-New-ConstitutionEnR03.pdf.

Muhsin, Rami, ed. 2008. *Nash'at al-Na'ib fi 500 Yawm. Na'ib al-Sha'b Dr. Jamal Zahran*. Cairo: n.p.

Musa, Salama. 1958. *Tarbiyat Salama Musa*. Cairo: Mu'assasat al-Khanji.

North, Douglass. 1990. *Institutions, Institutional Change and Economic Performance*. Cambridge: Cambridge Univ. Press.

Norton, Philip. 2013. *Parliament in British Politics*. 2nd ed. Contemporary Political Studies. New York: Palgrave Macmillan.

Nullmeier, Frank, and Martin Nonhoff. 2010. "Der Wandel des Legitimitätsdenkens." In *Prekäre Legitimitäten: Rechtfertigung von Herrschaft in der postnationalen Konstellation*, edited by Frank Nullmeier, Dominika Biegon,

Jennifer Gronau, Martin Nonhoff, Henning Schmidtke, and Steffen Schneider, 16–44. Frankfurt am Main: Campus.

Oevermann, Ulrich. 1991. "Genetischer Strukturalismus und das sozialwissenschaftliche Problem der Erklärung der Entstehung des Neuen." In *Jenseits der Utopie*, edited by Stefan Müller-Doohm, 267–336. Frankfurt am Main: Suhrkamp.

———. 1996. Konzeptualisierung von Anwendungsmöglichkeiten und praktischen Arbeitsfeldern der objektiven Hermeneutik. Manifest der objektiv hermeneutischen Sozialforschung. Manuscript, Frankfurt am Main.

———. 2000. "Die Methode der Fallrekonstruktion in der Grundlagenforschung sowie der klinischen und pädagogischen Praxis." In *Die Fallrekonstruktion. Sinnverstehen in der sozialwissenschaftlichen Forschung*, edited by Klaus Kraimer, 58–156. Frankfurt am Main: Suhrkamp.

Owen, Roger. 1969. *Cotton and the Egyptian Economy, 1820–1914: A Study in Trade and Development*. Oxford: Oxford Univ. Press.

Pawelka, Peter. 1985. *Herrschaft und Entwicklung im Nahen Osten: Ägypten*. Heidelberg: C. F. Müller.

Payling, Simon J. 2018. "Middle Ages: Parliament and Politics before 1509." *History of Parliament: British Political, Social, and Local History*. Accessed Oct. 19, 2018. https://www.historyofparliamentonline.org/periods/medieval.

Perthes, Volker, ed. 2004. *Arab Elites: Negotiating the Politics of Change*. Boulder: Lynne Rienner Publishers.

Philipp, Thomas, and Ulrich Haarmann. 1998. *The Mamluks in Egyptian Politics and Society*. Cambridge: Cambridge Univ. Press.

Pierson, Paul. 2000. "Increasing Returns, Path Dependence, and the Study of Politics." *American Political Science Review* 94 (2): 251–67. https://doi.org/10.2307/2586011.

Pioppi, Daniela. 2013. "Playing with Fire. The Muslim Brotherhood and the Egyptian Leviathan." *International Spectator* 48 (4): 51–68. https://doi.org/10.1080/03932729.2013.847680.

Rafi'i, 'Abd al-Rahman al-. 1982. *'Asr Isma'il*. 3rd ed. 2 vols. Cairo: Dar al-Ma'arif.

Ranko, Annette. 2015. *The Muslim Brotherhood and Its Quest for Hegemony in Egypt: State-Discourse and Islamist Counter-Discourse*. Wiesbaden: Springer VS.

Raymond, André. 2000. *Cairo*. Translated by Willard Wood. Cambridge: Harvard Univ. Press.

Reichertz, Jo. 2004. "Objective Hermeneutics and Hermeneutic Sociology of Knowledge." In *A Companion to Qualitative Research*, edited by Uwe Flick, Ernst von Kardorff, and Ines Steinke, 290–95. London: Sage Publications.

Reid, Donald. 1980. "Fu'ad Siraj al-Din and the Egyptian Wafd." *Journal of Contemporary History* 15 (4): 721–44.

Reinich, Jacques. 1977. *Middle East Contemporary Survey*, Vol. 2. Boulder: Westview Press.

Reus-Smit, Christian. 2007. "International Crises of Legitimacy." *International Politics* 44, 157–74.

Rhodes, R. A. W. 2006. "Old Institutionalisms." In *The Oxford Handbook of Political Institutions*, edited by R. A. W. Rhodes, Sarah A. Binder, and Bert A. Rockman, 90–108. Oxford Handbooks of Political Science. Oxford: Oxford Univ. Press.

Richards, Alan. 1982. *Egypt's Agricultural Development, 1800–1980: Technical and Social Change*. Westview Replica Edition. Boulder: Westview Press.

Richter, Carola. 2013. "Liberalisierungsprozesse im ägyptischen Mediensystem und ihre Bedeutung für den politischen Umbruch 2011." In *Revolution und Regimewandel in Ägypten*, edited by Holger Albrecht and Thomas Demmelhuber, 143–62. Baden-Baden: Nomos.

Rivlin, Helen. 1961. *Agricultural Policy of Muhammad Ali in Egypt*. Cambridge: Harvard Univ. Press.

Rizq, Yunan Labib. 1991. *Qissat al-Barlaman al-Misri*. Cairo: Dar al-Hilal.

———. 2000. "Democracy Is Born." *Ahram Weekly* (May 25), 483. Accessed Oct. 12, 2013. http://weekly.ahram.org.eg/2000/483/chrncls.htm.

Rohde, Achim. 2010. *State-Society Relations in Ba'thist Iraq: Facing Dictatorship*. London: Routledge.

Ruiz de Elvira, Laura, Christoph H. Schwarz, and Irene Weipert-Fenner. 2018. "Introduction: Networks of Dependency, a Research Perspective." In *Clientelism and Patronage in the Middle East and North Africa: Networks of Dependency*, edited by Laura Ruiz de Elvira, Christoph H. Schwarz, and Irene Weipert-Fenner, 1–16. London: Routledge.

Safran, Nadav. 1961. *Egypt in Search of Political Community*. Cambridge: Harvard Univ. Press.

Sawi, Ali el-, Abdel Hafiz el-Sawi, Mohamed Shuman, and Noha el-Mikawy. 2002. "Institutional Impediments to Economic Legislation." In *Institutional Reform and Economic Development in Egypt*, edited by Noha el-Mikawy and Heba Handoussa, 37–48. Cairo: American Univ. in Cairo Press.

Sawi, Ali el-, Ahmed Ghoneim, and Maha Kamel. 2005. *The Main Actors in the Law-Making Process for Economic Reform: An Assessment of their Strengths and Weaknesses to Participate in the Law-Making Process.* Bonn: Center for Development Research.

Sayyid, Jalal al-, and Sami Mahran. 1984. *Al-Barlaman al-Misri: Taqalid, Riqaba, Tashri'.* Cairo: Al-Hay'a al-Misriyya al-'amma li-l-kitab.

Sayyid, Mustapha Kamil al-. 1990. "Privatization: The Egyptian Debate." *Cairo Papers in Social Science* 13: 4.

————. 1996. "Parliamentarians and Issues of Privatization." In *Privatization in Egypt: The Debate in the People's Assembly,* edited by Wafaa Abd-El Elah, Wadouda Badran, and Azza Wahby, 301–27. Cairo: Center for Political Research and Studies—Faculty of Economics and Political Science.

Sayyid Marsot, Afaf Lutfi al-. 1977. *Egypt's Liberal Experiment: 1922–36.* Berkeley: Univ. of California Press.

————. 1984. *Egypt in the Reign of Muhammad Ali.* Cambridge: Cambridge Univ. Press.

Schedler, Andreas. 2006. "The Logic of Electoral Authoritarianism." In *Electoral Authoritarianism: The Dynamics of Unfree Competition,* edited by Andreas Schedler, 1–23. Boulder, London: Lynne Rienner Publishers.

————. 2009. "The New Institutionalism in the Study of Authoritarian Regimes." *Totalitarianism and Democracy* 6 (2): 323–40.

————. 2013. *The Politics of Uncertainty: Sustaining and Subverting Electoral Authoritarianism.* New York: Oxford Univ. Press.

Schmidt, Vivien A. 2010. "Taking Ideas and Discourse Seriously: Explaining Change through Discursive Institutionalism as the Fourth 'New Institutionalism.'" *European Political Science Review* 2 (1): 1. https://doi.org/10.1017/S175577390999021X.

————. 2012. "A Curious Constructivism: A Response to Professor Bell." *British Journal of Political Science* 42 (3): 705–13. https://doi.org/10.1017/S0007123411000470.

Schölch, Alexander. 1972. *Ägypten den Ägyptern! Die politische und gesellschaftliche Krise der Jahre 1878–1882 in Ägypen.* Beiträge zur Kolonial- und Überseegeschichte Bd. 9. Zürich: Atlantis-Verlag.

Schuler, Paul, and Edmund Malesky. 2014. "Authoritarian Legislatures." In *The Oxford Handbook of Legislative Studies,* edited by Shane Martin, Thomas Saalfeld, and Kaare W. Strøm, 676–96. Oxford: Oxford Univ. Press.

Schwartz-Shea, Peregrine, and Dvora Yanow. 2012. *Interpretive Research Design: Concepts and Processes*. New York, London: Routledge.

Shakir, Muhammad Habib. 1986. *The Holy Qur'an*. London: Routledge.

Shehata, Dina. 2010. *Islamists and Secularists in Egypt: Opposition, Conflict, and Cooperation*. London: Routledge.

Shehata, Samer, and Joshua Stacher. 2006. "The Brotherhood Goes to Parliament." *Middle East Report* 240 (Fall).

Shukrallah, Hani. 2005. "Egypt: Stormy Elections Close a Turbulent Year." *Arab Reform Bulletin*. Carnegie Endowment for International Peace. Accessed Nov. 1, 2019. https://carnegieendowment.org/files/Shukrallah.pdf.

Sonneveld, Nadia. 2006. "If only there was khul'. . . ." *International Institute for the Study of Islam in the Modern World Review* 17: 50–51.

Soudias, Dimitris. 2014. *Negotiating Space: The Evolution of the Egyptian Street, 2000–2011*. Cairo: American Univ. in Cairo Press.

Sowers, Jeannie Lynn, and Christopher J. Toensing. 2012. *The Journey to Tahrir: Revolution, Protest, and Social Change in Egypt*. London: Verso.

Springborg, Robert. 1979. "Patrimonialism and Policy Making in Egypt: Nasser and Sadat and the Tenure Policy for Reclaimed Lands." *Middle Eastern Studies* 15 (1): 49–69.

———. 1989. *Mubarak's Egypt: Fragmentation of the Political Order*. Boulder: Westview Press.

Stacher, Joshua. 2012. *Adaptable Autocrats: Regime Power in Egypt and Syria*. Stanford: Stanford Univ. Press.

Steinmo, Sven, Kathleen Thelen, and Frank Longstreth, eds. 1992. *Structuring Politics: Historical Institutionalism in Comparative Analysis*. Cambridge: Cambridge Univ. Press.

Streeck, Wolfgang, and Kathleen Ann Thelen, eds. 2005. *Beyond Continuity: Institutional Change in Advanced Political Economies*. Oxford: Oxford Univ. Press.

Subhi, Muhammad Khalil. 1939–47. *Tarikh al-Hayat al-Niyabiyya fi Misr min 'Ahd Sakin al-Jinan Muhammad 'Ali Basha*. Cairo: Dar al-Kutub al-Misriyya.

Tarouty, Safinaz el. 2015. *Businessmen, Clientelism, and Authoritarianism in Egypt*. New York: Palgrave Macmillan.

Tawil, Muhammad al-. 1992. *Al-Ikhwan fi al-Barlaman*. Cairo: al-Maktab al-Misri al-Hadith.

Thabet, Hala. 2006. "Egyptian Parliamentary Elections: Between Democratisation and Autocracy." *Africa Development* 31 (3): 11–24.

Thelen, Kathleen. 1999. "Historical Institutionalism in Comparative Politics." *Annual Review of Political Science* (2): 369–404.

Thornhill, Michael T. 2010. "Informal Empire, Independent Egypt and the Accession of King Farouk." *Journal of Imperial and Commonwealth History* 38 (2): 279–302. https://doi.org/10.1080/03086531003743981.

Tignor, Robert. 1976. "The Egyptian Revolution of 1919: New Directions in the Egyptian Economy." *Middle Eastern Studies* 12 (3): 41–67.

Toledano, Ehud. 1990. *State and Society in Mid-Nineteenth Century Egypt.* Cambridge: Cambridge Univ. Press.

Tollefson, Harold. 1990. "The 1894 British Takeover of the Egyptian Ministry of Interior." *Middle Eastern Studies* 26 (4): 547–60.

United Nations Development Programme, Institute of National Planning. 2008. "Egypt's Social Contract: The Role of Civil Society." *Egyptian Human Development Report.* Cairo: United Nations Development Programme.

Vatikiotis, P. J. 1969. *The Modern History of Egypt.* London: Weidenfeld and Nicolson.

Waterbury, John. 1983. *The Egypt of Nasser and Sadat: The Political Economy of Two Regimes.* Princeton: Princeton Univ. Press.

Weber, Max. 2010. *Wirtschaft und Gesellschaft: Grundriss der verstehenden Soziologie.* Reprint. Frankfurt am Main: Zweitausendeins.

Weipert-Fenner, Irene. 2011. *Starke Reformer oder schwache Revolutionäre? Ländliche Notabeln und das ägyptische Parlament in der 'Urabi-Bewegung, 1866–1882.* Berlin: Klaus Schwarz.

———. 2013a. "Am institutionellen Nullpunkt. Über die politischen und verfassungsrechtlichen Probleme in Ägypten." In *Jahrbuch des Göttinger Instituts für Demokratieforschung,* edited by Roland Hiemann, Daniela Kallinich, Robert Lorenz, and Katharina Rahlf, 218–20. Stuttgart: Ibidem Verlag.

———. 2013b. "Wegbereiter oder treibende Kraft? Die Rolle der Arbeiter in der ägyptischen Revolution." In *Revolution und Regimewandel in Ägypten,* edited by Holger Albrecht and Thomas Demmelhuber, 209–31. Baden-Baden: Nomos.

———. 2018. "Blurred Lines of Inclusion and Exclusion: Research Ethics for Political Sympathizers." In *Political Science Research in the Middle East and North Africa: Methodological and Ethical Challenges,* edited by Janine A. Clark and Francesco Cavatorta, 233–41. New York: Oxford Univ. Press.

Wendt, Alexander. 1987. "The Agent-Structure Problem in International Relations Theory." *International Organization* 41 (3): 335–70.

———. "On Constitution and Causation in International Relations." *Review of International Studies* 42: 101–17.

Whidden, James. 2013. *Monarchy and Modernity in Egypt: Politics, Islam and Neo-colonialism between the Wars.* London: I. B. Tauris.

Wintrobe, Ronald. 2007. "Dictatorship: Analytical Approaches." In *The Oxford Handbook of Comparative Politics*, edited by Carles Boix and Susan C. Stokes, 363–94. Oxford Handbooks of Political Science 4. New York: Oxford Univ. Press.

Wright, Joseph. 2008. "Do Authoritarian Institutions Constrain? How Legislatures Affect Economic Growth and Investment." *American Journal of Political Science* 52 (2): 322–43.

Yasin, Ashraf Muhammad Abdallah Hasan. 2005. "Majlis al-Shaab al-Misri. Dirasa fi al-fa'iliyya (1984–2000)." PhD thesis, Suez Canal University.

Youssef, Hassan. 1983. "The Democratic Experience in Egypt, 1923–1952." In *Democracy in Egypt: Problems and Prospects*, 2nd ed., edited by Ali Dessouki, 27–34. Cairo: American Univ. in Cairo Press.

Zaki, Moheb. 1995. *Civil Society and Democratization in Egypt, 1981–1994.* Cairo: Dar al-Kutub.

Index

Photos, figures, and tables are indicated by italicized page numbers.

IRENE WEIPERT-FENNER is a senior research fellow at the Peace Research Institute Frankfurt. She holds a PhD from Goethe University Frankfurt. In 2019 she served as a visiting professor of Middle Eastern Politics at the Philipps University of Marburg, Germany. Her research focuses on authoritarian regimes, democratization, and social movements in Egypt and Tunisia. Her articles have appeared in such peer-reviewed periodicals as the *Journal of North African Studies* and *Politische Vierteljahresschrift*. Weipert-Fenner is a coeditor of *Clientelism and Patronage in the Middle East and North Africa: Networks of Dependency* (Routledge, 2018; with Laura Ruiz de Elvira and Christoph H. Schwarz) and *Socioeconomic Protests in MENA and Latin America: Egypt and Tunisia in Interregional Comparison* (Palgrave Macmillan, 2020, with Jonas Wolff).